The Maggid of Dubno and his parables

Th

הקול
קול
יעקב

Maggid of Dubno
and his parables

by BENNO HEINEMANN

NEWLY REVISED EDITION

FELDHEIM PUBLISHERS

Jerusalem • New York / 5738 / 1978

ISBN 0-87306-156-x

First edition, 1967
Second edition, 1969
Third edition, 1973
Fourth edition, newly revised and reset, 1978

PHILIPP FELDHEIM Inc.
96 East Broadway
New York, NY 10002

FELDHEIM PUBLISHERS Ltd
POB 6525 / Jerusalem, Israel

Printed in Israel

□ AUTHOR'S PREFACE

In offering this book to the public, the author has attempted to fill an obvious need for an inspiring book for the Jewish home. There is a definite need for this type of literature among both men and women who cannot delve into the vast reservoir of the Talmud, and among those who have not as yet had the opportunity to study the works of the gread Maggid of Dubno. Last but not least, this book should prove of educational and inspirational value to our younger generation as well.

At the same time this work should be of interest, too, to those who have more specific Jewish learning and who seek a clearer and more profound knowledge of the customs and traditions of our people.

The many ingenious parables contained in this anthology should provide welcome recreation for the reader in themselves, even without specific reference to any particular Biblical verse. But their greatest asset lies in the fact that they are always direct and to the point, and magically explain even the most perplexing verses.

The distinctive feature of this anthology is that it has been arranged according to subject matter rather than in the customary order which is based on the sequence of weekly *Sidroth*. It is not meant to be a scholarly treatise, but is intended simply to be read at leisure in the Jewish home.

But we would not be doing justice to the name of the great Maggid of Dubno if we were to remember him only as a wonderful teller of parables. He was, in fact, a great philosopher, and it should be worth our while to attempt to trace his profound thoughts, of which we here have been able to select only a limited number.

At this time the author wishes to record his deep indebtedness to Rabbi Joshua Landau, his teacher, who shared the fate of so many of our brethren in the tragic events of recent years, but whose memory is still living. It was he who originally encouraged and inspired the author to begin work on this anthology, the result of many years of study.

The author desires to express his sincerest thanks also to Rabbi J. J. Horovitz, who, as the Rabbi of Letchworth, England, where the author spent the years of World War II, gave liberally of his vast store of learning for the preparation of this work and who wrote the introductory essay entitled "The Moshol in Midrash and Maggiduth."*

The author owes a special debt of gratitude to Mr. N. D. Deuchar of Letchworth, England, for the care and attention he gave to the original manuscript which was compiled and readied for publication in England some years ago.

Thanks are due also to Mrs. Rosalie Jung-Rosenfeld, who unselfishly gave her assistance in the process of changing much of the King's English of the original into the American idiom.

The author gratefully acknowledges the help and counsel of Miss Gertrude Hirschler, well-known translator of standard works of Jewish literature, who revised the entire text of the original manuscript so as to make it more understandable to the American reader.

Thanks go also to Rabbi Dr. Joseph Breuer and Rabbi Simon

---

*In other instances of transliteration, the author was guided by the Sephardic pronunciation. In the case of the word "Moshol," however, he did not wish to change the familiar Ashkenazic pronunciation.

Schwab for giving of their time to read over parts of this work and for their invaluable assistance and suggestions.

Finally, the author wishes to express his appreciation to the publishers and printers for their unfailing, constant courtesy and consideration.

BENNO HEINEMANN*

---

* Unfortunately Dr. Heinemann did not live to see his work in print. The manuscript was prepared for publication by his wife and children after his death on July 21, 1964   (י"ב אב תשכ"ד)

הח׳ ברוך גדליה בן הח׳ משה ז"ל

תנצב"ה

RABBI DR. JOSEPH BREUER
50 Overlook Terrace
New York 33, N.Y.

WADSWORTH 3-2682

יוסף ברייער
רב דק"ק
קהל עדת ישרון
נוא־יארק יע"א

ב"ה

The old traditional D'rasha which clothes its thoughts and ideas in appropriate parables (Meshalim) met its most famous master in the world-renowned "Dubno Maggid."

In a labor of love, consuming many years, Dr. Benno Heinemann has tackled the difficult task of sifting and arranging the wealth of topics contained in these D'rashoth.

While the spiritual giants of the eighteenth century respected the originality of the Maggid, the man on the street was magically attracted by his personality which, permeated by profound Jewishness, appealed intimately to the mind as well as to the heart. This is borne out by the beautiful selection of stories appended to the work.

It is certain that this anthology, so long overdue, will be widely read by old and young alike.

RABBI DR. JOSEPH BREUER

New York City

☐ FOREWORD
By Rabbi J. J. Horovitz*

THE MOSHOL IN MIDRASH AND MAGGIDUTH

מֵהֵיכָן זָכָה מֹשֶׁה לְקַרְנֵי הוֹד ? טִיפַּת דְּיוֹ נִשְׁתַּיֵּיר בְּקוּלְמוֹסוֹ וְקִנְחָה בְּרֹאשׁוֹ וּמִשָּׁם זָכָה
לְקַרְנֵי הוֹד. (ש"ר מ"ז)

"**How did Moses come to deserve the privilege of having a halo of light shine forth about his head when he descended from Mount Sinai? (see Exodus 34:3). Says the Midrash: After he had completed the last words of the Torah a drop of ink still remained on his quill. This drop he then passed over his head, and it was from that drop that the great light shone forth from him.**"

With this statement the Midrash means to show us the very basis of the greatness of a human being. At first reading it seems somewhat obscure, but, as we shall presently see, it is a most apt characterization of a great teacher.

He who simply amasses a wealth of ideas and then attempts to drum them into the immature minds of young students who are not

---

* Before World War II Rabbi Horovitz, now the spiritual leader of Congregation B'er Shmuel in Brooklyn, New York, was *Av Beth Din* of the Orthodox Communities of Unsdorf, Hungary, and Frankfort-on-the-Main.

yet capable of grasping them is not a great educator at all. The good
teacher is one who, while he himself has the ability to grasp and retain vast masses of knowledge, also has the power to transmit to his
students only such subjects, and only in such doses and form, as are
suited to their powers of comprehension.

In the Ethics of the Fathers, Chapter Four, Mishnah Twenty-
five, the transmission of knowledge to the young is compared to the
marking of clean paper with symbols in ink. Our Sages tell us that
when Moses, our great Master, taught the Torah to his disciples in
the wilderness, he had the ability to hold back the flow of ink so that
it should not pour forth to excess from his pen; in other words, he
had the talent of discrimination and discretion, to ensure that the
quantity of knowledge to be communicated to his disciples should
not be overly great, lest the whole effort of education prove a failure.
In this manner his teaching could penetrate the minds of all, even
those of little learning; hence even the least gifted of his disciples
could take their rightful place in the Jewish community. And as for
Moses himself, his dignity did not suffer because he transmitted his
own vast knowledge in the simple language that all of his listeners
could understand. In fact, it was his method of instruction — the
use of wise discrimination in what to tell his students and what to
retain for himself alone — that made him truly great. It was that extra drop of ink which Moses withheld and passed over his head un-
used that made his teaching spread the light of the Word of God
over all the world. This talent was the "halo about his head."

This method of instruction, which is not simply a show of the
educator's knowledge but is geared to the needs and capacity of the
student, has been followed by all of Israel's great teachers
throughout the centuries. In the Book of *Koheleth* (Ecclesiastes) we
are told of King Solomon, the wisest man of all ages, that *he also
taught the people knowledge; yea, he pondered, and sought out, and
compiled many parables (Mesholim)* (Eccl. 12:9). King Solomon
employed the *Moshol* in the same spirit as Moses cast the final drop
of ink away. Instead of indulging in intricate philosophical gym-
nastics and idle casuistry at the expense of their disciples, both
Moses and Solomon spoke in the language of the people. In the case

of King Solomon, the instructive device for this purpose was the parable or the *Moshol.*

In the Midrash we read that the Sages asked, "What is the meaning of the *Moshol?*" One of the answers is: "The Torah may be likened to a maze. Before people can pass through it, there must be one pioneer to pave the way; after that, everyone will be able to follow the trail he has blazed. In learning, the role of the pioneer is taken by the *Moshol.* Once the right *Moshol* has been devised, the Scriptural verse in question is clear and accessible to all who desire to explore it."

Another one of our Rabbis says that the greatness of King Solomon's wisdom lay in his ability to fashion simple *Mesholim* by means of which to convey the deepest and most abstract of thoughts to the unschooled. This is true wisdom, the Rabbi explains; therefore, since we know that Solomon was the wisest of all men, it is evident that he was also the most eminent author of parables and allegories.

In the Introduction to the Midrash of *Shir Ha-Shirim* — the Midrashic explanation of the Song of Songs — it is said, *Do not take the Moshol lightly, for through it man acquires the foundation of the words of the Torah.*

If one has lost a precious treasure of pearls or diamonds, one uses in the search for the valued object a tool which in itself is almost of no value — the candle. In the search for the treasures of the Torah, the place of the candle is taken by the *Moshol.* The *Moshol* in itself would be of little worth, but it is the Moshol that brings light to the darkness of mystery and inscrutability. A candle can be bought for a few pennies, but the light it sheds can be most profitable when put to good use. In like manner, the *Moshol* may be simple, but definitely successful when employed in the proper spirit. The more natural and direct the *Moshol,* the more striking is its efficacy.

Our greatest and most successful teachers have always been those who were able to disseminate the knowledge of the Torah to ever-widening circles. If his work is viewed in this light, then the Maggid of Dubno will shine forth as one of the most eminent disciples of Moses and thus as one of the most important scholars among

The Maggid of Dubno and his Parables

the teachers in Israel. By means of his *Mesholim,* which reveal deep insight into the very soul of his people, he succeeded in bringing even the most inscrutable aspects of our Law a little closer to the understanding of his contemporaries and thus helped supply their need for the strength and consolation inherent in the Word of God.

Therefore it is most important to preserve and cherish for all time the teachings of this renowned orator in Israel who, apart from his well-known learning and righteousness, was also a genius in pedagogy and rhetoric. To this end his teachings should be translated into all the languages spoken by Jews today so that the spiritual values which he left to future generations may become accessible to the broadest circles possible.

Thus the translation of the *Divrei Torah* of the Maggid of Dubno into the language of those who are not learned in Hebrew is actually a continuation of the work of the Maggid, who himself was a translator after a manner, rendering the profound and recondite thoughts of the Torah into the language of the average reader.

In view of what has just been said, this valued work of my friend Dr. Benno Heinemann is deserving of the highest recognition. For this book, the result of many years of diligent study and painstaking research, remedies an obvious deficiency, bringing the treasures of our Torah, as it does, to the Jewish public, at a time when, more than ever before, we are greatly in need of such teaching and guidance.

□ CONTENTS

PART TWO

THE MAGGID
OF DUBNO
AND HIS PARABLES

☐ Chapter One

☐ BIOGRAPHICAL SKETCH

We believe that, to most of our readers, the Maggid of Dubno, or "The Dubnoer Maggid," as he is better known in Jewish literature, will not be a stranger. This renowned rabbi was one of the most talented and best-known *Maggidim*, the itinerant preachers who, not too many years ago, would travel through Eastern Europe from town to town and deliver messages of instruction and exhortation in the synagogues to their fellow-Jews. Rabbi Yaakov of Dubno, in particular, had a special genius for moving his listeners to greater piety and devotion. He combined erudition and uncompromising rigor in his own observance of the Law with the gift of eloquent speech and the knack for meeting his listeners at their own level.

His full name was Rabbi Yaakov ben Z'ev (Wolf) Kranz. He was born in 1741 in the town of Setil, in the district of Vilna (in present-day Lithuania), and died in 1804 (17th day of Teveth 5565) in Zamosch, Poland. He was a contemporary and friend of the famed Gaon of Vilna, whom he survived by seven years. Whatever has been written to date concerning his life and work is based on simple oral tradition passed on from generation to generation. The one authoritative written source of information on which

1

to base our biographical data is the brief biographical sketch written by Rabbi Abraham Dov Berush Flamm, his most devoted disciple.* Rabbi Yaakov came of good stock. His father, Rabbi Wolf Kranz, who was his first teacher, enjoyed undisputed Rabbinical authority in the town of Setil, and his mother, Hinda, was herself the daughter of a scholar of note. He was also a descendant of the renowned Rabbi Abraham Abush, Rabbi in Frankfort-on-the-Main.

At the age of eighteen, Rabbi Yaakov went to Mezeritch, where he studied at the *Beth Hamidrash*. It was in Mezeritch that his oratorical talents first came to the fore. At this time he had already committed to memory more than nine tractates of the Talmud. Whenever he preached, the synagogue would be filled to capacity and eventually he was appointed the community's official Maggid. As such he expounded the Law and Jewish ethics in forceful and moving sermons. Two years later he moved to Zolkiev, and thereafter to Dubno, a town which remained his home for eighteen years and from which his by-name is derived. Eventually he made the acquaintance of Rabbi Elijah, the renowned Gaon of Vilna, who was to become his sincere admirer. While in Vilna on one of his visits to the Gaon, the Maggid was invited to become the rabbi and preacher of the Jewish community of Vlodava, Poland. He followed this call but remained at that pulpit for only one year. From Vlodava he moved to Chelm, where he stayed for two years. He

---

* In his Introduction to Rabbi Yaakov's *Sefer Ha-Middoth*. It would be well to point out here that the correct surname is Flamm or Flahm, but not Plahm, by which name some sources erroneously refer to him. Nor could he have been, as some sources have it, a "favorite pupil" of the Maggid, for at the time of the Maggid's death, Flamm was only one year old. Flamm assisted the Maggid's son Yitzchak in the preparation for publication of the first edition of *Sefer Bereshith*, part of the Maggid's classic *Ohel Yaakov*. Rabbi Yitzchak Kranz called Abraham Dov Flamm "the distinguished elder in wisdom, though youthful in years," of the Kehillah of Mezeritch.

Yet, even though he himself had never met the Maggid of Dubno, Rabbi Flamm always considered himself the spiritual disciple of the latter. He explained that his resolve to compile and edit the works of the Maggid had come to him at a moment of crisis, after he had accidentally fallen into a well that was under construction. When, by a miracle, he was rescued from almost certain death by drowning, the youthful Rabbi vowed to carry out this pledge. He edited a total of nine of the Dubnoer's major works, and annotated them with his own commentaries.

spent the last fifteen years of his life in Zamosch. At one time during these final years, he was recalled to the Jewish community of Mezeritch, but after only a few months he returned to Zamosch because Rabbi Yitzchak, his only son, still lived there and could not follow him to Mezeritch.

Like any true Maggid, Rabbi Yaakov did not confine his activities to the places in which he actually resided. Instead, he traveled through the length and breadth of Poland and Germany, visiting numerous towns and villages and capturing the hearts of Jewish audiences with his moving eloquence. He became famous particularly for his *Mesholim,* those parables of marvelous directness and classic simplicity with which he would illustrate the lessons he sought to teach. In addition to his great learning and eloquence, he was endowed with the rare talent of being able to treat commonplace subjects in an uncommon manner, finding a Scriptural verse and parable to suit almost every aspect of day-to-day living and conduct.

It had not been his intention to publish his sermons and commentaries. The task of compiling them and preparing them for publication after his death fell to his son Rabbi Yitzchak and to Rabbi Abraham Berush Flamm. In his introduction to one of these works, the *Sefer Ha-Middoth,* Rabbi Flamm explains that this was a most arduous task indeed, since the Maggid of Dubno had never written out any of his lectures or sermons. The Maggid had left only some sketchy notes. As a result, the two learned Rabbis undertaking this gigantic project had to decipher the notes and supplement them with material from personal memory (in the case of Rabbi Yitzchak) or from secondary sources of information.

A list of the books and anthologies containing the works of the Maggid of Dubno will be found in the short bibliography at the end of this volume.

If we consider the life Rabbi Yaakov led throughout his adult years, we will readily understand why he could hardly have given much time to the careful recording of his sermons and parables. His rigorous daily routine of prayer, study and teaching left him little time for other pursuits. He made it a practice to fast every Monday and Thursday, and if the following day was the eve of *Rosh Chodesh,* the "New Moon," he would fast on that day also, thus going without food for two consecutive days. Shortly before his death, the Maggid confided to a friend that, since his eighteenth year, he had never been asleep at midnight. Even if he had managed to retire prior to the midnight hour, he would rise from bed at the stroke of twelve to recite prayers and lamentations (*Tikun Chatzoth*), weeping bitterly all the while. He would then commence his studies and, before daybreak, repair to the *Mikvah* to perform his ritual ablutions. When the time came for morning prayers, he would put on his *Tallith* and *Tefillin* and not remove them until the late afternoon, at the time of the *Minchah* service. A heavy-set man, he would stand motionless during prayer, facing a wall and with head bowed, looking neither to the right nor to the left, a humble servant rendering homage to his Master. It is said that as he prayed, even on joyous occasions such as Sabbaths and Festivals, he would weep so copiously that the traces of his tears still showed on the reading desk after he had completed his devotions.

After morning prayers Rabbi Yaakov would study the Mishnah and Gemara until about noon; then he would go home, with his *Tefillin* covered, to take his first meal of the day. In the afternoon he would return to the House of Study and teach at his Yeshivah. Every day, he would stand at the *Amud,* the Reader's desk at the synagogue, to recite a few chapters from the Psalms. After his death the *Shammash* explained that these tearful prayers had been intended for those suffering from distress and oppression; it had been the duty of the *Shammash* to report to the Maggid any trouble or tragedy involving a member of the community.

But stern though he was in matters pertaining to observance of the Law, he was anxious that every possibility of relief within the framework of the Torah should be thoroughly explored in the case of problems affecting his fellow-Jews.

One such instance involved the case of an *Agunah.* This is the designation in Jewish law for a woman whose husband is missing but not officially proven dead. Such a woman is thus "neither wife nor widow" because she cannot remarry until a reliable witness can give evidence to the effect that her husband has died.

One such unfortunate woman had already consulted many great Rabbis, including those of Lemberg and Brody, but they could not come to a unanimous decision. Most of them were determined to give the *Heter,* but hesitated because of the important precedent involved. Eventually she came to her kinsman, Rabbi Abush, and asked him to present her case to the eminent Rabbi of Budshav. Rabbi Abush invited her to spend the Sabbath with his family, promising to fulfill her request after the Sabbath.

Just as Rabbi Abush was about to set out on his mission, a carriage stopped before his house and the Maggid of Dubno stepped out. He had come to the town on one of his periodic visits. The news of his arrival spread quickly and all the Jews of the town flocked to see and hear him. The *Agunah* stood aside, weeping, for she feared that her personal problem would now be ignored and forgotten. The Maggid, however, noticed her, and agreed to render his decision in her case. All that night Rabbi Yaakov remained awake in his room, studying the pertinent documents and information given him by Rabbi Abush, to see whether something could not be done to help the poor woman.

The next day, after morning services, the entire congregation went to the home of the town's Chief Rabbi where many erudite rabbis had assembled to honor the Maggid of Dubno. When the Maggid entered, they all fell silent, eager to hear his words of wisdom. Rabbi Yaakov, his eyes closed, was rapt in thought, seemingly oblivious of the gathering. Finally, he began to speak:

"*Rabbothai,* worthy Rabbis, I shall tell you a *Moshol.*" What the parable was has not been recorded. But obviously the scholars gathered at the Chief Rabbi's home were most impressed by what the Maggid had to tell them, for when he had finished, all the Rabbis were confirmed in their belief in the justification of the *Heter,* and they signed the Rabbinical dispensation which made the *Agunah* free to remarry. Such was the power that Rabbi Yaakov of Dubno wielded with the spoken work.

Rabbi Jacob Orenstein (1774-1839), the author of a work en-

titled *Yeshuath Yaakov,* tells of the powerful emotional impact of
the sermons delivered by the Maggid of Dubno.

At one time the Maggid paid a visit to the town of Jaroslav and
stayed for some time at the home of Rabbi Orenstein's father-in-
law. At the time, Rabbi Orenstein, together with another young student, lived there as a boarder. When the Maggid of Dubno would
deliver his daily sermon, both young men would leave their studies
to listen most attentively to what Rabbi Yaakov had to say. The day
before his departure from the town, the Maggid told them not to
come to his final sermon which he would deliver the next day. When
they asked the reason for this strange request, the Maggid replied:

"When I leave a town where I have stayed for some time, my last
sermon is stern and moralizing, filled with *Mussar,* with rebuke and
exhortation. I know you two are tender-hearted, and what I will say
tomorrow may cause you pain, Heaven forbid. Therefore I would
suggest that you devote the time to your holy books instead." The
two students, however, could not be dissuaded from going to hear
the last lecture of the illustrious visitor. Rabbi Orenstein records
that even at the very beginning of the sermon, he already shed bitter tears. His friend managed to restrain himself at the time but
was so overwrought by the Maggid's fiery oration that he was
emotionally shaken for a long time thereafter.

A few years before his death, Rabbi Yaakov took into his home a
young orphan named Solomon Kluger* who grew up to become the
famed rabbi and preacher of Brody. It seems that, one day, the
Maggid of Dubno, then living in Zamosch, found the boy in the
street, guiding a blind man. Even though he himself was not a
wealthy man, the Maggid took both the orphan and his sightless
companion into his home and provided them with food and shelter.
After the blind man's death, young Solomon remained with Rabbi
Yaakov. Some years later he left to study at the Yeshiva of Rabbi
Hochgelernter, and became the rabbi's star pupil, but he continued
to take private *Shiurim* with his foster-father. Much of Rabbi

----

* 1786-1869.

Kluger's successful work in the fields of *Halacha* and *Maggiduth* was directly attributable to what he had learned at the feet of the Maggid of Dubno.

Rabbi Yaakov was outstanding in both the study and the teaching of *Gemara,* often adding original interpretations. His striking *Mesholim* made even the most difficult problems lucid and clear. His parables are couched in terms of what his listeners saw about them; they abound with figures and characters that were part of daily living in those times, such as kings, princes and their servants, rabbis and coachmen, merchants and artisans. There are the healthy and the sick, the fathers and the sons. Particularly, over and over again, the rich man and the poor man are prominent characters. He was convinced that every human being had an important place in God's scheme on earth, and that fortunes change through the years in accordance with Divine plan. For this reason he was a staunch advocate of the poor and the oppressed.

The poor and the humble as well as the rich and the learned were great admirers of the Maggid of Dubno. As his fame spread, his name became known also in many other circles. Even Moses Mendelssohn, who met him in Berlin, referred to him as "the Jewish Aesop."

In this book we have attempted to give a selection of Rabbi Yaakov's great and variegated repertory of scholarship. In the first part we intend to show the uniqueness of his explanations, usually illustrated with *Mesholim,* while the second part brings out the universal nature of the Maggid's method, through his meetings with other great personalities and with communities.

☐ CHAPTER TWO

☐ WE AND ERETZ YISRAEL

☐ 1 — OUR TIES TO ERETZ YISRAEL

כִּי הָאָרֶץ אֲשֶׁר אַתָּה בָא־שָׁמָּה לְרִשְׁתָּהּ לֹא כְאֶרֶץ מִצְרַיִם הִיא אֲשֶׁר יְצָאתֶם מִשָּׁם.
(עקב)

"For the land which you are entering to possess it is not like the land of Egypt from which you have come."   *(Deut. 11:10)*

Why, indeed, has God given the blessed Eretz Yisrael to the Jews and placed the other nations elsewhere?

Said the Dubnoer Maggid:

Let me give you a *Moshol.* There was once a man who was blessed with a son of fine character and exceptional piety. The young man married, and in due course he, too, became the father of a son. The proud grandfather made elaborate arrangements to celebrate the infant's *B'rith Milah.* Now the youthful father was most content but he was sorely troubled by one question.

"Father," he asked the older man, "How will you seat the guests? If you will seat the rich in the places of honor and leave the poor to

8

take the far end of the banquet table I will be so distressed that the feast will give me little joy. I beg of you, let the rich sit at the far end this time, and give the poor the seats of honor, for are not the poor as worthy in the eyes of God as the rich?"

"I see your point, my son," the father replied. "But if I were to do as you ask it would give little joy to any of our guests. You see, our old custom of placing prominent guests at the head of the board and the poor at the foot is based on sound common sense. The poor are always hungry, and when you are hungry all you want is food and you care little where you sit. Not so the rich. They are well-fed and accustomed to the luxuries of life, and when you feel neither hunger nor thirst, and your body is content, you are free to seek better things. You still like good food, but most of all you covet honor, gracious service and the finer things of life. The rich do not come to banquets for the food. That they can have at home. What they relish is to be treated as guests of honor, and they will enjoy their dinner only if they are properly seated and elegantly served.

"Now the poor care nothing about such refinements. All they want is food, plenty of it, and the chance to enjoy it without being disturbed. Believe me, my son, they feel much more comfortable when they can sit in an inconspicuous corner where no one will care about their table manners and where they can smack their lips and take second helpings without anyone staring at them."

Such, said the Maggid of Dubno, is the difference also between Israel and the other nations. The heathens of old, like the poor at the rich man's table, sought only to satisfy their bodies. This they could do anywhere in the world, in places less important than the Holy Land. But the People of God has always wanted more than that. Judaism has always sought the higher aspects of living. The study of the Law of God, its observance and dissemination, is Israel's very life and soul. And ideals such as Torah, wisdom, the fear of the Lord, prophecy and the spirit of holiness can be fully achieved and realized only in Eretz Yisrael, of which our Sages say "even the air of the Holy Land makes one wise."

The people of Israel are to be the wealthy guests at the table of the Lord. That is why Divine Providence gave them the Holy Land as their dwelling place at the head of the table.

Of course, once they forsook their true mission and sought only to satisfy their baser urges and to ape their heathen neighbors, when *they went after things of nought and thus became nought themselves* (II Kings 17:15) the Lord sent them away from their place of honor. He exiled them from the Holy Land to alien lands, and they were compelled to dwell among their pagan tempters. Thus they must share the lesser dwelling places on earth with the heathens, until such time as Israel will return to God, and the words of the Prophet Isaiah will be fulfilled: *Beth Yaakov lechu venel'cha be'or Hashem.* "*O House of Jacob, come, and let us walk in the light of the Lord*" (Isaiah 2:5).

□ 2 — ERETZ YISRAEL AND THE DIASPORA

אֶרֶץ אֲשֶׁר ה' אֱ־לֹהֶיךָ דֹּרֵשׁ אֹתָהּ תָּמִיד עֵינֵי ה' אֱ־לֹהֶיךָ בָּהּ.   (עקב)

"A land which the Lord your God cares for: the eyes of the Lord your God are always upon it..."   *(Deut. 11:12)*

What difference is it to us whether we live in the Holy Land or some other country?

Said Rabbi Yaakov: The privilege of living in Eretz Yisrael may be compared to the good fortune of a son living happily with his father. Whatever the son will need, the father will gladly and lovingly provide for him, for how could a devoted father refuse his son's request if he sees the child standing before him, speaking to him face to face?

However, if the son were to be living not at home but in some far-off country, the situation would not be the same. Then the boy's requests would reach the father by letter or messenger only; the appeals would lose some of their intimate, urgent nature and it might well be that the father would not act as quickly and directly as he certainly would have if he could have heard his son's voice pleading with him.

So it is also with the people of Israel. When we dwell in the House of our Heavenly Father, in the Holy Land, we may expect our hopes and prayers to be heard and fulfilled much more speedily than anywhere else in the world. For did not King Solomon say: *"And listen to the supplication of Your servant, and of Your people Israel, when they shall pray toward this place; and hear it in Heaven, Your dwelling place"* (I Kings 8:30)?

It is written in the Talmud that the *Beth Hamikdash* on earth corresponds to God's dwelling place in Heaven above. Hence, those prayers offered in the Holy Land will be answered with an abundance of blessings, for, as we have just learned, "the eyes of the Lord are always upon this land." The Land of Israel is the source of everything that is blessed and good, and all the other nations of the world look to this center of divine radiance as the well-spring of their own prosperity.

At present we are like children who have been turned away from the House of their Father. We no longer receive our blessings directly from the hand of the Lord; instead, we must live on cuttings and gleanings from the opulent gardens of the other nations thus blessed by a gracious Providence. We fervently pray that the day may soon come when Israel will receive its blessed portion not second-hand, but obviously and directly from our Heavenly Father. Such joy, so evidently God-sent, will be infinitely greater than any pleasure we may now derive from the rich harvests *of grain and wine that the other nations gather in* (Psalms 4:8).

We are sadly in need of the direct support of our Father in Heaven, of the immediate acceptance of our prayers without any agent or intermediary such as the other nations of the world. Here again, said the Maggid of Dubno, a *Moshol* will serve to explain what I mean.

The only son of a rich man was arrested without just cause, and now he lay dejectedly in his prison cell without even knowing why he had been put there. At home he had never lacked the best of food and drink; now he had to content himself with turnips, water and

bread. Once he had recovered from the shock of his arrest, he began
to bombard his father with letters, begging him to send him some
decent food. When the first parcel from home arrived, the young
man tore it open anxiously. Imagine his disappointment when, instead of the delicacies which he had expected, he found nothing but
fresh bread, potatoes and cereals, and not even much of that. So he
wrote to his father, "Have you also joined my enemies now? Why
have you deserted me now when I need you most?" Some weeks
later, via secret channels, the answering message came. The father
had written: "Were you sitting at my own table now, you may be
sure that you would lack for nothing, for not even the finest of food
is too good for my son. But if I were to send you the meat and the
fish and all the fancy fare you want, it would never reach you. Why,
your prison guards would have eaten it all before you would ever see
it. And why should I help feed the evil men who torture my son?"

Such, too, is the situation of the Children of Israel at this time.
And for this reason God, our Father, does not give us our own portion now but allows us to depend on the bounty and prosperity of
the nations among which we have been exiled. But once the Messiah
will come, God will support and maintain His people in His own
land by His own direct Providence, without the intermediary of any
man or nation, as Joel the Prophet said long ago. *"Behold, I will
send you grain, and wine, and oil, and you shall be satisfied with it,
and I will no longer make you a reproach among the nations"* (Joel
2:19).

□ 3 — THE SANCTITY OF ERETZ YISRAEL

וְלֹא תָקִיא הָאָרֶץ אֶתְכֶם בְּטַמַּאֲכֶם אֹתָהּ כַּאֲשֶׁר קָאָה אֶת הַגּוֹי אֲשֶׁר לִפְנֵיכֶם. כִּי כָּל
אֲשֶׁר יַעֲשֶׂה מִכֹּל הַתּוֹעֵבוֹת הָאֵלֶּה וְנִכְרְתוּ הַנְּפָשׁוֹת הָעֹשֹׂת מִקֶּרֶב עַמָּם.
(אחרי מות)

"And the land will not vomit you out* when you defile it as it vomited out the nation that was before you. For whoever will do any of these abominations, the souls that do them shall be cut off from among their people."   *(Lev. 18:28-29)*

We would have expected to read "and the land will not vomit you out if you will not defile it." "The land will not vomit you out when you defile it" seems a contradictory statement.

Said the Maggid of Dubno: Let me explain this with a *Moshol.*

A rich man had an only son. In order to spur him on to more diligent study and to teach him to cope with competition, the father decided to take into his home an orphan boy who would be given every privilege in return for acting as his son's companion at study and at play.

Unfortunately, the young stranger proved a disappointment to his foster-father. He had little liking for study, neglected his lessons and so got into trouble constantly. In the end, his benefactor told him to leave the house.

Shortly thereafter the father discovered to his great chagrin that his own son was following in the footsteps of his former companion. He took the boy to task, berated him angrily and gave him a severe punishment. When he was about to send the boy back to his room, the latter complained: "Father," he asked, "would you be good enough to explain why you had to vent all your anger on me, your own son? Look at that orphan boy. He was no better than I, and yet all you said to him was 'Go away and fend for yourself.' Why couldn't you have been just as calm and lenient with me?"

"Foolish boy," the father replied impatiently. "Think before you speak! What was that orphan boy to me? I was glad to have him here as long as he was obedient and well-behaved. But when he got out of hand, I had to send him away. That was all. But it's different with you. You are my own son and I am deeply concerned about what will become of you. Why should I send you away from your

---

* This is the literal translation of what is usually rendered by "...that the land vomit not you also..."

own home? Will that make you better? No, my son. It is my duty to scold you and to punish you to make you mend your ways, for I am your father and it is my heart's desire to see you grow into a decent and happy man."

This *Moshol,* said the Maggid, should help us understand that verse in the Bible. We know from the Bible that the other nations, who had dwelt in the land of Canaan before the coming of the Children of Israel, would be expelled from the land as a punishment for having defiled it by their evil ways. But simple expulsion, such as this, would not be punishment enough for Israel, the "first-born son" of God. Therefore the Bible tells us: "O Children of Israel, if you, too, should defile the land you will *not* be expelled from it as were the other nations before you. *Your punishment will be much more severe.* The land will not cast you off, but instead, your very souls shall be cut off from among your people." And Verse 30 continues: *"Therefore you shall keep my charge in order not to practice any of the customs of the abominations which were done before you, and you shall not defile yourselves with them; I am the Lord your God."* In other words, "I am your Father. How then could I cast you off? But it is My full intention to chastise you until you will keep My commandments and no longer defile yourselves with your sins."

□ 4 — OUR MOURNING TURNED INTO JOY

שִׂמְחוּ אֶת יְרוּשָׁלַיִם וְגִילוּ בָה כָּל אֹהֲבֶיהָ.
שִׂישׂוּ אִתָּהּ מָשׂושׂ כָּל הַמִּתְאַבְּלִים עָלֶיהָ.   (ישעיה סו')

Every year, for a period of three weeks beginning with the 17th day of Tammuz and ending with the 9th of Av, the Jewish people goes into deep mourning for the Holy Temple in Jerusalem. We had two Temples; the first one was destroyed by Nebuchadnezzar, the King of Babylonia, the second was razed by Titus and his Roman legions. Now we have no place that can be called the Sanctuary of God on earth. But our prophets have given us God's promise that, in due time, we shall have a third Temple, which will remain for all eternity, and those who mourned the most bitterly for Israel's lost glory will have their grief turned into great rejoicing.

The Prophet Isaiah said:

"Rejoice with Jerusalem and be glad with her, all of you who love her; rejoice with her with great rejoicing, all of you who mourn for her." *(Isaiah 66:10)*

In other words, those who genuinely keep the "three weeks" of mourning for our Temple, who will forego all pleasure and entertainment in memory of Jerusalem, will be privileged in due time to rejoice in the rebuilding of our Holy City and the Sanctuary therein. But why say "Rejoice with *great* rejoicing"?

The Maggid of Dubno gave his answer in the form of a *Moshol:*

A man embarked on a long journey which was to take him to distant lands across the sea. After he had been gone for some time, reports reached his home town that his ship had met with an accident and that he had been drowned. His wife and children were prostrate with grief. His friends, too, were deeply shocked, and even those who barely knew him were momentarily stunned. As time went on, however, the memory of the man they had esteemed so highly grew dimmer in their hearts. But though the months passed, his immediate family never ceased to mourn for him.

Then, one day, the door of the man's house opened. Behold, there stood the man who they had thought was dead, very much alive! The good news quickly spread through the town, and soon the house was crowded with friends who came to express their joy at his safe return. Those who had known him but slightly were pleased for him and his family. But his intimates, who had felt genuine sorrow when he had been presumed dead, were more than merely pleased; they were overjoyed that their friend was still among the living. And his family, of course, were beside themselves with happiness. Those who had mourned the most for the lost traveler were the happiest now that he had returned.

The same applies to our own mourning for the Temple and for

Jerusalem, and to the happiness that will be ours when, in due time, both the City and the Sanctuary will rise again. Jeremiah said: *"And I will turn their mourning into joy and I will comfort them, and make them rejoice from their sorrow"* (Jeremiah 31:12). In other words: The exuberance of their rejoicing will be in direct proportion to the tears they shed when there was reason to mourn. All of Israel will rejoice when the Temple will rise again in Jerusalem, but the degree to which they will rejoice will depend upon the extent to which they wept before. And those of us who truly mourned for Jerusalem will then indeed "rejoice *with great rejoicing*" at its rebuilding.

Much the same idea is expressed in the *Shir Ha-Maaloth* which we sing on Sabbaths and holidays: *Hazor'im bedim'ah berinah yiktzoru. "Those who sow in tears will accordingly reap with joy"* (Psalms 126:5). The more genuine and heart-rending our tears for the lost Temple, the greater will be our joy and exultation at its restoration.

□ 5 — THE MIRACULOUS HARVEST

וְכִי תֹאמְרוּ מַה־נֹּאכַל בַּשָּׁנָה הַשְּׁבִיעִית הֵן לֹא נִזְרָע וְלֹא נֶאֱסֹף אֶת תְּבוּאָתֵנוּ. וְצִוִּיתִי
אֶת־בִּרְכָתִי לָכֶם בַּשָּׁנָה הַשִּׁשִּׁית וְעָשָׂת אֶת־הַתְּבוּאָה לִשְׁלֹשׁ הַשָּׁנִים. (בהר)

"And if you shall say: 'What shall we eat in the seventh year? For behold, we may not sow, nor gather in our produce.' Then I will command My blessing upon you in the sixth year and it shall bring forth produce for the three years."   *(Lev. 25:20-21)*

The Sabbatical year is one of those basic Jewish institutions that can be enforced only in the Holy Land.

Even as the Sabbath of rest comes at the end of a week of toil, so the Sabbatical year ends a period of six years during which the soil was diligently tilled. During that seventh year, the land is to lie fallow and is to be turned back to God, as it were, for during that year the beneficiaries of that soil are not only we ourselves, but also the poor, who may gather produce from it, and the cattle, which may graze upon it.

At first glance it seems strange that the Bible should have phrased this statement thus. The people ask, "What shall we eat in the seventh year?" And the answer is, "I will give you blessings in the sixth year sufficient to supply you with food for three years." Would it not have been simpler to state, "I will bless you so abundantly during the sixth year that you will have no food problems whatsoever during the seventh"? Why, altogether, the question and the answer?

First of all, we must realize that God's blessing may take various forms. He may make the yield of the sixth year so abundant in actual quantity that there will be a sufficient amount of grain to last throughout the Sabbatical year. That would be the *B'rachah basadeh*, the actual blessing in the field. But then there is also the *B'rachah beme'av*, the blessing which relates to our bodily assimilation of the food we eat. Here the quantity of grain supplied is immaterial; the blessing lies in the fact that, whatever the quantity of food we receive, it will satisfy our bodily needs and our hunger. Of these two blessings, the latter is very definitely greater than the former. True, a physical surplus of grain sufficient to last for three years would represent a major miracle, but at the same time it would impose an almost inhuman burden of cutting, gathering, threshing, grinding and processing, for it would represent the harvest of three years all coming in one single season. But of the *B'rachah beme'av* it is said: *"The blessing of the Lord makes rich and does not bring further toil"* (Proverbs 10:22). It satisfies us without imposing upon us the strenuous toil that would be involved in the *Birchath hasadeh*. Now the extent to which we will thus be "satisfied" depends entirely on our *bitachon*, our trust and confidence in God. If the people of Israel will trust in God and observe His Laws, the bodily blessing will be sent to them; they will not need to do additional work, and yet they will be fully satisfied, as it is written in the Torah: *"And you shall do My statutes and keep My ordinances and do them and then you shall dwell in the land in safety. And the land shall yield its fruit, and you shall eat and be satisfied and dwell in safety on it"* (Lev. 25:18-19).

But if their faith in God, their *Bitachon,* should lessen and they will ask *Mah nochal,* "What shall we eat?" then they will forfeit this, the greater blessing of the two. In that case they will receive *B'rachah basadeh* only. By a miracle, their fields will produce three times the normal yearly yield of crops, but such a surplus can "satisfy" them only if they can gather it all before it spoils, and this gigantic ingathering operation will involve thrice the work required in an ordinary year's harvest. But if you have *Bitachon,* you will be blessed with that miraculous harvest which satisfies abundantly without back-breaking toil.

□ 6 — GOD'S EARTHLY RESIDENCE

וַיִּיקַץ יַעֲקֹב מִשְּׁנָתוֹ וַיֹּאמֶר אָכֵן יֵשׁ ה׳ בַּמָּקוֹם הַזֶּה . . . מַה־נּוֹרָא הַמָּקוֹם הַזֶּה אֵין זֶה
כִּי־אִם בֵּית אֱ־לֹהִים . . .   (ויצא)

"And Jacob awoke from his sleep, and he said, 'Surely the Lord is in this place, and I did not know it.' And he was afraid and he said, 'How awesome is this place! This is none other than the House of God, and this is the Gate of Heaven.' "

(Gen. 28:16-17)

Now why did our Father Jacob use such complicated language here? He says, "This is none other than the House of God," instead of simply, "This is the House of God." Besides, he has already said before, "Surely the Lord is in this place." Why, then, all the repetition?

To understand this properly, let us first attempt to answer the age-old question — why do we ascribe greater holiness to the *Beth Hamikdash,* the Holy Temple, than to any other place? For do we not always say that *"the earth is full of the glory of God"* (Isaiah

6:3), that every nook of this world must be considered as God's own dwelling place? Why, then attempt to pin-point the residence of our God in one place, the Sanctuary? Why does Jacob imply that only *"this* place" — and none other — is "full of awe"? And why are we told that tradition, when it tells us *"This righteous man came to the place where I dwell" says the Lord (Chullin* 91b), means the place where the Temple in Jerusalem was eventually erected?

Said Rabbi Yaakov:

Let us deal with this problem with the help of a little *Moshol.* A man once came to the capital of his country and was taken on a sight-seeing tour. At one point his guide announced with gusto, "And now we are approaching the residence of the King." The tourist expected to be shown a great imposing palace, but, instead, the guide pointed to a number of smaller buildings, all situated in a beautiful park, but none as impressive as one might expect a king's palace to look. "In this row of houses," said the guide, "live the King's officials. Over there are the homes of the royal physicians, and the most beautiful house in that group in the residence of the king's own Physician-in-Waiting. This one here is the place where the Gentlemen of the Bedchamber live." Finally, they came to one building at which the guide stopped, saying, "And this is the King's residence."

"Indeed?" said the tourist, surprised. "Why, was not everything you have shown me thus far part of the King's residence? Why stop at this one house of all the others and point it out to me as 'The King's Residence'?"

And the guide replied: "Certainly, this whole estate really does belong to the King, and it is through his grace that the members of his Court may live here. But this one building is the personal residence of the King himself. Any member of the Royal Court has unlimited access to any and all of the other houses on the grounds, but none may enter this one mansion except on special occasions and with special ceremony."

So, too, is it with our world and our Holy Temple. We know that *the whole world is God's royal dwelling-place* (Isaiah 6:3) which, by His grace, *He has assigned to man* (Psalms 115:16) as his sphere of activity. But in addition, He has chosen one place on earth which belongs to Him alone and which none may enter except on those occasions and under those conditions which He Himself has ordained. This is the *Beth Hamikdash,* the Holy Temple in Jerusalem, the spiritual center for the worship of God, which, though at present in ruins, will be rebuilt in due time to last for all eternity.

The place where Jacob found himself in his dream was the very site at which, hundreds of years later, the Holy Temple was erected. And even then, as he lay beneath the starry skies there in the wilderness, Jacob sensed that this was a special place. "Surely the Lord is in this place," he exclaimed, "for His presence and His glory fill the entire universe; the whole earth is the Palace of our King." But "how awesome is this one place in particular! This one spot is none other than the House of God, the special royal dwelling-place which God will not share with any other being." And realizing this, Jacob added, "and this is the Gate of Heaven."

□ 7 — OUR RIGHT TO ERETZ YISRAEL

גֵּר־וְתוֹשָׁב אָנֹכִי עִמָּכֶם.   (חיי שרה)

"I am a stranger and a settler among you; give me a burial property among you..."   *(Gen. 23:4)*

A "stranger" and a "settler" at the same time — what a strange statement for Abraham to make to the sons of Cheth! But the Midrash has rendered it quite plausible by explaining it as follows: Abraham said to the sons of Cheth, "If you will agree to sell me the land then I will regard myself as a *stranger,* and will pay for it. But if you should refuse me, then I shall act as a *settler,* and lay claim to it, for, in fact, I have a legal right to your land, since God has said to me, '*I shall give this land to your descendants*'" (Gen. 12:7).

And this is the *Moshol* which our Maggid liked to give to make the point quite clear.

A wealthy merchant who owned a spacious and well-built house decided to leave his home and to settle in some far-off land. So that the house might serve some useful purpose while he was gone, he decided to turn it over to a young fellow-townsman who enjoyed a good reputation in the community. In the agreement drawn up between the two men in the presence of a notary the rights of the new tenant were explicitly enumerated. These rights were extensive, but all subject to the proviso that the tenant must never be insolent to his benefactor and must never deny him any request that he might make of him in connection with the house. The tenant agreed to this stipulation, the deed of transfer was duly signed, and the original landlord sailed away.

After an absence of many years, he decided to return to his home town and went directly to his former property. He asked to see the new tenant and told him that he wanted to remain for a few weeks. He would be perfectly satisfied with one room on the second floor for that period, he said. His request was readily granted.

Four weeks passed. By this time the young landlord had become impatient and asked the old man just how much longer he intended to stay. " 'A few weeks' are over, old man," he declared insolently. "It's high time for you to be on your way."

But instead of losing his temper, the old man calmly replied, "You seem to have forgotten that this is my house. I built it, you know, and I have the right to stay in it as long as I wish."

The young man, however, remained adamant and finally the matter was taken to court. At first the judges were inclined to decide in favor of the new tenant. But then the old landlord asked them to give one more careful reading to the original deed of transfer. "I think there is one stipulation in that document that should settle this matter once and for all," he declared.

The judges did as he had asked, and in the end the decision which they handed down was in favor of the former landlord. When the young man angrily protested that this was a miscarriage of justice, the judges answered: "No; the law is on the side of this old man. If you had agreed to allow him to live in this one small room upstairs even until the end of his days, he would have acted the part of a courteous, considerate 'stranger' and you would have remained the sole proprietor of the house. He would never have questioned your rights of ownership. But instead, you have violated the one condition under which he ceded this property to you. You were insolent to him and refused to show him the consideration to which he was entitled as the original owner of the house. Therefore it is you, and not he, that must leave the premises immediately, and by order of this court all the rights of ownership and settlement now revert to him."

Much the same is true in the case of Abraham. God had assigned him as the "landlord" of the Holy Land (Gen. 12:7) and added *"and in the fourth generation they shall come back here, for the sin of the Amorite is not yet complete"* (Gen. 15:16). When Sarah died, Abraham did the same thing that the old man in our parable had done; he went to the new "landlords," the Amorites, and said to them, *"Give me a burial property among you so that I may bury my dead one from before me* (Gen. 23:4). If you agree to give me the ground, then you are upright, honest men and I am nothing more than a *stranger*, more than willing to render due compensation for whatever land you will let me have. But if you will be obstinate and attempt to send me away, you are men of insolence, *and the measure of your sin will be complete*. Then, in accordance with the promise given me by God, I will assert my legal claim to this country and act the part of the *settler*, the rightful owner of all this territory."

Thus spoke Abraham, and his statement holds true to this very day. For as the hatred of the nations among whom we dwell increases in violence, so the measure of their iniquity steadily fills. And when that measure is full, the Lord will restore to us our legal right to our Holy Land and our exile will be at an end—we hope it will be soon.

☐ Chapter Three

☐ THE SABBATH

☐ 1 — Genuine Sabbath Observance

וַיַּקְהֵל מֹשֶׁה אֶת־כָּל־עֲדַת בְּנֵי יִשְׂרָאֵל וַיֹּאמֶר אֲלֵהֶם אֵלֶּה הַדְּבָרִים אֲשֶׁר צִוָּה ה' לַעֲשֹׂת
אֹתָם. שֵׁשֶׁת יָמִים תֵּעָשֶׂה מְלָאכָה וּבַיּוֹם הַשְּׁבִיעִי יִהְיֶה לָכֶם קֹדֶשׁ שַׁבַּת שַׁבָּתוֹן לה'.
(ויקהל)

**"And Moses assembled all the congregation of the Children of
Israel and said to them, 'These are the words which the Lord has
commanded that you should do them. Six days shall work be
done, but on the seventh day there shall be to you a holy day, a
Sabbath of solemn rest to the Lord...' "** *(Exod. 35:1-2)*

In *Yalkut,* an anthology of selections from the Midrash, we are told
in this connection: *"Said the Holy One, blessed be He: 'Make
yourselves great assemblies and speak publicly before them about
the laws of the Sabbath on the Sabbath Day.' "* Moses made sure
that the people of Israel would devote their Sabbaths and Festivals

23

to the diligent study of the laws and customs ordained for these holy days.

In other words, it is obvious that God gave us our Sabbaths and Festivals in order to afford us an opportunity to make up for all those times during the week when we neglect or forget to study His Law because of the pressures of our daily work to make a living. These sacred landmarks in our calendar cycle should serve to help us attain once more that high spiritual plane at which the Children of Israel stood as they received the Law on Mount Sinai. In fact, tradition has it that the Law was given to the Jewish people not on a weekday, but on a Sabbath.

Hence the Sabbath is not simply a day of respite from work, to be marked by recreation so that we may "enjoy life." Why, if we were so to squander the holy day given us by God, then, truly, our very inmost being would have cause to tremble at the rebuke of the prophet Isaiah, who cried out in the name of the Lord: *"Your New Moons and your appointed seasons are hateful to My soul"* (Isaiah 1:14). If God is not to repudiate your Sabbaths you must keep them not in accordance with your whims and pleasures but solely in accordance with His will. The physical rest we enjoy on the seventh day is not an end in itself; it is only a means to afford us the strength to observe this day as we should — by the study of our Torah and by devoting ourselves to our homes and families, fostering the spiritual and religious edification of those nearest and dearest to our hearts.

Rabbi Yaakov had a trenchant *Moshol* on this subject.

There was once a man who suddenly had to leave his country and go to a far-off island where it was impossible to receive news through direct channels from his home and family. Whenever a stranger came to the island, the man would contact him, ask him where he had come from, and whether by any chance he had any news to tell him of his dear ones at home. After many months of futile searching, he finally found a beggar who went from door to door soliciting alms and whom it turned out he had known in his old home town. The expatriate eagerly plied the poor man with questions about his family, but the latter told him that he had no time for such things since he had to go about the island all day long in search of sufficient alms to keep body and soul together.

"Tell me, my good man," the anxious husband and father inquired, "how much money do you collect each day?"

"Three to four pieces of gold," replied the man.

"Look," our friend quickly said, "Here I'll give you four pieces of gold this very minute. In return for this I am engaging your services for one day, to stay with me all day long and to tell me all you know about my family."

The beggar agreed, and the two made an appointment to meet on the day before the mendicant would board a ship to return home. The day arrived, but hardly had he begun to talk when he suddenly nodded and fell asleep. When he finally awoke, he told our friend, his employer, that he felt much too weak to go on answering his questions and that he was in need of a solid meal before he could resume his report. His request was granted. He ate and drank to his heart's content while his host sat by him and left him undisturbed. Finally, he had eaten his fill. But instead of continuing his account of recent happenings in his home town, he said that he had eaten too much and would have to take a brief nap before he would be able to answer any more questions. Now the patience of our friend had worn thin and he said with great anger: "Look, my good man, I engaged your services for the whole day to have you tell me what you know about my family. I certainly made it worth your while; I gave you at least as many pieces of gold as you could have earned begging during all this time; maybe more. All I asked in return was that you reserve this whole day for me. Instead, you've done nothing but eat, drink, and sleep, until you've practically wasted the day which you should have devoted entirely to me. You seem to forget that, for this day, I am your master and I have a right to your attention."

We, too, would do well to keep this message in mind. All week long we are busy with our own pursuits, but on the seventh day we are expected to devote all our efforts and energies to our Heavenly Father, for it is written, *"Six days shall work be done, but on the seventh day there shall be to you a holy day, a Sabbath of solemn rest unto the Lord."* For this reason the Lord gave us a double ration of bread in the wilderness each Friday, and even today repays our extra expenses for the Sabbath, so that our minds and spirits may be free to abstain from weekday work and to devote ourselves to Him alone. And it behooves us, too, not to follow the sad example of the beggar who ate and drank his master's food and enjoyed his master's bounty but forgot that, in return, he owed his master at least one full day's attention and service.

□ 2 — THE SABBATH — A HEALING FOR THE SPIRIT

אֵלֶּה מוֹעֲדֵי ה'.   (אמור)

"These are the appointed seasons of the Lord."   *(Lev. 23:4)*

This means that these are the seasons which God has fixed for Israel, festive days which He Himself eagerly anticipates because, if observed as they should be observed, they will help His own people grow in purity and holiness. Had these Sabbaths and Festivals been intended solely for our own pleasure and enjoyment, we would have been told that "these are *your* appointed seasons." Instead, the Bible is quite explicit in stating that our Sabbaths and holidays are seasons that must be dedicated not only to ourselves but also to God.

If, therefore, God should see that we squander His holy Sabbath in fleeting pleasures and idle play, He will exclaim in anger, *"Your New Moons and your appointed seasons are hateful to My soul; they are a burden to Me; I am weary of bearing them"* (Isaiah 1:14).

In this connection, the Maggid of Dubno liked to tell his audiences a *Moshol* as follows:

There was once a rich man with several children who were all afflicted with a baffling ailment. Since money was no object, the father retained an outstanding physician who took up residence in his home and devoted all his skill and knowledge to finding a cure for the strange illness that had struck the children. Eventually, after much effort and research, the doctor was able to devise a new remedy which brought about a miraculous improvement in the condition of his little patients. Naturally, the happy father did everything in his power to show his admiration and appreciation for the skilled physician who had made his children well. Unfortunately, this happy state did not long continue. Some time later, the children were taken seriously ill once more. Again the doctor managed to find a drug to ease their suffering. The only trouble was that this time the children refused to take the medicine, and their condition grew steadily worse. The father went about downcast, and whenever he happened to see the doctor, he glared at him with ill-concealed wrath. One day the physician could no longer restrain himself and asked his employer, "Why should you be angry with me? Is it my fault that your children refuse to take the one medicine that could cure them?" And the worried father replied, "Doctor, it isn't really that I am angry with you. It is just that every time I see you I have to think how stupid and absurd all this is. If no doctor and no medicine could help my children, then I'd have to resign myself to their illness and be grateful that it is no worse. But here I have you, living with me in my very own house, and when I think of the wonderful drug you prepared which could help my children so much if only they would obey me and take it, the frustration and the exasperation I feel is almost more than I can bear."

Let Israel, too, remember this parable. We are the children of God, and the Sabbath is the healer that can restore our spirit, if only we use and keep it as directed. Instead, so many of us are like stubborn children who refuse to accept the one remedy that could heal us. We waste our Sabbath with foolish, trifling play, and therefore God is angry and He cries out that Israel's Sabbaths and holidays are only a burden and that He is utterly weary of them.

Actually, it is not the Sabbath that has angered God. But whenever God thinks of our Sabbath, He remembers our stubborn refusal to accept the healing which it could afford us. The wrath that overcomes Him when He beholds our folly is vented, first of all, on the innocent Sabbath which we have failed to keep.

□ 3—THE SABBATH AND OUR TRUST IN GOD

זָכוֹר אֶת־יוֹם הַשַּׁבָּת לְקַדְּשׁוֹ. שֵׁשֶׁת יָמִים תַּעֲבֹד וְעָשִׂיתָ כָּל־מְלַאכְתֶּךָ. וְיוֹם הַשְּׁבִיעִי
שַׁבָּת לַה׳ אֱ־לֹהֶיךָ.   (יתרו)

**"Remember the Sabbath Day to sanctify it. Six days you may
labor, and do all your work (consider all your work as done). But
the seventh day is a Sabbath to the Lord, your God..."**
(Exod. 20:8-10)

These words clearly and distinctly convey to us the sanctity, the
dignity and the basic importance of the Sabbath commandment.
Not only actual work, but even the very mention of work or weekday
activity is forbidden. Once the Sabbath has begun, all the cares of
the workday week are to depart from our minds as if they had never
existed. Thus, Sabbath observance in the true sense of the word is a
supreme expression of trust in God. We are to remember that God
Almighty is fully capable of helping every human being, as the
Psalm puts it: *"Cast your burden upon the Lord and He will sustain
you"* (Psalms 55:23). For one day in the week commit your cares to
God and let Him put things right for you.

The Maggid of Dubno explained this by one of his classic
Mesholim:

A poor man bearing a heavy bundle on his shoulders was walking
on the highway. When a rich man drove by in his carriage and offered to give him a lift, he very happily accepted the offer. Imagine
the surprise of the wealthy man, however, when he turned to glance
at his companion and saw that the traveler was still holding his
heavy load upon his shoulders. "My good man," the owner of the
carriage cried out, "What are you doing? Why don't you put your
sack down on the seat or on the floor?"

"If you please, sir," the humble traveler replied, "you have been
kind enough to me already. Your carriage has to bear the weight of
my body even now. How could I presume to burden you with my
bundle too?" At this his host laughed heartily. "Foolish man," he

said. "Why strain your back? Don't you see that it's all the same to me whether you hold your parcel on your shoulder or whether you put it down beside you? It's still in the carriage and whatever you do, the carriage has to carry its weight."

The same is true of us Jews, the Maggid said. Our Heavenly Father keeps us all the time; He bears our burdens and supplies our wants throughout the entire year. Why, then, should we fear that the little burden of providing for our livelihood on the Sabbath, when we do not work, should be too much for Him? Let Him assume the burden also of our Sabbath, and forget your workday cares when the Day of Rest arrives at the end of the six days of toil.

Only he who has perfect trust and confidence in God can truly observe and enjoy his Sabbath as a Day of Rest. He will know that he really need not work on the Sabbath, for Divine Providence will provide for his wants on the Sabbath, even as it helped him struggle through the week of weary labor.

Now we shall have a better understanding also of the Sabbath Law found in the Book of Deuteronomy: *"Observe the Sabbath Day, to keep it holy as the Lord has commanded you to do."* This means that the Sabbath must be sanctified entirely to God, scrupulously observed in all its details and never desecrated by thoughts of weekday cares. And we are told: *"And remember that you were a slave in the land of Egypt, and the Lord your God brought you out from there...therefore the Lord your God commanded you to keep the Sabbath Day"* (Deut. 5:15). This means that our own relationship to God on the Sabbath should be that of faithful servants who, having done their work well throughout the week, may now trustingly commit their cares to their Master.

□ 4 — SABBATH OBSERVANCE
    AND THE RESPECT DUE OUR PARENTS

(קדושים)   אִישׁ אִמּוֹ וְאָבִיו תִּירָאוּ וְאֶת שַׁבְּתֹתַי תִּשְׁמֹרוּ אֲנִי ה' אֱ־לֹהֵיכֶם.

"You shall fear, every man, his mother and his father, and you shall keep My Sabbath Days: I am the Lord your God."

(Lev. 19:3)

Why, we ask, should these two basic precepts, which actually constitute the Fourth and the Fifth Commandments, be put side by side here? The Talmud answers that this is to teach us that the fear of our parents must not exceed our fear of God. Should our parents ever demand of us that we act contrary to the Law of God, then we must place our duty to God before the debt we owe our parents. For example, a parent does not have the right to command his child to profane the Sabbath, for *"I am the Lord your God; and all of you (including fathers and mothers) are duty-bound to honor Me"* (Yevamoth 6).

Said the Maggid of Dubno:

Let me give you a *Moshol* so that you may understand what this means. Once upon a time there were three friends who agreed to part for one year, each of them going to another city to learn some useful trade. When the year was over, the three met to relate what they had done and what they had learned during that period. The first one reported that he had invented a *mirror* with the help of which one could see anything one wanted to see, no matter how far away. The second artisan said that he had devised a marvelous *vehicle* that could travel any distance, even thousands of miles, in one moment's time. And the third young man told his friends that he had produced a *medicine* that could cure any illness of body or mind.

The three decided to pool their skills so as to be able to use their marvelous inventions more effectively in the service of mankind. One day the inventor of the amazing mirror looked at his instrument and noted that there was great excitement in a far-off city because the daughter of the king there was seriously ill. The three immediately climbed into the miraculous vehicle which carried them to the city instantaneously. The third man then gave some of his wonder drug to the ailing princess, who promptly began to recover. Naturally there was great rejoicing in the city and the king announced that he would give his daughter in marriage to the man who had saved her life. But now the three friends began to argue with one another, for each of them felt that without his contribution the princess could never have been saved. In the end the matter was brought before the princess herself. The wise young woman thought for a moment, and then she said, "Of course, it is quite true that all of you are of equal merit, because not one of you could achieve very much without the cooperation of the other two. But if I am to make a final decision as to who it was that helped me the most, I must not look in the past but only into the future. Tell me, of what use could the magic mirror be to me in the future? Or even the marvelous carriage that travels so fast? I am afraid that I'll hardly have the opportunity to avail myself of either. But as for the miracle medicine, I will have to continue taking it for a long time to come. Therefore I think that the merits of the man who invented this wonderful drug are greater than those of his friends, and it is he who shall be my husband."

This, said the Maggid, is true also of man. There are three partners who each have an equal share in the creation of any human being: "God, the father, and the mother" (Niddah 6). If even one of these three should not contribute, there can be no life. But once the child has been born, we must think not of his past but of his future. After a certain number of years, we gradually outgrow our dependence upon our parents and must master life for ourselves. But until the day we die we could never do without the assistance of Heavenly Providence. All our needs are supplied by God, and we could not live for even one moment without His care and guidance. And therefore it is quite obvious that, if ever there should be a conflict between what God has commanded us to do and what our parents demand of us, we must decide in favor of the requirements of God: "Everyone of you shall fear his mother and his father, but you must keep My Sabbath Days. I am the Lord, the God of all of you; both you and your parents are equally duty-bound to honor Me."

□ 5 — How to Honor the Sabbath Properly

הֲלוֹא פָרֹס לָרָעֵב לַחְמֶךָ . . . וּמִבְּשָׂרְךָ לֹא תִתְעַלָּם . . . וְקָרָאתָ לַשַּׁבָּת עֹנֶג . . . אָז
תִּתְעַנַּג עַל ה' . . . וְהַאֲכַלְתִּיךָ נַחֲלַת יַעֲקֹב אָבִיךָ. (הפטרת יום כיפור)

**"Is it not to deal your bread to the hungry . . . and that you should
not hide yourself from your own flesh? . . . And call the Sabbath a
delight . . . then you will take delight in the Lord . . . and I shall
feed you with the heritage of Jacob your father . . ."**

(Isaiah 58:7-14)

In these verses the Prophet cites the basic laws of kindness side by
side with the high ideals represented by the Sabbath. This is to
teach us that the observance of the fundamental religious precepts
of humaneness are paramount in importance to that of the Sabbath. The Law of God requires us to observe both in equal measure.

Rabbi Yaakov had an ingenious *Moshol* to convey this basic
point of Jewish ideology.

A very wealthy man had two sons in a distant province. One son
was rich like his father; the other, unfortunately, was poor. When
their sister was to be married, the father sent out the following invitation to his wealthy son with the request that he inform his less
fortunate brother: "You and your brother, together with your
families, are expected at the wedding, and I will gladly reimburse
either of you for all the expenses you may incur to honor me." The
rich son was delighted. He and his wife began preparations at once,
selected the most exquisite clothes for themselves and the fanciest
possible attire for their children. "Why save money," he thought, "if
Father will pay all my expenses?" They hired a gleaming carriage to
bring them to the wedding and it was a never-to-be-forgotten sight
to see this family set out for the wedding of their sister. But in all
the excitement they had forgotten to inform their poor brother
about the invitation, and it was only at the last moment that they
remembered him. And so, on their way out of the city, they briefly
stopped at his humble abode and, since there was not much time,

the man jumped into the carriage as he was, barefooted and in his old shabby clothes.

The happy father beamed with pride when he saw the splendid carriage drive up with his son, daughter-in-law and grandchildren dressed in all their wedding finery. But who was that beggar in rags who was the last to get out of the carriage? The father's joy changed to shock and acute embarrassment when the man in tatters turned out to be none other than his second son.

After the wedding was over and the last guest had departed, the rich son presented his father with an itemized bill and asked that he reimburse him for his expenses as soon as possible. But the father replied, "I shall do no such thing. You don't seem to remember what it was I promised you. I promised that I would reimburse you for any expenses that you might incur *to honor me* at my daughter's wedding. But did you honor me? Not at all. In fact, you brought me shame. Had you wanted to honor me, you would have done what any decent human being would do; you would have seen to it that your poor brother, too, had proper clothes to wear. That would have been a show of kindness and charity worthy of your father. Don't try to convince me that your own wedding finery was put on to honor me. The money you spent on all the fancy dress and carriage was spent only to give *you* pleasure, and there is no reason why I should pay for your foolish extravagances."

Do you see, said the Maggid, our own Father in Heaven has also promised us that He will compensate us for any expenses we might have in honoring Him, particularly in the proper observance of His Sabbath. The *Gemara* (Betzah 15b) tells us that "The means of day-to-day support are fixed for each man at the beginning of each year: all, that is, except the reimbursement for expenses incurred in the observance of Sabbaths and Festivals." Whether or not we will be compensated for those expenditures depends entirely on whether or not they were incurred in a sincere effort to honor God. And how can we best show Him that honor in which He takes pleasure? Only if we allow the needy to partake in our delight in the Sabbath. If we spend lavishly on food and drink for the Sabbath but then refuse the poor a place at our table, or give no thought to providing for

their Sabbath needs, then we have spent the money not in honor of
God but simply for the satisfaction of our own greed and we cannot
very well expect Him to pay for that. But, *"He who is gracious to
the poor lends to the Lord, and He will repay his good deed for him"*
(Prov. 19:17). If we are truly distressed at the want and poverty
around us and prove our feelings by practical action, God will consider our contributions to charity as a loan to Himself which He will
repay by reimbursing us for any expenditures we might have in connection with the proper observance of His Sabbath.

This, then, is the meaning of the verses from Isaiah which were
quoted at the beginning of this chapter. If we share our bread with
the hungry we will suffer no loss thereby; on the contrary, such
humaneness on our part will enable us truly to "call the Sabbath a
delight" in honor of God. For He will then nourish us with the inheritance of Jacob, with riches beyond measure, because "I, the
Lord, have promised it."

□ 6 — THE SABBATH — DUTY AND DELIGHT

אַךְ אֶת שַׁבְּתֹתַי תִּשְׁמֹרוּ כִּי אוֹת הִיא בֵּינִי וּבֵינֵיכֶם לְדֹרֹתֵיכֶם לָדַעַת כִּי אֲנִי ה'
מְקַדִּשְׁכֶם.   (כי תשא)

**"Only keep My Sabbaths, for it is a sign between Me and you
throughout your generations, that you may know that I am the
Lord Who sanctifies you."**   *(Exod. 31:13)*

"Only keep My Sabbaths" — This statement is in need of
explanation. Why the qualifying *Ach*, *"only"*? Besides, why mention
the Sabbath alone when making it known that "I am the Lord Who
sanctifies you"? Is it not a fact that, whenever we fulfill any commandment of the Lord, we say *Asher kiddeshanu bemitzvothav*
"Who hast sanctified us by His commandments"?

Rabbi Yaakov tells us that, actually, it is not an easy thing for us nowadays to observe all the commandments of God with all our hearts without ever experiencing a sense of hardship, or feeling that we are being inconvenienced. But this was not always so. Rambam (Maimonides) points out that, originally, man was so created that the desire to perform the *Mitzvoth* of the Lord was a basic drive in his nature, like the craving for food, drink and sleep. In other words, he found the performance of *Mitzvoth* as pleasant and attractive an activity as the gratification of the other fundamental functions that are necessary if life and health are to be preserved. But when man fell victim to temptation and ate of the fruit of the Tree of Knowledge of Good and Evil, he changed, and even though the fulfillment of God's commandments is just as essential to life and well-being as food, drink and sleep, he was no longer driven by a compelling urge to comply with them. The limbs of his body, too, had changed; they were no longer as strong as before and now a special effort on our part is often needed to fulfill the *Mitzvoth* of God. However, the Torah and our Prophets tell us that there will come a time, at the End of Days, when human nature will be restored to its pristine purity and the impulse to perform God's *Mitzvoth* will once again be as strong within us as the craving for the physical essentials of living. At that time we shall once again fulfill all the Divine commandments with zest and infinite pleasure. As our Rabbis taught: "In the days of the Messiah, the Holy One, blessed be He, will make the arguments in favor of the *Mitzvoth* as sweet as honey in our mouths."

However, we must remember that the commandment to observe the Sabbath had not yet been given man at the time of his first sin in the Garden of Eden, and therefore the Sabbath remains unaffected and untainted by the consequences of our error. Hence the commandment of Sabbath observance still contains elements of earthly pleasure; we are bidden to enjoy good food and drink, and to wear festive clothing. It is a *Mitzvah* in which the basic requirements are in keeping with the satisfaction of man's physical cravings. "The Sabbath in its perfect purity," as our Sages have taught us in their memorable words, "is a reflection of the splendor of the World-to-come."

To convey the idea of the purity of the Sabbath, the Maggid would cite the following *Moshol:*

A father once bought exceptionally fine material and requested a tailor to make from it a suit, a cap, and an overcoat for his only son. Now the tailor was very busy and could not fill the whole order at once, and therefore he delivered each article separately. When the boy had received his pants, vest, jacket and cap he put them on and ran outside to show his new clothes to his playmates. But boys will be rough, and his young friends pounced on him and he fell into the mud by the side of the road, so that his clothes became dirty and were badly torn. The boy sadly returned home, only to receive a thorough scolding from his father for his carelessness till he felt thoroughly crestfallen.

A few days later, the tailor delivered the final installment of the outfit — the overcoat. The father called his son, gave him the coat and said, "My son, I am willing to forget your carelessness with the rest of your clothes. But I want you to remember to be more careful with this coat than you were with the suit. The coat is new, clean and fits you well; therefore, I beg of you, keep it in good order so that you will have at least something left of the expensive outfit I had made for you."

So, too, our Heavenly Father has spoken: "You have been careless in your pursuits and your sins have tainted all the *Mitzoth* that can be fulfilled in the six working days. The only *Mitzvah* that has retained its power and its purity is that of the Sabbath, which, when man first yielded to temptation, had not yet been received by him, for it was still in the hands of its Maker. Hence, of all the *Mitzvoth,* only the Sabbath has remained pure; that is why I beg of you, *Only keep my Sabbaths,* keep them and make them holy. For the *oneg shabbath,* the true delight in the Sabbath, is all you have left to remind you of the pleasure you should have taken in the fulfillment of the other commandments which I have given you."

And so the verse continues, *for it is a sign between Me and you.* For, of all the joys with which we have been blessed, the Sabbath is the one sign, the one pure reminder that is truly Divine. It is the sacred symbol of the delight which we will take in all the *Mitzvoth* in the World-to-Come. Hence more than any other *Mitzvah* the Sabbath, with its *Neshamah Yetherah,* its additional soul, can make us realize, beyond all doubt, *"that I am the Lord Who makes you holy."*

□ CHAPTER FOUR

□ YOM TOV THOUGHTS

□ 1 — WHAT IS SIMCHA?

שִׁבְעַת יָמִים תָּחֹג לה' אֱ־לֹהֶיךָ . . . וְהָיִיתָ אַךְ שָׂמֵחַ. (ראה)

**"Seven days you shall keep a feast unto the Lord your God...and
you shall be only joyful."***   *(Deut. 16:14-15)*

"Joyous worship" has always been the keynote of our Festivals,
particularly of Succoth, of which our Rabbis said that if our rejoicing is genuine it will endure undiminished right through the night of
the very last day of the Feast (Talmud *Succah* 48a and *Pesachim*
71).

    Actually, this type of *Simcha* or rejoicing contains two separate
components. On one hand, there is a sense of spiritual delight in our
closeness to God; on the other hand, we are explicitly commanded

---

    * This is the literal translation of what is usually rendered by "...and thou
shalt be altogether joyful."

38

to mark our Festivals with the enjoyment of more earthly pleasures such as good food and drink. There is no denying the fact that much of the pleasure and delight we associate with our Festivals is really due to the little non-spiritual luxuries in which we indulge on *Yom Tov* in accordance with the precepts of our Sages.

Rabbi Yaakov was quick to point out that both of these components are essential to the proper observance of our Festivals. A hungry body cannot experience real joy. It is only when the body has been refreshed by the physical nourishment that the spirit can feast on the nearness of God. Only then can we soar up to true happiness, to the ecstatic bliss of intimate communion with God such as is intimated in the Song of Songs: *"I am my Beloved's and my Beloved is mine"* (Song of Songs 6:3).

However, the desire and need to refresh our bodies, the better to be able to do the will of our God, should not be permitted to degenerate into base gluttony. If we were to bend all our physical and spiritual energies to the gratification of our greed we would soon be led to cast off the yoke of our Master and to go astray (Deut. 31:20)—*"and Jeshurun grew fat and kicked"* (Deut. 32:15). If physical pleasures to excess were the main object of *Yom Tov,* we would certainly all be delighted on the first *Yom Tov* night as we would sit down to our sumptuous dinner. On the second day, however, our appetites would be somewhat abated, and finally, by the time the Feast would come to an end we would have no joy left at all, for by then, after eight days of uninterrupted feasting, not even the most delicious morsels could tempt us. But if we follow the dictates of our teachings and practice moderation, realizing that we cater to our appetite only the better to be able to delight in the Lord, then the joy of our souls will steadily increase and continue until the very end of the holiday. This is what is meant by the Biblical command *"and you shall be only joyful."* The Torah tells us, "Eat and drink well on your festivals but remember that you do so only in honor of the Holiday. If you will feast your bodies in moderation, then only will the delight of your spirit steadily increase *" 'and you shall be only joyful,'* until the very last moment of the Festival."

□ 2 — "Gladness and Feasting"

עַל־כֵּן ֹהַיְּהוּדִים הַפְּרָזִים וכו' ... שִׂמְחָה וּמִשְׁתֶּה וְיוֹם טוֹב. (אסתר ט' י"ט) לְקַיֵּם
עֲלֵיהֶם ... לַעֲשׂוֹת אוֹתָם יְמֵי מִשְׁתֶּה וְשִׂמְחָה וּמִשְׁלֹחַ מָנוֹת אִישׁ לְרֵעֵהוּ וּמַתָּנוֹת
לָאֶבְיוֹנִים. (אסתר ט' כ"ב)

"Therefore the Jews of the villages, who dwell in the unwalled towns, make the fourteenth day of the month of Adar a day of gladness and feasting, and a good day, and of sending portions one to another."   *(Esther 9:19)*

Such was the ordinance in the *Megillath Esther* concerning the observance of the Feast of Purim. But, a few verses further on, where it is specified that Purim is to be a feast "for future generations," we read:

"...To enjoin them...that they should make them days of feasting and gladness, and of sending portions one to another, and gifts to the poor."   *(Esther 9:21-22)*

Is it not strange that, in the first instance, "gladness" should be mentioned first, and "feasting" only thereafter, while, only a few verses further on, "feasting" comes first and "gladness" second?

But here, too, the Maggid of Dubno was prepared with an explanation.

Try to imagine for a moment, he said, how the Jews felt on the day when King Ahasuerus rescinded the order of Haman to kill them all and, instead, condemned his wicked minister to death by hanging. The evil dictator was dead and the Jews were free once more. Do you believe that they really needed meat or wine to make them glad on that day? If they dined festively on that first Purim Day in history, it was because they were already glad, nay, overjoyed, before they ever sat down at the festive board. Therefore, in the very first ordinance pertinent to Purim, "gladness" is first, and "feasting" only comes after.

But then the *Megillah* turns to the "future generations" that would celebrate Purim in the years to come. Those generations would be in exile, troubled by persecution and oppression even as they gathered to celebrate the miraculous rescue of their ancestors in the days of Mordecai and Esther. Preoccupied by their present suffering, they feel little joy and if they are to observe Purim with good cheer they must first have a festive meal to put them in the right spirit. Therefore, the *Megillah* implies that, in those times, there would have to be "feasting" on Purim before there could be any "gladness."

And why does the phrase *"gifts to the poor"* occur only in the second instance and not at all in the first? In view of what we have just said, the reason is quite evident. On that first Purim Day, the rejoicing in our miraculous deliverance was universal; rich and poor alike were glad. But now, in these troubled times of exile, the poor must be given a cause for rejoicing by means of our charity. As long as we are in *Galuth*, in exile, there is little genuine joy for us and therefore we must resort to means of our own to stimulate at least a semblance of that rejoicing which prevailed on the first Purim Day.

□ 3 — PLEASURE — PHYSICAL OR SPIRITUAL?

וְשָׂמַחְתָּ בְּחַגֶּךָ.   (ראה)

"And rejoice in your feast."   *(Deut. 16:14)*

Thus we are commanded to rejoice in our festivals by partaking of festive food and drink and by donning holiday apparel. But are such earthly, material pleasures all there is to the observance of our sacred festivals? And if not, why does the Holy Law of God specifically command us thus to demonstrate our rejoicing? Why this great stress on material joys, on *gashmiuth*, materialism, when the principal feature of our festivals actually is *ruchniuth*, spirituality, the elevation of the soul?

This is the *Moshol* with which Rabbi Yaakov sought to reconcile this apparent paradox:

There was once a lame man who greatly resented being unable to leave his home. Now this man had a friend who, though strong and able otherwise, was quite deaf. One day it occurred to the lame man that if he and his friend would do certain things together, it would be of advantage to both of them, one making up for the physical shortcomings of the other. And so it was agreed that the deaf man would be at his lame friend's disposal all day and carry him through the town on his shoulders, while the latter would act as a guide. One day, when they were thus out together, they passed a place where there was delightful music and dancing. Now the lame man was very fond of music and he wanted to stop awhile to enjoy the lilting tunes to which he himself could not dance. But how could he make his friend, who heard not a sound, stand still for a few moments? Suddenly he knew what he had to do. In his pocket he happened to have a small bottle of gin with a tiny cup. He took out the bottle, filled the little cup and offered it to his bearer. The latter then stopped long enough to drain the cup, and before he could walk on, the lame man on his shoulders offered him a second drink, and then a third. By this time the deaf man had become somewhat tipsy and began to dance and to enjoy himself. And the lame man, too, benefited, for not only could he stop at this place and listen to the music but even dance on the shoulders of his partner, who by now had become quite nimble and lively. In this way, each of the partners was well-content.

So, too, said Rabbi Yaakov, it is with the *Neshamah,* the soul, and the *Guf,* the body. The *Neshamah yetherah,* the "additional soul," which, according to the Talmud (*Betzah* 15a and *Taanith* 27b), joins us on our Sabbath days, seeks *ruchniuth.* But the soul become truly joyous only if the body, too, cooperates; therefore it is necessary to gladden the body with good food, drink and clothing to achieve that true and proper harmony of pleasure (rejoicing) which is expected of us on our festivals.

□ 4 — "...IF THE WAY IS TOO LONG FOR YOU..."

וְכִי יִרְבֶּה מִמְּךָ הַדֶּרֶךְ כִּי לֹא תוּכַל שְׂאֵתוֹ כִּי־יִרְחַק מִמְּךָ הַמָּקוֹם אֲשֶׁר יִבְחַר ה'
אֱ־לֹהֶיךָ לָשׂוּם שְׁמוֹ שָׁם. (ראה)

On certain Holidays, such as the last day of Passover, we read from
the Torah that portion which deals with tithing, or more specifically, with *Maaser Sheni*, the "second tithe" which had to be set aside
in certain years from the yearly produce, and which was to be eaten
by the owner himself, in Jerusalem, as a "meal before God." Under
certain circumstances, specifically enumerated in this portion of the
Law, the landowner did not have to bring the tithe itself from his
home town to Jerusalem; instead, he could sell it at home, and use
the money in Jerusalem for the purchase of food which he then ate
there.

**"And if the way is too long for you, so that you are not able to
carry it (the tithes of your grain, wine and oil) because the place
is too far from you, which the Lord your God shall choose to set
His Name there, when the Lord your God shall bless you. Then
sell it for money...and go to the place...And spend the money
for whatever your soul desires...and eat it there before the Lord
your God, and rejoice, you and your household."**

(Deut. 14:24-26)

In other words, the Torah recognized two specific conditions as
hardships sufficiently severe to exempt the landowner from bringing
the actual produce of his field to the Temple. These were: 1) un-
usually distant dwelling place and 2) unusual difficulty in transpor-
tation of the food because of unusual size or quantity. But why,
then, does the Torah mention the hardship of great distance twice;
first *"and if the way is too long for you,"* and then again *"because
the place is too far from you"*?

My *Moshol* will make it easier for you to understand, said Rabbi
Yaakov of Dubno.

A diamond dealer once sent a boy to fetch him two large bags full
of diamonds. After what seemed to the dealer an inordinately long

time for this brief errand, the boy returned with two bags on his shoulder, panting and near exhaustion. The merchant turned to his assistant in alarm: "I'm afraid he's done something wrong," he whispered. "I think he took out the diamonds and filled the bags with stones instead."

"Whatever makes you think so?" asked the other man.

"Have you ever heard of anyone giving in to fatigue when he carried precious diamonds on his shoulders? He must have stolen the diamonds and what he is bringing not is nothing but a heap of rocks and stones." And behold, when the bags were opened, it turned out that the diamond dealer had been right.

Now, said the Dubnoer, most of us don't cheat our employers, and we certainly don't deliberately steal. But we all can learn something from what the merchant said to his friend. "Have you ever heard of anyone giving in to fatigue when he carried precious diamonds on his shoulders?" If we perform the commandments of God willingly and joyously, we will not mind the hardships they may entail, for we will carry our load gladly and lightly, since the *Mitzvoth* of our Torah are even more precious than diamonds. It is only if we consider every *Mitzvah* an imposition on our freedom and perform it grudgingly that we will wilt under the burden as we would under the crushing weight of stones. This is what our Torah means: Barring genuinely unusual hardship, *"if the way is too long for you"* so that you do not think you will be able to bear the burden imposed by the *Mitzvah,* then it is only *"because the place* is too far from you,"* because you have gone so far away in mind and spirit from your Heavenly Master that He cannot bless you. For one who is eager to reach a destination, no place is too far!

□ 5 — SIX FESTIVE DAYS

(אמר) אֵלֶּה הֵם מוֹעֲדֵי שֵׁשֶׁת יָמִים תֵּעָשֶׂה מְלָאכָה וּבַיּוֹם הַשְּׁבִיעִי שַׁבַּת שַׁבָּתוֹן.

---

* *Hamakom,* the Hebrew for "place," is also used to denote God as the "Omnipresent."

"The appointed festivals of the Lord which you shall proclaim to be holy convocations—these are My appointed seasons. Six days shall work be done; but on the seventh day is a Sabbath of solemn rest, a holy convocation. You shall do no manner of work; it is a Sabbath to the Lord in all your dwellings."

(Lev. 23:2-3)

The passage then continues, *"These are the appointed festivals of the Lord..."* and proceeds to discuss Passover and then the other festivals of the Jewish year. Therefore the opening paragraph, at first glance, would seem strangely incoherent. The first verse explains that the passage will deal with the Festivals of the year. Then there is a verse, seemingly without connection with the text, relating to a "Sabbath of solemn rest," and after that the Law resumes the discussion of the *Yomim Tovim.*

But the Maggid of Dubno has left us quite a plausible explanation which he himself had learned from the great Gaon of Vilna. He says: The "six days" on which "work shall be done" do not, in this case, refer to the six days of the week, but to the six major Festivals of the Jewish year. According to Biblical Law, our calendar has seven Holidays; two days of Passover (the first day and the seventh day), two days of Succoth (the first day and the eighth day), one day of Shavuoth, one day of Rosh Hashanah, and the Day of Atonement. Of these seven Festivals, the first six are those on which the Law permits certain work, relating to the preparation of food for the Festival, to be done. But the seventh of these, Yom Kippur, is a *"Sabbath of Sabbaths"* on which it is mandatory to abstain even from this type of work. In fact, a subsequent portion of our Biblical Chapter (verses 28-30) explains that, on the Day of Atonement *"you shall do no manner of work...,"* nor must you eat because whoever shall either *work or eat* on Yom Kippur will receive one of the harshest penalties: *"his soul shall be cut off from his people."*

The "seventh day," the "Sabbath of solemn rest" mentioned in Verse 3, is not the weekly Sabbath, then, but the annual Day of Atonement, which in fact is specifically classed as "a Sabbath of solemn rest" also in Verse 32 in the passage containing the law explicitly pertaining to Yom Kippur.

Of all the festivals of the Jewish year, God has given special distinction and sanctity to Yom Kippur, the "Sabbath of solemn rest" when we must abstain not only from all work but also from all food and devote ourselves entirely to Him.

In this light a passage of the Festival liturgy becomes clear. We read there: *"And Thou hast made a distinction... between the seventh day and the six days of labor... and the seventh day Thou hast sanctified above the six days on which (certain) work may be done..."*—Why the seeming repetition?

Here, too, the first phrase refers to the actual work week which has been separated from the Sabbath. The second phrase, however, refers to the six festivals on which some work is permitted, in contrast with the holy Yom Kippur day which is sanctified above them.

CHAPTER FIVE

☐ ON WOMEN AND MARRIAGE

☐ 1 — TRUE LOVE

וַיַּעֲבֹד יַעֲקֹב בְּרָחֵל שֶׁבַע שָׁנִים וַיִּהְיוּ בְעֵינָיו כְּיָמִים אֲחָדִים בְּאַהֲבָתוֹ אֹתָהּ. (ויצא)

"And Jacob served seven years for Rachel, and they seemed to him but a few days in his love for her."   *(Gen. 29:20)*

Now if Jacob was really "in love" with Rachel in the commonly used sense of the word, how is it that the seven years *"seemed to him but a few days"?* In such cases even one day's separation from the beloved seems like a year. How, then, could Jacob have managed to spend seven years apart from Rachel and yet feel as if all those years had been only days?

The answer, said Rabbi Yaakov, is that the love of our Patriarch Jacob for Rachel was of a higher quality. Most of our behavior is conditioned by one or the other of two factors: either we act in accordance with what will be best for us in the long run, or else we do whatever will bring us the most pleasure in the immediate present.

Ordinarily these two courses of action conflict with one another, for the desire for immediate pleasure, *chefetz*, is a creature of blind instinct, while *cheshek*, the wise planning for what will benefit us most in the long run, though not necessarily at this moment, depends on rational and mature thought. Thus instinctive impulse must of necessity conflict with mature reason.

Now in the case of love and marriage, the lover driven solely by *chefetz* will be impatient; he will want marriage and its comforts at this very minute and will rebel at the thought of any more "waiting." But the man who allows his actions to be guided by reason will carefully think things over, determine whether the time is ripe, and consider whether what he is about to do will bring happiness to all concerned not only now but in the long-range future as well.

In the personality of our Patriarch Jacob, *chefetz* and *cheshek,* instinct and reason, were blended in perfect harmony. True, Rachel was a lovely young woman; we are told that *"Rachel was of beautiful form and fair to look upon"* (Gen. 29:17). But was it simply physical attraction that caused Jacob to love Rachel? No! says the Torah, by telling us that he was capable of waiting for her for seven full years, *"and they seemed to him but a few days."* This is certainly not the nature of instinctive love, where a *few days* would seem like a few years; it is rather the description of a carefully planned course of action guided purely by reason.

Jacob, our father, knew that Rachel was his divinely chosen wife, and that she was also to be the mother of the future Jewish people. Together, they would set the pattern for the future generations of Israel who would continue to carry on the sacred traditions of the Patriarchs.

And now we can understand the words *"in his love for her."* If someone is very fond of sweets and delicacies, does he eat them because he loves *them*? No! It is because he loves *himself!* His greed is not prompted by reason.

The love of Jacob for his partner in life was not a selfish love of *himself* as instinctive love would be; it was *"his love for her"* as the mother of the Jewish people, as the divinely chosen partner, with whom his mission in life could be accomplished.

How fortunate are we! How wonderful is our lot! How noble our heritage!

□ 2 — THE WIFE'S MISSION

(בראשית)   לֹא־טוֹב הֱיוֹת הָאָדָם לְבַדּוֹ אֶעֱשֶׂה־לּוֹ עֵזֶר כְּנֶגְדּוֹ.

"And the Lord God said, 'It is not good that the man should be alone; I will make him a helper to oppose him.' "*   *(Gen. 2:18)*

"A helper to oppose him"—what a contradictory statement! But only so at first glance. The Rabbis in the Talmud have a ready explanation for this apparent paradox. "If the husband is worthy," they say, "the wife will be a *help* to him; if he is unworthy she must *oppose* him" (Yevamoth 63).

Rabbi Yaakov said: No human being is immune to sin or error. But, what is worse, there is hardly any one among us who does not attempt to whitewash his wrongs or even to prove them right. We would rather deceive ourselves than admit to guilt; we would rather be right in the eyes of others than truthful with ourselves, as we read in the Book of Proverbs: *"Every way of man is right in his own eyes"* (Prov. 21:2), or, as the Mishnah puts it: *"A man may examine every suspicion of plague in any other person but never in himself"* (Negaim 2:5). Metaphorically, one is quick to note the faults of others, but not his own, because he cannot be objective about himself.

Now, we can see the faults of others, even though they cannot see their own. And therefore reason must tell us that we, too, have faults even though we ourselves may not know them. Who, then, is to tell us where we have erred? The prophet Michah said: *"It has been told to you, O man, what is good..."* (Micah 6:8). This means,

---

* This is the literal translation of what is usually rendered as "...and I will make him a help-meet."

"Others have told you, O man, what is good in you and what is not." And who is that "other person" best suited to tell you your faults frankly and freely? It is the woman whom God has given you as your wife. It is her task to be a mirror to her husband, as it were, so that he may see his shortcomings through her. If he does not do so, she must stand opposite him as the loving critic, admonishing him and even scolding him if necessary to help him rid himself of his faults.

This then, is what our Torah means when it says, "I will make him a helper to oppose him": If the husband is worthy, his wife will be his helper, his better self to make his life complete; but if he is unworthy, she must serve as his implacable opponent to lead him back to the right path.

□ 3 — THE VERDICT OF THE MARKETPLACE

וַיִּקַּח הָעֶבֶד עֲשָׂרָה גְמַלִּים מִגְּמַלֵּי אֲדֹנָיו . . . וַיַּבְרֵךְ הַגְּמַלִּים מִחוּץ לָעִיר אֶל בְּאֵר
הַמָּיִם לְעֵת עֶרֶב לְעֵת צֵאת הַשֹּׁאֲבֹת.   (חיי שרה)

"And the slave (Eliezer) took ten camels, of the camels of his master (Abraham)...and went to Mesopotamia to the city of Nahor...And he made the camels kneel down outside the city by a well of water at evening time, the time when women go out to draw water."   *(Gen. 24:10-11)*

And there, at the well, Eliezer waited to find information about a maiden who would fit to be the wife of Isaac, the son of Abraham.

Why should the slave have chosen this place to learn about the maiden? Might it not have been much better instead to go straight to an inn or to the place where the elders of the town could be found, men of years and wise judgment whose opinions would certainly be more reliable than the verdict of the place where camels are fed?

Said Rabbi Yaakov: Rav Huna said, "If a man plans to marry a certain woman and he hears the dogs barking, he will prick up his ears to hear what they have to say" (Midrash).

Had Eliezer gone to the inn and spoken to the elders there, he would never have received a frank answer to his questions. Men of refinement have a certain reserve and are inclined to withhold their opinion of others. Certainly they would hesitate to speak evil of a girl even if she had indeed given cause for gossip. But not so the common people who gather at the feeding place to exchange news of the day. There, indeed, you can hear the "dogs barking," there is *lashon hara*, gossip and scandal-mongering aplenty and all you need do is mingle with the crowds and listen attentively to what they say. Eventually the talk will turn to the girl of whom you wish to know more and, when it does, you may learn many things about her that the wise old men of the city would never have told you.

□ 4 — MARRIAGES ARE MADE IN HEAVEN

אַרְבָּעִים יוֹם קֹדֶם יְצִירַת הַוָּלָד בַּת קוֹל יוֹצֵאת וְאוֹמֶרֶת בַּת פְּלוֹנִי לִפְלוֹנִי.
(סוטה ב')

"Forty days before a child is created, a voice calls forth from Heaven, saying: 'The daughter of So-and-So shall marry So-and-So.' "   *(Talmud, Sota 2)*

The above quotation implies that any independent effort on the part of human beings to arrange a marriage is of little value, for everything will come to pass as was ordained by Heaven long before either party to the marriage was born.

Why, then, need many young people avail themselves of the services of a *Shadchan*, an intermediary, to help them find their mates? The answer is simple: If the intermediary is successful in his search, it is because he has acted not as an individual, but as an instrument chosen by a Higher Authority for this purpose.

If a hammer, or a saw, or some other tool could think, it might very well come to believe that the piece of furniture upon which it had labored was of its own making, and forget the skillful artisan who plied and guided it. But this would be unjustified conceit. In the same manner, the *Shadchan,* too, is not himself a maker of marriages; he is only a tool, carrying out the plans laid down by Providence.

"Planning" and "foresight" as commonly interpreted are idle illusions, for all our plans and our endeavors can be successful only if they are in accordance with God's own plans for us.

□ 5 — TRYING TO PREVENT A MARRIAGE

וָאֹמַר אֶל אֲדֹנִי אֻלַי לֹא תֵלֵךְ הָאִשָּׁה אַחֲרָי. (חיי שרה)

"And I said to my master: Perhaps the woman will not follow me."   *(Gen. 24:39)*

Rashi comments: The word *Ulai* (meaning "perhaps") is spelled here in a shortened form, without the letter *vav,* so that actually it may be read as *Elai* (meaning "to me"). Eliezer had a daughter of marriageable age and he would have liked to see Abraham come to him and, on behalf of his son Isaac, beg him for the hand of his daughter. Therefore, when he told Laban and Bethuel of Abraham's wish, Eliezer gave them a word-for-word account of what Abraham had told him and what he had answered, and he implied, "And I thought: *Elai, to me* you will have to come to seek a wife for Isaac; the woman whom you want will certainly never follow me."

Said Rabbi Yaakov: Eliezer had agreed to act as the go-between for his master Abraham in this matter, even though he would much rather have married his own daughter to Isaac. Why, then, did he repeat to Laban and Bethuel all the questions and doubts which he had discussed with his master before leaving? And why did Rashi concentrate on this second quote, rather than on the original? The reason is obvious. Let me illustrate with a *Moshol.*

A merchant had an agent whom he sent to the fair in the big city twice a year to buy large quantities of goods. By the time the next fair opened, the goods bought at the previous fair would be all paid for and the agent would buy more merchandise, on the same terms of credit. This was the procedure the merchant followed for many years. But then, one day, he said to his agent:

"This time buy the largest quantity of stock that they can sell to you at the fair."

"But they'll never sell so much merchandise to me on credit," replied the agent. "Besides, I don't know how you will ever be able to pay for it all."

"That is none of your business," retorted the merchant impatiently. "Your only concern is to carry out my orders."

The agent saw that it was useless to reason with his employer and set out for the fair. But he still had no desire to be party to any such deal as the merchant had proposed. Thus, when he arrived at the fair, he contacted the wholesaler with whom he had always dealt and said to him:

"Look, my master has asked me to buy from you the largest possible quantity of goods I could get from you on credit. This would be a much greater purchase than any we have ever made before. I pointed out to him that I doubted very much that you would let us have so much merchandise on credit, and, besides, I am not at all sure that the financial situation of our firm would even permit us to engage in such a transaction. But my employer became quite angry and said that he did not need my advice, and that I had better carry out his orders without questioning them."

Naturally, after this story, the wholesaler wasn't very anxious to make the deal the merchant would have wanted, and refused to sell him any merchandise at all.

Eliezer followed the same course in his negotiations with the father and brother of Rebecca. He had been forced to carry out his master's orders, but he had no real desire that his mission should be successful. He therefore told them, word for word, of the conversation he had had with Abraham, hoping in this manner to be able to influence Rebecca's family so that they would have no desire to pursue the matter of Abraham's proposal any further. And therefore, he implied, Abraham would have to come *Elai, to me* and ask me to let my own daughter marry his son.

☐   6 — WOMEN AND JEWISH LAW

(קדושין א׳ ז׳)   כָּל מִצְוַת עֲשֵׂה שֶׁהַזְּמַן גְּרָמָה אֲנָשִׁים חַיָּבִים וְנָשִׁים פְּטוּרוֹת.·

"The observance of all the positive ordinances that are associated with a definite time (of day or of year) is incumbent on men, but not on women."   *(Kiddushin 34a)*

We all know that the Jewish people were given a total of 613 commandments, *Taryag Mitzvoth,* by Divine plan. We were taught, too, that it is only by observing these commandments strictly and wholeheartedly that we can have a chance of attaining perfection, morally and ethically. In fact, those who observe the lofty ideals expressed in the 613 commandments are the pillars upon which rest the survival and the future existence of all of our world.

These *Mitzvoth* may be divided into several distinct categories. There are those that are linked with a definite *location;* for example, the *Mezuzah,* which must be attached to the doorposts of our homes, thus lending them truly Jewish sanctity and dignity. Other commandments are inextricably linked with the *Holy Land,* and can be observed nowhere else, such as *Shemitah,* the Sabbatical Year, *Yovel,* the Jubilee Year, and so forth.

And then there are other commandments still which lend sanctity and inspiration to its observers at some given *time.* Among these are the wearing of *Tefillin* and *Tzitzith,* the taking up of the *Lulav* and *Ethrog* and the sojourn in the *Sukkah.*

Each generation his its own mission in life, and is assigned a definite period of time in which to fulfill it. And this time has meaning only if they who live in it heed the messages that God bids them hear at certain definite periods during their days and years on earth.

"The Holy one, blessed be He, has told Adam what each generation is to represent and what its task on earth is, each according to its abilities and special qualifications" (Sanhedrin 38b). For every age there is a generation fit to meet the needs and to solve the problems of the time. Now what are these tasks, and who is to perform them?

Said the Maggid of Dubno:

A certain merchant goes to the same fair each year at the same season. And every time he takes with him an assistant to carry his baggage and to drive his carriage. People say that he is accustomed to going to this one fair and always at this one stated time because no other place and no other time would meet his specific requirements. What the merchant does, then, is governed by a set time and a set place. But for the assistant, time and place have meaning only insofar as they concern his employer; his task is dependent directly only upon the wishes of his master. All he must remember is to follow his employer wherever the latter may wish to go in connection with his executive duties.

This, said the Maggid, quite properly illustrates the difference between the task that *man* must perform and the duties that are in the province of *woman*. Man is the crowning work of Creation and, as such, has been given a basic task to fulfill. It is the male that must bear the *Ol Torah*, "the yoke of the Law," and the *Ol Mitzvoth*, "the yoke of the Commandments of God"; it is incumbent upon him alone to fulfill certain major religious laws which this Divinely-assigned "yoke" entails. These are the obligations that are dependent upon time and place in human life even as are the changeless laws of the universe in nature.

Not so the woman. She is not considered by the Torah as an independent individual; she is, instead, the valued assistant of her husband, accompanying him through life, following him wherever he may go, and making a home for him so that he may be able to fulfill the tasks assigned him by God. Hence her life is governed not by laws of time and place, but only by the needs of the man whose cherished helpmeet she is. And therefore according to Jewish Law, she is exempt from the performance of those religious duties that are associated with a definite time.

□ 7—WOMEN AND THEIR JEWELS

וַיָּבֹאוּ כָּל־אִישׁ אֲשֶׁר נְשָׂאוֹ לִבּוֹ . . . וַיָּבֹאוּ הָאֲנָשִׁים עַל הַנָּשִׁים.   (ויקהל)

"And they came, everyone whose heart stirred him up, and everyone whose spirit moved him, and brought the Lord's offering, for the work of the tent of meeting... And they came, both men and women, as many as were willing of heart, and brought golden bracelets, earrings and signet-rings, and armlets, all jewels of gold ..."   *(Exod. 35:21-22)*

It seems that the women came forward themselves to bring their jewelry, but since, according to Jewish law, one may not seek or accept inordinately large donations from women, their husbands had to come with them to signify their consent to this action.

But why should the Biblical account should go into such detail with regard to the people who made the donations, and what ornaments they contributed for the erection of the Sanctuary in the wilderness? Is it proper at all to call so much attention to such contributions? The fact of the matter is that those who make donations *l'shem shamayim,* for no other motive but "the honor of God," have no desire that their actions should be widely publicized.

The answer is that in this case the Torah took special care to stress the enthusiasm shown for this holy task not only by the men but also by those of whom, ordinarily, little might have been expected by the way of donations—namely, the women of Israel.

But how can we really know whether these gifts were truly voluntary? Was it not the word of God that the Sanctuary should be built? Might it not be more logical to think that all this outpouring of wealth was only a demonstration of somewhat reluctant compliance with the behest of the King of kings?

First of all, the Torah explicitly tells us that both the men and the women did not attempt to stand back or limit their donations; on the contrary, they eagerly thrust themselves forward to give of their wealth (Exod. 35:22).

Then there is the abundance of gifts that poured in. The people were all so imbued with holy zeal and enthusiasm for the task at hand that a stop had to be put to the contributions: *"The people are bringing much more than enough for the service of the work"* (Exod. 36:5).

Moreover, the gifts actually represented the most treasured possessions of the donors. Had the people just sought to acquit themselves of a burdensome duty, they would have made a token contribution of money, or they might have donated some things that were of little value to them. Instead, they gave liberally of those treasures which they had acquired by dint of hard labor. They acted in accordance with the statement in the Book of Proverbs: *"Honor the Lord with your own substance, and with the first fruits of all your produce"* (Prov. 3:9). Nor did they seek to rid themselves of defective goods. In keeping with the precept in Leviticus, *"Whatever has a blemish, that you shall not bring; for it shall not be acceptable for you"* (Lev. 22:20), their gifts were perfect and without a fault or blemish. Both in the quality and in the quantity of their donations, the children of Israel far surpassed the standards set by the Torah. *"The Children of Israel brought a free-will offering to the Lord; every man and woman, whose heart moved them to bring for all the work which the Lord had commanded, by the hand of Moses, to be made"* (Exod. 35:29). Imbued by the fervent desire to demonstrate their utter surrender to the will of God, the women led the way and sacrificed their most precious possessions, their gold and jewelry. What more proof could there be that their contributions were not forced but entirely spontaneous?

And now there is another question. At an earlier date (Exod. 32:2) we read that Aaron asked the Children of Israel to give of their most valuable jewelry. At that time, however, it was not for the building of a Sanctuary, but for the casting of a golden calf to be worshipped as an idol in defiance of God's Law. He had told their menfolk: *"Break off the golden rings which are in the ears of your wives, of your sons and of your daughters and bring them to me"* (Exod. 32:2). How is it that Aaron, the leader of his people, should have asked for such generous donations for an ignoble purpose such as this?

The answer is simple: While men care little for such baubles, Aaron knew that women set much store by jewelry and ornaments. It was obvious, then, that the women would not readily permit their husbands to deprive them of their cherished treasures. It was Aaron's hope that the attempts of the men to wheedle these jewels from their wives and children would result in quarrelling and bickering, so that the work of making the idol would be delayed until his brother Moses would return from the top of Mount Sinai.

Be it said to the credit of the women in Israel that they were reluctant, then, to part with their ornaments. And their reluctance was due not to any foolish love of finery, but solely to their fierce loyalty to their God, for we learn from the Biblical account that when it came to the building of a Sanctuary to the true God, not only the men, but the women too, came in large numbers to give of their treasures.

The Midrash to *Parshath Ki Thisa* tells us, "With their earrings they sinned (when they made the golden calf) and it was with their earrings that they showed themselves willing (to further the building and decoration of the Sanctuary)." When the appeal came to make contributions for the erection of the Sanctuary, the Children of Israel sought to atone for their worship of the golden calf by offering for the Sanctuary the same type of jewelry which they had sought to use for the crime of idolatry not so long before.

No appeal had been made to the women at all, and yet they took the initiative in making sacrifices so that the Sanctuary might be built and made as beautiful as possible. This readiness to surrender their best-loved possessions for God, as opposed to their reluctance to give them away for idolatry, may well be remembered as one of the most outspoken protests against crude paganism in our history, led by the valiant women of the People of Israel.

□ 8 — UNDER FALSE PRETENSES

וַיְדַבֵּר חֲמוֹר אִתָּם לֵאמֹר שְׁכֶם בְּנִי חָשְׁקָה נַפְשׁוֹ בְּבִתְּכֶם תְּנוּ נָא אֹתָהּ לוֹ לְאִשָּׁה.
(וישלח)

**"And Chamor spoke with them, saying 'The soul of my son
Shechem delights in your daughter. I pray you, give her to him as
a wife!' "**   *(Gen. 34:8)*

This is the chapter dealing with the violation of Dinah, the
daughter of Jacob. Here we read the proposal of Chamor, the father
of Shechem, and of the terrible vengeance exacted by Dinah's
brothers for Shechem's act of misconduct. Why, we may ask, did
the brothers take such drastic action when his father declared the
young man's readiness to make amends?

But note the word which Chamor used to describe his son's feelings for Dinah. The term he employed is a form of *cheshek*. This
verb denotes a liking based on reason, on considerations more
rational than would be implied by the term *chefetz,* which in such
cases carries a definite connotation of purely physical, animal
desire.

Now let us try to understand what it was that incited the
brothers of Dinah to such fury that they took such fearful
vengeance. Shechem had violated Dinah, the daughter of Jacob.
The sons of Jacob had thought that Shechem's actions had been
motivated by simple, natural impulses and that Dinah's noble descent had had nothing to do with the crime. Now Chamor, the father
of Shechem, knowing something of the high standards of morality
held by the family of Jacob, sought to extenuate the whole affair in
order to avoid trouble. Therefore he took care to explain to the girl's
family that the motive of his son Shechem had not been *chefetz* but
cheshek. What his son had done, he said, was not a simple act of
rape. No, *chash'kah nafsho bevit'chem,* it was not his body but his
"intellect" that had wanted Dinah. His mind had told him that this
girl, the daughter of a great father and of honorable family, would
be a most suitable wife for him. He had been carried away not by

base emotions or animal lust but only by a sincere desire to become a member of the clan of Jacob.

How was it, then, that Dinah's brothers could see through the transparency of the excuse and be aroused to wild anger?

Said the Maggid of Dubno:

Let me give you a *Moshol* to show you what I mean. A man once gave a great banquet to which he invited many distinguished guests. He seated them according to their rank and station and of all the delicacies that were placed before the assembled guests, the elders, of course, had first choice before the younger folk were served. But there was one young man who refused to wait his turn and grabbed one of the choicest morsels at the very beginning. At first the host was annoyed, but then he relented, telling himself that the boy's rude behavior had been due only to thoughtlessness, and that he had just happened to pick up the first piece that had offered itself. But when another dish was passed around, and again the boy deliberately fished the biggest and most appetizing portion from the platter, the host could no longer contain himself. Turning angrily on the offender, he said, "At first I believed that you had only made a mistake out of carelessness, but this time I watched you and saw that you deliberately picked and chose among the dishes, and knowingly grabbed for yourself the best that there was. Your actions were not the result of thoughtlessness, but rather the consequence of deliberate audacity."

Shechem, the son of Chamor, was no different from the young lout in this story. Had Chamor not offered this transparent excuse for his son's misdeed, the brothers would have continued to think that Shechem's conduct had been due to natural temptations, and they would have been less harsh in their retaliation. But when Chamor compounded the offense by asserting that his son had been carried away not by the maiden's charms but only by the desire to ally himself to the house of Jacob, the forbearance of Jacob's sons was at an end. Obviously, this was not the right way for a person to seek admittance to the family of Jacob. It therefore became quite clear to the sons of Jacob that Shechem's act was perpetrated not on unrestrainable impulse, but deliberately and with evil intent.

This, they felt, was deserving of death. He had sought not to share in the honor of the house of Jacob but solely to dishonor it. Thus it was more than clear that Shechem was now proposing marriage to Dinah under false pretenses, and Simeon and Levi felt called upon to avenge the fearful wrong done to their sister and to the house of Jacob.

CHAPTER SIX

□ OF KINGS, PRIESTS AND LEVITES

□ 1 — "... A KINGDOM OF PRIESTS"

וְעַתָּה אִם שָׁמוֹעַ תִּשְׁמְעוּ בְּקֹלִי וּשְׁמַרְתֶּם אֶת בְּרִיתִי וִהְיִיתֶם לִי סְגֻלָּה מִכָּל־הָעַמִּים כִּי־
לִי כָּל־הָאָרֶץ. וְאַתֶּם תִּהְיוּ־לִי מַמְלֶכֶת כֹּהֲנִים וְגוֹי קָדוֹשׁ ... (יתרו)

**"Now, therefore, if you will truly listen to My voice, and keep My
covenant, then you shall be My own treasure from among all
peoples; for all the earth is Mine. And you shall be to Me a
kingdom of priests and a holy nation. These are the words which
you shall say to the Children of Israel..."** *(Exod. 19:5-6)*

The wording here is quite peculiar. Why not *"... then you shall be
My own treasure from among all peoples — a nation of priests and a
holy nation..."* Why the repetition in the second sentence that
literally reads *"And you, you shall be to Me..."*

The Maggid of Dubno explains this with an apt *Moshol:*

A fabulously wealthy widower decided that the time had come for

62

him to remarry. He was determined, this time, not to choose a woman from an affluent family but only a maiden from a poor home. Thus his final choice fell upon one of his own maidservants, and he said to her: "My girl, until now you have been a mere servant of mine, one among many. Now I have chosen you to become mistress over my entire household. You are a lady now, but remember, your new position entails heavy responsibilities. While you were my servant, you had to attend only to the one small task assigned you in my home. You cooked, or perhaps you were made to clean my rooms. But, as my wife, your duties are no longer confined to any one chore; you are now in charge of the whole household as its mistress, and you must see to it that all the servants do their work to my full satisfaction, for if they do not, I must hold you responsible.

"Now you may wonder, with all the added duties and work, what advantages there are to being my wife and running my home. Know, then, that I will love and honor you; that you will receive full credit for whatever is right in my home, and that I will treat you in public with all the respect and deference due to the lady who is the chatelaine of my mansion.

"Yet, remember always that this is no cause for you to become haughty and arrogant, or to take matters into your own hands and lead the life you want. On the contrary, now that everything in my home is under your command you must show even greater devotion to your duty than you did when you were nothing but a mere maidservant. Remember always that I have made you a lady only because you are much more duty-bound to abide by my wishes than any one of the maidservants whom you supervise. This is part of our marriage contract. It is only if you will thus be faithful to me that you will remain my own treasure whom I have chosen from among all women."

Thus, too, did the Lord speak to Israel. *"...And I have set you apart from the peoples that you should be Mine"* (Lev. 20:26); *"...and to raise you above all nations"* (Deut. 26:19).

The Lord has exalted the Children of Israel above the other nations. He has promised them a special kind of love, a bond of close kinship to unite God and His people. But the high privilege of such a relationship with God should not cause Israel to become unduly proud. On the contrary, it should make every Jew doubly aware of the great duties and responsibilities involved. Israel became a people by reason of having been chosen as such from all other nations by none other than God Himself. For this reason, the survival of Israel as a nation, too, is dependent on whether or not Israel abides by the standards set for it by God. Any deviation from the commandments of God must have fatal consequences for Israel's survival.

The prophet Amos says: *"You only have I known of all the families of the earth; therefore I will call you to account for all your sins"* (Amos 3:2).

By fulfilling our mission on earth, which is unreserved obedience to the will of God, we make our contribution to the survival and welfare of all mankind and help bring about a better understanding of the meaning and the purpose of this world. Therefore we Jews must remember always that we are actually bound by sheer necessity to serve God as He sees fit, even as He told us on Mount Sinai: *"And you will be to me a treasure...My* promise to you is that I will make you My cherished treasure, My chosen people among all the nations of the earth, the one closest to me. But you, *you shall be to Me a kingdom of priests and a holy nation. Your* part in the maintenance of our sacred contract will be unconditional surrender to the service of God and to the faithful observance of His commandments."

Therefore the stress is on, *"And as for* you, *you shall be to Me a kingdom of priests, and a holy nation,"* distinguished not by wealth and power but by a sacred obligation to serve your Master in Heaven who will love and cherish you in return.

□ 2 — THE JEWISH CONCEPT OF KINGSHIP

כִּי לה׳ הַמְּלוּכָה.   (תהלים כב׳ כ"ט)

הַשְׂכֵּל וְיָדֹעַ אוֹתִי כִּי אֲנִי ה׳ עֹשֶׂה חֶסֶד מִשְׁפָּט וּצְדָקָה בָּאָרֶץ. (הפטרה של ת"ב)

"For the kingdom is the Lord's..."   *(Psalms 22:29)*

"...that he understands and knows Me, that I am the Lord Who exercises mercy, justice and righteousness on earth; for in these things I delight, says the Lord."   *(Jer. 9:23)*

If the kingdom is indeed the Lord's how can a human being even aspire to a throne and the prerogatives of Jewish kingship?

In attempting to answer this question, let us remember that God often chooses men as the instruments for performing His will. Much of the good, God has carried out by a *tzaddik*, a righteous man; whilst much of the ill He must send to the world is brought about through the agency of a *rasha*, a wicked man. Hence the *tzaddik* is a servant whose mission is to do good and the *rasha* is termed a "bad" servant,* a servant whose mission is to do evil.

A strange statement indeed. But the Maggid of Dubno was quick to explain it by means of one of his classic *Mesholim:*

A man once committed a crime in a city, and the law directed the Sheriff to confiscate a valuable fur coat from the criminal's home in the hopes that this might prevent him and his family from attempting to leave town. Now it happened that the Sheriff's wife saw the beautiful coat in her home and her delight knew no bounds. Thinking that it was a gift from the City Fathers, she immediately went to the Council chambers to express her appreciation. But the Aldermen only gaped at her in surprise, and finally one of them said to her, "Come now, did you really believe that the fur coat belonged to you? When your husband took the fur coat from its owner, he did so only in execution of a Court warrant. The mere fact that he was told to expropriate it does not mean that it is rightfully either yours or his."

In the same manner, said Rabbi Yaakov, Nebuchadnezzar, the conqueror of Jerusalem, had been granted victory over the people of

---

* This term is employed in Midrash Eichah with reference to Nebuchadnezzar, the King of Babylonia, who brought about the destruction of the First Temple.

Israel only as part of God's plan to punish the Jewish people for its misdeeds, and not as a means of self-aggrandizement. Therefore he had no cause to boast of his prowess in battle, even as the prophet Jeremiah said: *"And let not the mighty man glory in his might"* (Jer. 9:22).

King Ahasuerus, too, made the mistake of "glorying in his might," as is intimated in the Book of Esther, where we read, *"...when the King Ahasuerus sat on the throne of his kingdom"* (Esther 1:2). He thought of the empire over which he reigned as *his* kingdom and not as the kingdom which had been entrusted to his keeping by God, the true King of all the Universe.

The concept of kingship held by Judaism is quite different. A Jewish king must always be conscious of Who it is to Whom he owes his position. He must conceive of his mission in such a manner *"...that he understands and knows Me, that I am the Lord Who exercises mercy, justice and righteousness on earth, for in these things I delight, says the Lord"* (Jer. 9:23). In other words, God has vested the human king with a portion of His own majesty to authorize him to act on earth in accordance with the will of the King of the Universe. A Jewish king must know at all times that his kingship is actually only a trusteeship; he is not a free agent but only the executor of God's will on earth. That is why the kings in Jewish history were called "shepherds." For even as a shepherd has no right to dispose of his flock as he pleases, but watches over it only in behalf of the employer who committed the sheep to his care, so a king, too, must not deal with his subjects in accordance with his own wishes but must rule them in conformity with the will of his Master Who put them into his keeping. A Jewish king, then, is nothing but a viceroy of God on earth.

When we see a king of one of the nations of the world, we are bidden to pronounce a blessing: "Blessed be He Who has *given* of His glory to flesh and blood." But when and if we should come to see a Jewish king, the blessing to be recited is "Blessed be He Who has *imparted* of His glory to them that fear Him," for the Jewish king is *not* considered a ruler in his own right but only God's instrument for establishing and maintaining the rule of the King of the Universe on earth. In similar vein, we are told of King Solomon: *"Then Solomon sat on the throne of the Lord"* (I Chronicles 29:23). It was not the throne of Solomon. Solomon acted only as the agent of the King of kings.

Other kings may use their position to increase their own power. In fact, they may feel it their duty to do so, for any country is in need of a warlord who is mighty and brave.

But not so the Jewish king. He needs none of the trappings of military might, for the Jewish people already has a Supreme Warlord. *"The Lord is a Master of war"* (Exod. 15:3). And the Lord fights His good fight not with the sword and the lance but with the power of His great Name. Therefore a king in Israel need concern himself little with problems of battle and military strategy, nor need he wield force in his dominion over his people. These things he must leave to God. His own authority depends solely on the dignity of his conduct and on his ability to teach men, far and wide, the fear of the Lord. *"And all the peoples of the earth shall see that the Name of the Lord is called upon you, and they shall be afraid of you"* (Deut. 28:10). This means: When the other nations will behold the King of Israel spreading the fear of the Lord far and wide, they, too, will become subject to the influence exerted by the personality of the Jewish ruler and listen to his teachings.

A Jewish king is duty-bound not only to protect his people against the onslaughts of idolatry from without, but especially to safeguard the observance of God's Law within his own country. He himself must set an example to his subjects by studying, obeying and cherishing this Law, and he must teach it to his subjects in turn. The first subject of the King in Israel must be none other than the king himself. *"...And he shall write for himself a copy of this Law...that he may learn to fear the Lord his God"* (Deut. 17:18-19):

And since he is God's messenger on earth, the agent who puts God's law into practice here below, we must act in accordance with the precept in the Book of Proverbs which tells us that the fear of God and loyalty to the king are one and the same (Prov. 24:21).

The essence of kingship according to Jewish ideology, then, is the realization of God's kingdom on earth, and the welding of the people into one united whole by no other power than that of the Law of God. If he abides by these high standards, the king in Israel can do a great deal of good for all of mankind as the messenger of God on earth.

□ 3 — OUR ROYAL FAMILY

אָמַר רַבִּי יוֹחָנָן בֶּן זַכַּאי אַשְׁרֵיכֶם יִשְׂרָאֵל בִּזְמַן שֶׁאַתֶּם עוֹשִׂין רְצוֹנוֹ שֶׁל מָקוֹם אֵין כָּל אוּמָה וְלָשׁוֹן יְכוֹלִים לִשְׁלוֹט בָּכֶם, וּבִזְמַן שֶׁאֵין אַתֶּם עוֹשִׂין רְצוֹנוֹ שֶׁל מָקוֹם הַקָּדוֹשׁ בָּרוּךְ הוּא מוֹסֵר אֶתְכֶם בְּיַד אוּמָה שְׁפֵלָה אֲפִלּוּ בְּיַד בְּהֶמְתָּן.   (כתובות ס״ו)

"Rabban Yohanan ben Zakkai said, 'Happy are you, O Israel. As long as you perform the will of God no nation or people can rule over you; and when you fail to perform the will of God you are delivered into the hands of a degraded nation, and even into the hands of their beasts.' "   *(Kethuboth 66b)*

A strange statement indeed. Why should Israel deem itself a "happy" nation if it is in danger, in case it breaks any of God's Laws, of being delivered up to the mercies of a "degraded" people?

Then there is another puzzling question. If we turn to the Second Book of Samuel, we will read that Nathan the Prophet spoke to King David as follows: "The Lord tells you that the Lord will make you a house. When your days are completed and you will sleep with your fathers, I will set up your seed after you...and I will establish the throne of his kingdom forever. I shall be to him as a father, and he will be to Me as a son; if he commits a sin, I shall chasten him with the rod of men, and with the afflictions of the children of men; but My mercy will not depart from him, as I took it from Saul, *whom I removed before you*" (II Samuel 7:11-15).

It is quite obvious from Nathan's entire statement that Saul had been deposed and David appointed king in his stead. Why, then, are we told once more at the end, in connection with Saul, 'whom I removed before you"?

Now this entire paragraph is a promise to David that he will be king over his people and his descendants after him forever. Why, then, was it found necessary to add the dire warning about the chastisement David will receive "if he commits iniquity"? After all, the context of these passages clearly indicates that this is not a chapter in which the Prophet admonishes David.

Of course, it must be remembered that these promises of God were all meant to be valid only under the condition that the Royal Family fulfills His Law. Once the members of the House of David will stray from the path of faith and lose sight of their unique task and duty, God will be compelled to chastise them most severely. Yet, He will never abandon them entirely, but will discipline them to teach them how to fulfill their destiny.

Indeed, although the Jewish people were deprived of political independence, God never replaced the Dynasty of David with another system of government strong enough to endure forever and thus permanently unseat the House of David.

Rabbi Yaakov illustrates this point with one of his clever *Mesholim:*

A wealthy merchant traveling in a country far from his home suddenly found himself without ready cash. What was he to do? It so happened that he had a few valuable articles in his possession and he gave them to an agent to sell. Among the prospective buyers there were numerous lovers of art who were eager to offer large sums for what the merchant had to sell. But the latter made sure that the art treasures would be sold not to one of these wealthy connoisseurs but only to an ordinary dealer who regarded these articles as nothing more than means of making a living. When questioned about this, the merchant replied: "I have no desire to give my treasures away forever. If I had sold these beautiful objects to the sophisticated and knowledgeable art lovers, they would have made all these things part of their private collections and I would never have been able to buy them back again. Now my need for money is only temporary, so I thought it best to sell my treasures to a plain art dealer to whom the articles are of value only so long as he can make a tidy sum by selling them again. Once I can secure more money from home, I will offer him a larger sum than he paid me originally, and he will be more than glad to sell my things back to me."

This one Moshol, said Rabbi Yaakov, should be adequate to explain all the questions we have raised.

Samuel had said to Saul: *"The Lord has torn the kingdom of Israel from you today, and has given it to a neighbor of yours who is better than you. And also the glory of Israel will not lie nor repent..."* (I Samuel 15:28-29). It was too late for Saul to repent of his grave error, and so the Lord had no desire to "take Saul back" after he had been chastised. David is *"better than you,"* he is better than Saul and because of his near perfection his kingship will endure forever.

David was an outstanding Jewish personality. Therefore, God hastened to assure him that, even if some of his descendants should stray from the right path and God would therefore have to remove them from their kingly office, their position would still not be as hopeless as that of Saul *"whom I, the Lord, removed before you, David."* If members of the House of David should go astray, they would be replaced, but only temporarily, and their replacements would not be men of higher rank and station than the Davidian dynasty, but only lesser rulers who could be removed quickly once the Davidians had properly repented of their transgressions. Even as the merchant in our story saw to it that he would not have to part with his treasures forever, so the Lord, too, seeking to make sure that the House of David would not be lost to Him, left a door open so that the repentant Jewish people could return to Him and thus to their rightful place.

Therefore Rabban Yohanan ben Zakkai was quite right when he called Israel a "happy nation." Other nations and other dynasties that stray from the commandments of the Lord are "removed" forever and replaced by rulers better than the ones preceding. But not so Israel and the House of David. Israel has been quite literally assured of survival, come what may. As long as Israel and the House of David keep faith with their God, they are invincible. And even if they should sin, they are delivered not to the mercies of a superior power, but only to "the hands of a degraded nation" who, being so much inferior to the House of David, could hardly be expected to remain in power forever. Therefore, once the House of David repents of its misdeeds, the "degraded nation" will have to step aside and return Israel and the House of David to their former glory.

□ 4 — THE PRIVILEGES OF PRIESTHOOD

וְכָל־תְּרוּמָה לְכָל־קָדְשֵׁי בְנֵי־יִשְׂרָאֵל אֲשֶׁר־יַקְרִיבוּ לַכֹּהֵן לוֹ יִהְיֶה. וְאִישׁ אֶת קֳדָשָׁיו
לוֹ יִהְיוּ אִישׁ אֲשֶׁר־יִתֵּן לַכֹּהֵן לוֹ יִהְיֶה. (נשא)

"And every heave-offering of all the holy things of the Children of Israel which they present the priest shall be his. And every man's hallowed things shall be his—whatever any man gives to the priest shall be his." *(Num. 5:9-10)*

This Biblical ordinance is immediately followed by *Parshath Sotah*, the laws pertinent to the determination of the guilt of a wife suspected of adultery. Asked the Talmud: Why should legislation dealing with marital infidelity follow so closely upon the stipulations relative to *Terumoth*, heave offerings to the priests, and *Maasroth*, tithes which had to be given to the Levites? What association is there between these two distinctly separate groups of legislation? And the Talmud answers: This is to teach you that if you should willfully withhold the gifts rightly due the priests, your punishment will be that you will be forced to make use of their services in a most unpleasant matter; you will have to go to the priest to have him determine by due process of law, as specified, whether or not your wife has been guilty of adultery. This involved a most humiliating ceremony (Num. 5:11-28).

Now we must ask a question in our turn. Why, of all things, should failure to render the priest his rightful due be punishable in this particular manner? Could there not be other penalties for such willful negligence?

This is the *Moshol* of Rabbi Yaakov: A brilliant scholar, who was an expert in all fields of knowledge, lost his fortune and had to travel about to make a living. Everywhere he went he was received with respect and admiration and people would listen to his lectures with great interest. Once he came to a village where the townfolk were obviously quite simple. When they asked him what his profession was he told them that he was a country doctor who could heal all types of wounds and ailments. A friend of his, hearing this, asked why he had been so modest in stating his capabilities. Said the learned doctor, "I may be a scholar, but these people have neither culture nor learning. If I would have told them of all my scholastic achievements they would never have understood. Erudite speeches will do no good here. So I had to find some way that they would understand my work and what I meant to have them know. And so I spoke to them in terms which even they could easily understand."

Quite the same is true of the priest. The *Kohen* is not an ordinary person; he is an exceptional man and therefore favored with many privileges. It is he who officiates before the Lord in behalf of his people, and the Prophet Malachi said: *"For the priest's lips should keep knowledge, and they should seek the Law at his mouth, for he is a messenger of the Lord of Hosts"* (Malachi 2:7). It is he who has to offer up Israel's sacrifices and by this means entreat the blessings of Heaven for the Jewish people. It is within his function, too, to purify individuals and to bring offerings. Among his many other duties there is also that of administering the bitter waters to a *Sotah*, a suspected faithless wife, to determine whether or not she has truly been guilty of adultery, as suspected.

The wise and the educated understand the high position of the *Kohen* and honor him accordingly. And the Torah rightly assumes that anyone withholding from the priest the dues to which he is entitled must be a boor who is incapable of understanding the importance and holiness of the office of priesthood. Such a man must be told what God means to have him know in blunt and straightforward language which even he would readily understand. Therefore he will be put into the sad position of being compelled to use one of the priest's services for a matter that is understood all too well even by the most uneducated — a case of suspicion of adultery involving his own wife. It is in this unfortunate manner that he will first come to learn more about the great responsibilities entailed in priesthood and thus come to respect him who holds this sacred office.

□ 5 — THE PRIESTLY BLESSING

דַּבֵּר אֶל אַהֲרֹן וְאֶל בָּנָיו לֵאמֹר כֹּה תְבָרְכוּ אֶת בְּנֵי־יִשְׂרָאֵל אָמוֹר לָהֶם. יְבָרֶכְךָ ה'
וְיִשְׁמְרֶךָ. יָאֵר ה' פָּנָיו אֵלֶיךָ וִיחֻנֶּךָּ. יִשָּׂא ה' פָּנָיו אֵלֶיךָ וְיָשֵׂם לְךָ שָׁלוֹם. (נשא)

"Speak to Aaron and to his sons, saying: 'In this manner shall you bless the Children of Israel: You shall say to them, May the Lord bless you and keep you; may the Lord cause His face to shine upon you, and be gracious to you; may the Lord lift up His countenance toward you, and grant you peace.' "

(Num. 6:22-27)

Why, asks the Maggid of Dubno, does the Torah add *"You shall say to them"?* Is this repetition necessary?

There is another question, too. When the Priests pronounce their Priestly Blessing at the synagogue they do not face toward the Holy Ark, as is done at all other services. Instead, they face the congregation. Is this proper? Does not the *Birchath Kohanim,* the priestly blessing, symbolize a prayer to God to bless His people, and should not those who pray to Him face the Ark rather than turn away from it?

And the Maggid of Dubno proceeds to answer the question which he himself has posed. Once again he cites one of his famous *Mesholim:*

A father, angered at his son's bad conduct, and unable to reason with the boy, finally and with great reluctance sent him away from home and told him that he could count on no support from his family. The boy found no means of earning a livelihood and went about scantily clad and hungry. Very soon his clothes were nothing but tatters, and the boy went to one of his father's neighbors and asked him to go to his father and get at least some clothing for him, if nothing else. The neighbor promptly contacted the boy's father and said to him, "Have pity on your son; winter's here and he doesn't even have decent clothes to keep him warm." Much to the neighbor's surprise, the father nodded assent and said, "That's just what I wanted to discuss with you. I was going to ask you how I could get some clothes to my son." Seeing his neighbor's amazement, he added, "Do you really think that you must come to me and ask me to provide for my own son? He's my own flesh and blood and his happiness is as dear to me as my own. It was only because of his conduct that I had to act as if I no longer cared for him. Now if you should really want to help him, don't talk to me but go to him and appeal to his conscience, and let him know that if only he will mend his ways I will take him back and supply all his needs as any loving father would do."

The same, said the Maggid, is applicable also to our own relationship with our Father in Heaven. Is there really any need for a *Kohen* to turn to God and, as an intermediary, ask Him to bless and favor the people of Israel? Is it not God's desire to show us His lovingkindness at all times, simply *"because he delights in loving-kindness"* (Micah 7:18)? It is only because of our sins that we cannot enjoy the favor of His mercy at all times.

Now we can understand why the Priests turn towards the congregation and the meaning of the appeal implied by *"You shall say to them."* The Lord said to Aaron and his sons: In this manner shall you bless the Children of Israel: You shall turn, not to Me, but to *them*, and tell them: "May the Lord bless you"...in other words, may you so behave that you will be worthy of receiving from God, your Father in Heaven, all the gifts and blessings He has provided for you."

□ 6 — "MAY THE LORD BLESS YOU..."

כֹּה תְבָרֲכוּ אֶת בְּנֵי יִשְׂרָאֵל.   (נשא)

"In this manner shall you bless the Children of Israel..."

(Num. 6:23)

Asks the Talmud (Sotah 38a): "What does the Torah mean by specifying *'In this manner'?"* And the answer is: "It means that the Priests must employ in their blessing only those words specified in the Torah, without any modification."

But why should the Torah attach such importance to letter and form?

At the end of Tractate Uktzin we read: *"The Holy One, blessed be He, found no vessel that could hold Israel's blessing, except Peace, for it is written* (Psalms 29:11) *'The Lord will give strength to His people; the Lord will bless His people with peace' "* (Uktzin III: 12).

"A vessel that could hold Israel's blessing...!" Why did not our Sages call peace "a vessel that could pour forth abundant blessings to Israel"? Would that not have been more appropriate? But here again the Maggid of Dubno explains the unusual turn of phrase by a simple *Moshol.*

Take a washtub made of planks of wood held together by an iron hoop. If the boards remain intact and the hoop holds them together so that there is no crack or space between the boards, any liquid poured into the tub will remain there and none will be lost. But let there be even the smallest crack between the boards, and the water will leak out until, eventually, there will be none left in the tub.

Now what the hoop does for the tub, peace does for the people of Israel. God found no better means to weld the Jews together than *Shalom,* peace. Even as the crossbar of the Sanctuary, the *b'riach hatichon,* held together all the boards of the Holy Tabernacle, so mutual love, peace and friendship forge a firm bond that binds the people of Israel into one united whole, and it is only in this state of peace and ideal harmony that Israel can retain the blessings of sanctity and independence with which it has been endowed.

That is why God commanded Aaron and his sons: *"in this manner shall you bless them.* You may ask why I insist that you abide by the text 'The Lord bless *you* and keep *you...'** when, actually, you are pronouncing this blessing not over one person, but over a multitude of people. Know, then, that My insistence on this fine point is not unfounded. When you stand before My people to bless them, you must remind them that, in order to survive and prosper, Israel must view itself not as a mass of individuals, but as one perfect and united whole, welded together by bonds of peace and friendship. Therefore repeat it without deviation, as I have taught you: 'The Lord bless you and keep you...' "

□ 7 — THE PRIESTHOOD OF MOSES AND AARON

כָּל אַרְבָּעִים שָׁנָה שֶׁהָיוּ יִשְׂרָאֵל בַּמִּדְבָּר לֹא נִמְנַע מֹשֶׁה מִלְשַׁמֵּשׁ בִּכְהוּנָה גְדוֹלָה.
(ויקרא רבה י"א)

"...Throughout the forty years that Israel was in the wilderness, Moses did not refrain from performing the functions of the High Priest."   *(Midrash)*

The above quote is based on a verse in the Book of Psalms, where we are explicitly told that Moses as well as Aaron was among the Priests of God (Psalms 99:6).

But it seems that this verse from the Psalms was not sufficient evidence for Rabbi Berachya, who, in the name of Rabbi Shimon, in the above *Midrash,* derives the same fact from a passage in the Book of Chronicles which reads: "The sons of Amram: Aaron and Moses. And Aaron was separated, that he might be sanctified as most holy, he and his sons forever, to offer before the Lord, to minister to Him, and to bless in His Name forever. But as for Moses, *the man of God,* his sons are named among the tribe of Levi" (I Chronicles 23:13-14).

---

* 'you' is in the singular in the Hebrew.

Why, questioned the Maggid of Dubno, did Rabbi Berachya find it necessary to seek evidence of Moses's priesthood from a Biblical verse which, unlike the explicit statement in the Psalms, only alludes indirectly to the fact that Moses, like his brother Aaron, had exercised priestly functions?

Tradition tells us that, when God told Moses *"And bring near to you Aaron your brother and his sons ... that they may minister to Me in the office of priesthood ..."* (Exod. 28:1), Moses was grieved because this meant that he, Moses, was not to be the High Priest of his people. It seems that the official appointment of Aaron rather than Moses to the High Priesthood was meant as a punishment to Moses for having dallied for seven days at the burning bush, saying *"send anyone else but me"* before finally agreeing to do God's bidding and go out to set his people free. Later, when, during the Seven Days of Dedication which marked the consecration of the Sanctuary in the wilderness, Moses still performed some of the functions assigned to the High Priest, God told him, "This high office will no longer be yours but will go to your brother Aaron." And tradition has it that Moses was very sad indeed when he was thus reprimanded.

But all of this seems quite strange, for we are also told that, in fact, Moses did perform the functions of the High Priest throughout the forty years that Israel spent in the wilderness. We are told, too, that Moses acted in this official capacity garbed in plain white clothes. Now why did he not wear the special prescribed garments in keeping with the honor due the Sanctuary?

Our sages say that "The majesty of kingship on earth is similar to that of (God in) Heaven" (*Berachoth* 58a), and so the Maggid of Dubno felt justified in citing a *Moshol* in which he employed the honor due a human king as an analogy for the homage due God. He said: A king on earth has many ministers of state and many officials, and each one of them is responsible for the administration of another department of government. Each minister has his own functions, and each of them has special robes which he must wear when he comes before the king at certain appointed times. But most kings have one minister who is closer to them than the rest of the cabinet, a man who enjoys the king's full confidence, who need not wear any special costume when he comes before the king and who may, in fact, come to him at any time, without previous appointment. In the official hierarchy this minister is not assigned to any specific office, but he is nevertheless higher in rank than all his colleagues.

This analogy, said the Maggid, may be applied to the relationship of Aaron and Moses to the King of the Universe. Aaron was a High Priest, but still he could come before God only at appointed times. We read in the Book of Leviticus that *"he* (Aaron) *will come not at all times into the holy place"* (Lev. 16:2). Moreover, he could come before God only in special priestly attire, as it is written *"With this shall Aaron come into the holy place"* (Lev. 16:3-4). When in the Sanctuary, he had to wear the holy vestments which were the official insignia of the High Priest (see Exod. 28:4 ff).

The position of Moses, however, was different. Of him we read *"My servant Moses is not so; he is trusted in all My House"* (Num. 12:7), and the Midrash says that he was allowed to enter the Sanctuary at any time he so desired. In fact, from the very statement that Aaron could not enter there at any time, it was deduced that the opposite was true in the case of his brother Moses. Moreover, when Moses came into the Sanctuary (and he was permitted to go there even though he was not the official High Priest of his people at all) he did not have to don any special vestments. He was considered so close to God that he could come before Him even in plain white garments.

This is why the Midrash tells us: Officially, Aaron held the exalted office of High Priest. Yet, Moses did not refrain from performing High Priestly duties when he felt this to be necessary. True, God had told him that he could never be the High Priest, but, since he was an intimate of God, he could take a liberty which even the High Priest was not permitted; he, Moses, could enter the Sanctuary at any time and even in simple dress, without incurring the extreme penalty from Heaven.

But then it seems somewhat difficult to reconcile all this with the statement that Moses was sad when Aaron, and not he, was appointed High Priest. He may not have been the High Priest, but was it not obvious that his position in the hierarchy of God was far superior even to that of Aaron?

And this is the reason why Rabbi Berachya cited the passage from the First Book of Chronicles. Aaron was to be the High Priest of Israel for all future generations, as it is written *"And it shall be to him and to his descendants after him, the covenant of an everlasting priesthood"* (Num. 25:13). But this was not to apply to Moses. Aaron was the official High Priest; therefore his descendants after him would be priests. Moses may have been the intimate of God, but while he was High Priest in practice, he was not so in rank, and therefore, *"as for Moses, the man of God, his sons are named among the tribe of Levi."* The sons of Moses held only the rank of Levites.

Thus the special character of the Priesthood of Moses is an important point which could not have been inferred merely from the verse in the Book of Psalms.

□ 8—THE POSITION OF THE LEVITES—STRANGE BUT UNIQUE

לֹא יִהְיֶה לַכֹּהֲנִים הַלְוִיִּם כָּל־שֵׁבֶט לֵוִי חֵלֶק וְנַחֲלָה עִם יִשְׂרָאֵל . . . ה' הוּא נַחֲלָתוֹ. (שופטים)

"The Priests, the Levites, all the tribe of Levi, shall have no portion nor inheritance with Israel...the Lord is their inheritance..." *(Deut. 18:1-2)*

If we study the provisions made by the Torah for the livelihood of the Priests and the Levites, we have good cause to wonder at what, at first glance, seems bizarre. Aaron and his sons held priestly office and received certain material privileges as a result. The Levites, too, occupied a position of distinction among the Jewish people and had certain important functions to fulfill as representatives of the King of kings among His people. They, too, had no land or property of their own, and were dependent for their sustenance on the tithes given to them by the people.

Comes the question: Every acre of land throughout the world is God's own; why, then, could He not have assigned some land for the specific use of the Levites? Why did the Levites have to live on handouts like the poorest of the poor?

Said the Maggid of Dubno: An obvious reason for this would be that the minds of the Levites had to be kept clear for their spiritual calling and that, therefore, they were to be freed of the necessity of earning their livelihood by tilling their own soil. Therefore the rest of the people of Israel were duty-bound to make provision for them by giving them certain portions of their yearly produce.

But if this would be the sole reason, then it would seem almost unfair that the whole people of Israel should be burdened with the support of a favored class. It was certainly within God's power to employ other means for the support of the Levites. For example, He could have supplied them with food by supernatural means, like the fall of manna in the wilderness. In view of all this, the above reason cannot be, and is not, the answer to our quest for more specific information.

Let us, therefore, study the other explanation which, though at first glance it seems less plausible than the one given above, is nevertheless the true explanation for the manner in which God provided for the tribe of Levi.

The Prophet Malachi said: *"Bring the whole tithe into the storehouse, that there may be food in My House, and try Me now herewith, says the Lord of Hosts, if I will not open for you the windows of heaven, and pour out a blessing for you so that there shall be more than (mere) sufficiency"* (Malachi 3:10).

In other words, God says: "If you will fulfill your obligations. O Israel, and bring all your tithes into the storehouse of the *Beth Hamikdash*, the Sanctuary, for the use of the Priests and Levites, you may put Me to the test and see whether I will not bestow upon you the greatest of blessings, more than you ever could have expected. Or as our sages add—*"until your lips grow tired from saying: 'It is enough' "* (Taanith 9a).

But why should God bestow upon us such great blessings so generously? Are we indeed deserving of them?

You must understand, said the Maggid of Dubno, that God's ways of rendering help are quite different from those of man. Man is subject to the iron-clad rule of time in all that he does. If he fails to perform his duty at the appointed time, it may be too late forever. In cases of illness, for example, even a few minutes' delay in consulting a doctor may mean death or permanent invalidism. And medicine, too, cannot work immediately. It takes time before it can take effect and heal the patient. But the help given by God is not tied to such obviously natural factors. We cannot judge it by our own standards of what is appropriate or logical. He works in sudden, unexpected ways above the laws of nature. When our mother Sarah was told at the age of ninety that she would give birth to a son, she thought that this was well-nigh impossible; but God wrought a miraculous change in her so that, in but an instant's time, her body was that of a young woman of thirty, and He chided her for her doubts, saying, *"Is there anything too wonderful for the Lord (to perform)?"* (Gen. 18:14). "Do you think, O Sarah, that I, the Lord, am subject to the rule of time even as you are to the laws of nature?" We on earth are inclined to judge probability on the basis of the laws of nature, but not so the Lord, Who originally ordained these laws and can cancel them by a *Nes,* a supernatural act, at any time and for any purpose He sees fit.

Thus, for example, every *Rosh Hashanah* God Himself determines what the fortunes of each man on earth will be and how much he will earn during the year to come. But man, doubting the supernatural power of God, will never cease to seek new methods to safeguard his livelihood. He overestimates his actual needs and is constantly at work trying to increase his earnings. He attempts to override the laws of life set down by God Himself. But, in the end, he will find that it is impossible for him to engage in a race with the Holy One, blessed be He. Man is subject to the law of inertia; he cannot bring the mounting avalanche of his desires to a standstill. Only God can stop and recommence His Divine work whenever He sees fit.

But such is human nature, and the average man is engulfed by it. The Kohanites and the Levites, however, are a special class in themselves, and their concept of life and living must be on a higher level than that of other men and women. By their own conduct and by their way of life they must show their people that their own aspirations are not subject to standards generally prevalent among ordinary people. They must always hold before all of Israel a higher spiritual God-centered standard, in keeping with Him Who appointed the sons of the tribe of Levi to be His. *"The Priests, the Levites, all the tribe of Levi, shall have no portion nor inheritance with Israel; they shall eat the fire-offering of the Lord and His inheritance. And they shall have no inheritance among their brothers; the Lord is their inheritance, as He has said to them"* (Deut. 18:1-2). In other words, their distinction of serving God was to be their greatest and their most precious possession.

The strange position of the Levites in Israel will be better understood by a *Moshol.*

A wealthy merchant had to make a lengthy voyage, and took with him all his ten sons. In order to avoid additional, unnecessary expense, he left all his servants at home, planning to have all the necessary housekeeping chores done by his sons. The trouble was, however, that the merchant and nine of his ten sons did not know how to cook. Only one of the sons had been trained in the household arts, but the boy was inclined to be selfish and not to have too much concern for the welfare of his family. The father feared that the boy, if forced to cook, would want to make do with the least amount of work possible, and would therefore cook only enough food for himself. Therefore the father made sure that all the utensils taken along would be large. Thus the spoiled young man would actually be forced to prepare large quantities of food. For if he would attempt to use such huge pots and pans for cooking quantities just sufficient for his own personal needs, the food would no more than cover the bottoms of the utensils and it would quickly burn. Thus the boy would be compelled to fill the vessels with enough meat, soup and vegetables to provide for the entire family.

The Levites, said Rabbi Yaakov, may be compared to the young man who was the only one in the family who knew how to cook. The Levites, too, have an ability that the rest of Israel does not possess, namely, by virtue of their nearness to God, to bring down the blessings of heaven for their people. Now if each Levite would have a field of his own, he might yield to the temptation to be selfish and would give attention to his own produce only. Therefore, in order to make sure that they would not pray for themselves only, the Levites, as servants of the Lord, were to have "no portion and no inheritance in Israel." All the Israelites are in need of God's blessing for their crops on which their very lives depend, and it is the task of the Levites, who are so near to God, to pray to Heaven for all Israel, so that blessings may come from Heaven in large measure. Thus the welfare of the Levites is dependent on the prosperity of their brothers.

And as for the rest of Israel, they, too, will not find their obligation to the Levites an intolerable burden. If a man can produce just barely enough for his own existence, he has no time to occupy himself with things of the spirit. But by virtue of his obligation to provide for the Priests and the Levites he will be blessed in his turn, and thus he will be able to provide for himself more than amply and be enabled to aspire to greater things.

This is what the Prophet Malachi meant by the statement we have read earlier in this chapter. He said. "If you, O Israelites, will be willing to deliver up a portion of your produce to the *Kohanim* and Levites, the bearers of your civilization, God will give you in return much more than you would need for your own requirements. This abundance in your fields, in turn, will assure the prosperity also of the Levites, and so all of Israel will live together in peace and plenty."

After the rebellion of Korah had been quelled, God sought to give another proof that He Himself, and none other, had chosen Aaron and the tribe of Levi to minister to Him. The staffs of all the tribes were laid down in the Tabernacle (Num. 17). And it came to pass on the next morning that the rod of Aaron had blossomed forth and bore fruit. Thus it became evident to all of Israel that it was the Lord Who had singled out the tribe of Levi (Num. 17:23). From this we learn that the blessing of growth and abundance is dependent upon the tribe of Levi. Therefore, in making the prescribed contribution to the upkeep of the Levites, Israel does no more than insure its own prosperity.

□ CHAPTER SEVEN

□ BIBLICAL PERSONALITIES

□ 1 — ADAM

אָמַר הַקָּדוֹשׁ בָּרוּךְ הוּא : אָדָם הָרִאשׁוֹן הִכְנַסְתִּי אוֹתוֹ לְגַן עֵדֶן וְצִוִּיתִיו וְעָבַר עַל צִוּוּיִי וְדַנְתִּי אוֹתוֹ בְּגֵרוּשִׁין וּבְשִׁילוּחִין וְקוֹנַנְתִּי עָלָיו אֵיכָה שֶׁנֶּאֱמַר וַיֹּאמֶר לוֹ אַיֶּכָּה — אֵיכָה כְּתִיב. (מדרש איכה)

"Said the Holy One, blessed be He; 'I introduced the first man into the Garden of Eden and I gave him a command to follow, but he transgressed it. I therefore banished him and sent him away, and I mourned over his sin, crying out 'Eichah,' as it is written in Gen. 3:9, 'and He said to him: Ayekkah.' " *(Midrash Eichah)*

The vocalization commonly given to the letters *Aleph, Yud, Kaf, Heh,* is such that it is read *Ayekkah,* "Where are you?" But, in fact, the same letters, with different vowels, may spell also the word "*Eichah,*" meaning "alas," with which the Book of Lamentations opens. This is the semantic basis for the passage we have quoted above from the *Midrash Rabbah.* The Maggid of Dubno, with an ingenious *Moshol,* pointed out that the Biblical account of Adam's expulsion from the Garden of Eden may well have included both of the above two meanings. He tells us:

A man who owned several inns and lodging houses in a small town decided to entrust all these concerns to the management of his only son. "These inns are all flourishing concerns," he told his son, "and now they will all be yours. But there is one condition which I must attach to this gift: never entrust any partner or associate with the operation of the inns. You must remain the sole person in charge." In this fashion the father sought to protect his young and inexperienced son from being cheated by the unscrupulous characters of whom there were many in the province.

Unfortunately, the son did not heed his father's advice, and when a neighbor offered to assist him he hired him. In fact, he even gave the neighbor a room in one of the inns. When the father heard of this he wrote the young man a terse note of only one word: *Ayekkah?* meaning "Where are you? What is your place in the management of the inns and what is the position of the neighbor you have taken in?"

The father's fears were well justified, for the neighbor soon maneuvered himself into the position of sole manager. Eventually he made himself a partner of the concern, and in the end the son of the original owner found himself turned out into the street without a penny, even as it is written in Deut. 28:43, "The stranger that is among you will go up above you very high, and you will come down very low."

When the father heard of his son's sad fate, he wrote him another note, again of one word only: *Eichah* — implying, "Alas, what has become of you! Oh, if only you had followed your father's advice!"

This *Moshol* may well be applied to Adam, the first foolish son in world history. His Father Who had created him had put him in charge over all the earth, providing that he would not let himself be swayed by evil. However, Adam associated himself with the Adversary. And God called out to him in the Bible: *"Ayekkah?* Where are you? You have given the upper hand to the Evil Impulse. Where are you now?"

But Adam refused to heed the call of God and continued his relationship with the Adversary. And the result was that the Lord had to cry out to him: *"Eichah,* alas, what has become of you! You have scorned God's command and have let your enemy overpower you," and God drove him out from the Garden of Eden.

And this is the meaning of the Midrash—I therefore banished him and sent him away and I mourned over his sin, crying out *'Eichah!'*—alas. But I had to do this only because I was forced to warn him earlier saying *'Ayekkah'*—where is your place?

□ 2—NOAH

אֵלֶּה תּוֹלְדֹת נֹחַ אִישׁ צַדִּיק תָּמִים הָיָה בְּדֹרֹתָיו אֶת הָאֱ־לֹהִים הִתְהַלֶּךְ־נֹחַ.   (נח)

"These are the developments of Noah. Noah was a righteous man and perfect in his generations; Noah walked with God."

(Gen. 6:9)

The Biblical account tells us how conspicuous Noah was among his contemporaries by virtue of his goodness as opposed to the depravity of all the men around him. Therefore, when God finally decided to blot out man from the face of the earth, Noah and his family were saved from the raging flood in which all other men were swept away. And when the waters had receded, the Lord gave a special blessing to Noah (Gen. 9:1, 2, 7).

The Rabbis teach us that it was God's desire to give His particular blessing to the very first act that Noah might perform after he would leave the Ark and step on dry land for the first time since the Flood. Unfortunately, the first thing that Noah did on landing was nothing so holy or exalted as might have been expected; we are told that he degraded himself by planting a vineyard (Gen. 9:20), thus giving man, for the first time, that drink which, though it gladdens the heart, is also so often the cause of much sin and shame.

Rabbi Chisda says that the grapes began to grow on the vines on the very day on which Noah had planted the vineyard, so that he even drank of the wine on the very same day and disgraced himself (Sanhedrin 70).

Thus Noah was guilty not only of drunkenness, but of a sin even greater than that, as our Maggid explains in a very interesting *Moshol:*

A man on a journey happened to meet a great and saintly Rabbi. And he asked the sage, "O Master, give me a blessing," for he was certain that whatever the Rabbi might say would come true. Said the Rabbi: "May it be the will of God that the first thing you do when you come home will grow and endure."

The man immediately began to consider what that first act after his homecoming should be. He decided that it should be the piece-by-piece counting and weighing of all his money, for he thought that the Rabbi's blessing thus employed would make him rich and prosperous.

As soon as he entered his home, he asked his wife to give him the bags in which he kept his money. Quite bewildered by her husband's urgency, the poor woman could not immediately locate the bags, and when he continued to hurry her, she became suspicious and bluntly refused to give him the money. A very unpleasant scene followed. Husband and wife hurled invectives at one another and quarrelled all day long, so that they forgot all about counting the money. And so it happened that, since the good Rabbi's words always came true, the blessing was turned into a curse, and bickering and discontent became the portion of this family forever after.

And so it was with Noah. When the waters of the Flood receded, God remembered Noah and sought to bestow upon the new world an added measure of mercy and kindness through the acts of Noah which He hoped would be guided only by the noblest of motives. Noah was to play a leading part in the rebuilding of the flood-ravaged world and in the rearing of a new generation of men. Therefore the Lord blessed him, saying that the very first act he performed on dry land would succeed and prosper in great measure.

Unfortunately Noah's first act on land was not motivated by lofty intentions. But since the word of God is irreversible, the blessing remained in force and hence was squandered on the vineyard. Instead of having to wait for years before being able to partake of the fruit of the vine, Noah could enjoy his harvest on the very day that he had planted the seeds.

Vayachel Noach—"*And Noah began, and planted a vineyard...*" (Gen. 9:20). The Midrash and Rashi are quick to point out that *Vayachel* may also mean "And Noah degraded himself," for in the Hebrew language both these verbs have the same root. Instead of performing an act of eternal value to the coming generations of mankind, Noah planted the seeds of a fruit which was to bring so much trouble and sorrow to his descendants. Therefore Noah's sin was grave indeed; not only had he "degraded himself" by becoming intoxicated, but he also squandered God's blessing instead of using it for the purpose for which the Lord had intended it.

□ 3 — ABRAHAM — HE CALLED THE LORD HIS MASTER

אָמַר רַבִּי שִׁמְעוֹן בֶּן יוֹחָאי מְיוֹם שֶׁבָּרָא הַקָּדוֹשׁ בָּרוּךְ הוּא אֶת הָעוֹלָם לֹא הָיָה אָדָם שֶׁקְּרָאוֹ לְהַקָּדוֹשׁ בָּרוּךְ הוּא אָדוֹן עַד שֶׁבָּא אַבְרָהָם וּקְרָאוֹ אָדוֹן. (ברכות ז)

Rabbi Shimon ben Yochai says: "Since that day when the Holy One, blessed be He, created the world, there had been no one who had called the Holy One blessed be He, 'Master' (Lord), until Abraham came and called Him 'Master' (Lord), as it is written: 'And he (Abram) said, O Lord God, how will I know that I will inherit it?' " *(Gen. 15:8)*

"...And Daniel, too, was heard only because of Abraham, as it is written: 'Now therefore, O our God, hear the prayer of Your servant and his supplication, and cause Your face to shine upon Your Sanctuary that is desolate, for the Master's sake' *(Daniel 9:17)*. Instead of saying, 'for Your sake,' Daniel said, 'for the sake of Abraham who called You Master.' " *(Berachoth 7b)*

To explain this statement in the Talmud, the Maggid of Dubno would give the following *Moshol:*

A young nobleman inherited his father's title and became the Lord Mayor of a large city. However, he knew almost nothing of the mechanics of government since he had devoted all of his youth to the study of poetry and the fine arts. Hence he was ignorant of even the elementary principles of administration and did not know how to wield the authority which had been vested in him as mayor. A distinguished citizen offered him his services; he advised the mayor on the varied problems of administration and helped him institute a proper system of taxation to implement the program of the city government.

Many years later a grandson of this distinguished citizen was found guilty of violating the city tax law and was sentenced to prison. It was then that an old official remembered that the law which the offender had broken was the very law that had been instituted many years before by none other than the grandfather of the defendant.

The Alderman arose and addressed the Court as follows: "All our prosperity which we enjoy today, we owe to the noble efforts of this young man's grandfather who devised for us that tax law which his grandson has now violated. Now therefore deal kindly with the defendant this once and let him go free." And so the sentence of the accused was suspended.

Behold, said the Maggid, our Patriarch Abraham may well be compared to the distinguished citizen in our story. Before the coming of Abraham, God ruled the world in a fashion quite different from His present ways. In those ancient times, the inhabitants of the earth were not treated according to their deeds, but were given lavishly of God's bounty and lovingkindness which, most of the time, they had done little to deserve. Abraham was the first man to proclaim the sovereign authority of God on earth, and to assert that man must serve God. He was the first man to call God "Master" and in so doing he made all men subject to the yoke of Heaven. Ever since, God has judged men in accordance with the righteousness or the evil of their conduct.

We, the people of Israel, have sinned grievously, but, as Daniel says (Daniel 9:17), we have a right to beseech God to be merciful and to let us go free of the punishment of which we would be deserving, because we are the descendants of Abraham, who was the first to acknowledge and to spread the supreme sovereignty of the One God.

☐ 4 — "ABRAHAM WAS ONE"

אֶחָד הָיָה אַבְרָהָם. (יחזקאל)

כָּל מִי שֶׁנֶּאֱמַר בּוֹ "הָיָה" מִתְּחִלָּתוֹ וְעַד סוֹפוֹ הוּא צַדִּיק. (בראשית רבה ל')

"Abraham was one..."   *(Ezekiel 33:24)*

The Midrash comments:

Rabbi Yochanan says: *"The use in the Holy Writings of the word 'hayah' ('he was') in connection with a person indicates that this person was righteous all the days of his life."*

Can this be true also in the case of Abraham? We know that during the first years of his life he worshipped idols. Tradition differs as to the time of life at which Abraham first came to know the true God and gave up paganism. Some authorities claim that this happened when he was three years old; others hold that he did not become a servant of the One God until he was forty-eight years of age. At any rate, it is a known fact that there was a period of some years during which Abraham was a heathen. How, then, can it be said of such a person that he led a righteous life from the day of his birth until the day he died?

Rabbi Chanina and Rabbi Yochanan said: "Abraham came to recognize the One God when he was forty-eight years of age, *in order to bring the whole world to return to the worship of God.*"

This statement poses a second question: If Abraham himself had been a heathen, how could he "turn people toward God" so shortly after his own abjuration of idol-worship?

With the following *Moshol* both of these questions will be answered:

A very erudite rabbi, of great wealth and noble descent, held the office of honorary Town-Maggid (Town Preacher) in a small place. It was his great reputation as a powerful orator that caused his election to that position. Eager to do his best, he delivered splendid sermons and gave inspiring lectures on our Law and Ethics, but somehow his fiery words of remonstrance failed to bring about the desired effect upon the members of his community, and all the evils and vices against which he thundered from the pulpit of the synagogue still flourished like weeds in the town. The people began to wonder why the Rabbi proved so ineffectual. Some said, "It is easy for him to bid us to be honest and charitable, to study, and to be religious and devote our energies to things of the spirit. He is wealthy and he cannot understand that other people must work hard for a living and just do not have the energy left to study and to think at the end of a day's work. And we cannot afford to give up an hour from our daily pursuits to study."

Then the townsmen engaged a new rabbi, also a great scholar, known far and wide for his piety and devotion to learning. Unlike his predecessor, however, this man was poor and had never known anything but poverty all his life. But somehow he, too, failed to inspire his audience with the will and the resolve to become better than they had been before. This time the people put the blame on the fact that the new preacher could hardly be expected to talk in their language, for he had always led a life of austerity and had never found it necessary to wage a struggle against the temptations of earthly pleasures.

In the end the townspeople decided that their next preacher would not be a formally ordained rabbi at all. Their choice fell upon a merchant who, through no fault of his own, had lost all of his money. This man had enjoyed an outstanding reputation not only for his business acumen but also for his extensive knowledge of the Torah and the intricacies of Talmudic Law. He represented an ideal combination of erudite learning and practical wisdom. He was able to speak to any audience in their own language, and, as a result, they readily took his words to heart.

The moral of this story holds true for Abraham as well. We are told in the Torah *"You shall surely rebuke your companion"* (Lev. 19:17). This simply means that a man may remonstrate only with his peers, who live in the same circumstances as he. If a person pleads poverty as an excuse for neglect in performing the commandments of the Torah, he should be reminded of the example set by Hillel, who sacrificed his last penny and even endangered his life in order not to miss one single lecture at the Talmudical Academy (Yoma 35b). In other words, the teachings of Hillel, who was a poor man all of his days, should be employed to teach the poor, while the rich should be instructed with the aid of the teachings of Rabbi Elazar ben Charsom, who was well-known as a fabulously wealthy man.

Now the power of Abraham, too, lay in the fact that when he remonstrated with the idol-worshippers, he could speak to them as to his peers. Had he been a servant of the True God from the day of his birth onward, he could never have spoken so effectively and convincingly as to carry away his audiences by the power of his own conviction. Therefore the very fact that he himself had originally been an idol-worshipper was instrumental in leading his contemporaries to the One God.

Hence, regardless of whether Abraham had worshipped idols for forty-eight years or only for three, those years of paganism were eventually utilized in the service of the True God, and thus of true righteousness. Therefore we are fully justified in calling Abraham a perfect *tzaddik;* he served the cause of righteousness all the days of his life. This is the reason why Abraham was actually rewarded even for his years of idol-worship, and the Prophet was entirely right to use the word *"hayah"* when speaking of the life of Abraham, the first real Jew.

□ 5 — SARAH AND HAGAR

וַתֵּרֶא כִּי הָרָתָה וַתֵּקַל גְּבִרְתָּהּ בְּעֵינֶיהָ. (לך לך)

"...and when she (Hagar) saw that she had conceived, her mistress (Sarai) was lowered in her eyes."   *(Gen. 16:4)*

According to the Midrash, Hagar was the daughter of the king of Egypt. Abram had gone to Egypt with his wife, Sarai, in order to escape the famine in the land of Canaan. After the unpleasant episode with the Pharaoh described in Gen. 12:10-20, the people of Egypt escorted Abram out of their land, together with *"his wife and all that he had"* (Gen. 12:20). At that time Pharaoh said, "I would rather give my daughter Hagar as a handmaid to the house of Abram than as a wife to any other man." Thus, when Abram and his household left Egypt, Hagar went with them as a maid-servant. As implied by her very name,* Hagar had been given to Abram and Sarai by way of "compensation" for the advances which Pharaoh had made to Sarai thinking that she was the sister, and not the wife, of Abram.

At first, Hagar seemed a loyal servant who regarded Sarai as her mistress whose wish was her command. But when she became pregnant while Sarai remained barren, the maid's attitude changed. She reminded herself of her own royal descent and became haughty and arrogant. Therefore "her mistress was despised in her eyes," and eventually Hagar ran away. And the angel of the Lord found her in the wilderness and said to her *"Hagar, handmaid of Sarai, from where did you come? And where are you going?"* And she replied *"I am fleeing from the presence of my mistress Sarai"* (Gen. 16:8). Whereupon the angel of the Lord said, *"Return to your mistress and submit yourself to her"* (Gen. 16:9).

The angel addressed Hagar as "handmaid of Sarai," but in her answer Hagar speaks of Sarai as her "mistress." In view of what we know about Hagar's attitude to Sarah it seems somewhat strange that, in speaking to an angel of the Lord, Hagar should still call Sarah her "mistress."

The Maggid of Dubno asked this question and answered it with a simple *Moshol:*

---

* Hagar is related semantically with the word *Agra* meaning "wages" or "compensation."

Once there was a wealthy man who would travel each year from Lemberg in far-off Galicia to Leipzig, the great German city, to attend the annual fair. He would always be accompanied by a coachman who drove his carriage and acted as his master's valet. Since the great distance could not be covered in one day, they would stop in Prague and spend the night at an inn there before resuming their journey the next day. Now on one of these stopovers it happened that the coachman arose in the middle of the night, tiptoed into the bedroom of his sleeping master, put on the latter's fancy suit, took all of his belongings, and left his own coachman's livery and boots behind. The next morning the coachman, thus attired in his master's clothes, pretended to be the nobleman and commanded his master to get the carriage ready. Nothing that the latter told him could prevail upon the coachman to abandon his game and to resume his duties. In order not to waste time and run the risk of missing the very first day of the fair, the merchant ceased to argue with his valet and took the reins of the carriage himself while the coachman, garbed in his master's rich attire, lounged in the seat behind him.

As soon as they arrived in Leipzig they went to the Rabbi, each attempting to prove that he was the real master and that the other was the coachman. The Rabbi, not knowing either of the two men, was perplexed, but after only a minute's hesitation he said to them, "You will both have to sit and wait in the antechamber. It may take me some time to decide which of you is which. Sit down, and be ready when I call you."

After two hours had passed, the Rabbi sent his beadle out and he called loudly: "Let the coachman come to the Rabbi!" Almost by instinct the real coachman promptly rose and responded to the call. Thus the case was solved.

The same was true in the case of Hagar. When she became pregnant while Sarah was still barren, she looked upon her mistress with disdain and treated her with contempt because she imagined that by virtue of her royal birth she was superior to Sarah. Therefore the angel of God called her *"Hagar, handmaid of Sarai!"* and, as if by instinct, Hagar replied, "I flee from the face of Sarai, *my mistress.*"

As soon as these words escaped from her lips, Hagar, there in the wilderness, remembered her true position of servitude. Thus the angel of God, by addressing her as "the handmaid of Sarai," had reminded her of her true position just as the Rabbi had reminded the coachman in his antechamber who his real master was.

□ 6 — ISAAC AND REBECCAH

(תולדות)   .וַיֶּאֱהַב יִצְחָק אֶת־עֵשָׂו כִּי־צַיִד בְּפִיו וְרִבְקָה אֹהֶבֶת אֶת יַעֲקֹב

"And Isaac loved Esau, because he ate of his venison; but Rebeccah loved Jacob." *(Gen. 25:28)*

How was it possible that Isaac and Rebeccah could differ so basically in their attitudes toward their two sons?

The Midrash explains that the words *Ki tzayid befeev* actually do not mean "because he ate of his venison" but "there was hunting in his (Esau's) mouth"; in other words, Esau had the uncanny ability to cheat and deceive his father Isaac with empty words. For example, he would ask, "Father, what is the procedure for setting aside tithes of straw and salt?" even though he knew quite well that these two commodities were exempt from the tithing law. He asked the question only to make his father think that he was more anxious than most others to make sure that he obeyed the law in its every detail. And the aged Isaac really believed this and therefore loved Esau more than he did Jacob (Midrash Tanchuma).

How was it that Isaac could be duped so easily while his wife Rebeccah knew Esau for what he really was?

Said the Maggid of Dubno: "Isaac had been raised in the home of Abraham and Sarah, where truthfulness and sincerity prevailed at all times. Deceit and hypocrisy, therefore, were so utterly unknown and foreign to him that he could not detect dishonesty in another person, and certainly not in Esau. He took the young man's sanctimonious questions at face value and loved him for his apparent desire to delve into the intricacies of the Law and to observe its every letter. Rebeccah, on the other hand, had been reared in the house of Bethuel and Laban where trickery, perfidy and hypocrisy were everyday commodities. She herself was an honest woman, but, remembering the things she had seen happen in her own childhood home, she was easily able to see through Esau and to recognize him for what he really was. That is why she loved Jacob, who was Esau's opposite, a young man of honesty, sincerity, and genuine piety."

The Midrash remarks: "The more she (Rebeccah) heard the voice of Jacob, the more she *continued to love him.*" This Midrash will be better understood if we read the *Moshol* which Rabbi Yaakov would cite in this connection.

A certain community once elected as its town preacher a man who was not very learned but whose erudite style of preaching made a good impression on the audience with the first sermon.

The second sermon, however, was not nearly as brilliant as the first one had been, and every succeeding sermon was worse than the previous one, until the congregation simply ceased to attend the lectures altogether. Then the men who had hired him realized that the would-be rabbi actually had very little to offer. His first few learned discourses had been recited by rote, word for word, and once his pitifully scant repertory of learning had been exhausted, it was obvious that he had nothing left that would appeal to an audience.

Eventually, a new rabbi was appointed. This man, though not so eloquent of speech as might have been hoped for, had been a star student at the Talmudical Academy and was a scholar of great erudition and integrity. His trial sermon was simple and modest; he did not seek to impress his audience with his vast knowledge. Gradually, however, his sermons increased in volume and in quality, so that more and more people came to attend his lectures and the Rabbi soon enjoyed the respect and affection of the entire community.

This little parable, said Rabbi Yaakov, may be applied also to Esau and Jacob. Esau actually knew little of Jewish law and, what was worse, he was quite indifferent to it. Yet, in order to impress his

father, he sought to give a display of his zeal and of his very limited
knowledge. Now we note that, in connection with Isaac's love for
Esau, the Bible uses the past tense, *"and Isaac loved Esau"* but
this love did not last. When describing Rebeccah's affection for
Jacob, in the same verse, however, it employs a present form, which
should be literally translated as "Rebeccah *continued to love
Jacob."* Esau had temporarily succeeded in hoodwinking his father,
and therefore his father loved him, but that love could not last, for
eventually, even though he was blind, the aged man found out what
Esau really was. Jacob had quite a different personality. His
knowledge of the Law had been acquired at the School of Shem and
Ever, and he had never ceased studying and striving to perfect
himself with regard to learning and observance. Jacob was not content with whatever knowledge he might have gleaned in the past; to
him constant study in the present was of paramount importance.
Therefore, too, the Torah employs the present tense to describe
Rebeccah's love for Jacob, a love which only increased as the years
went by and the proud mother came to see more and more the
genuine sterling qualities of her younger son.

□ 7 — Isaac's Blessing

(תולדות)   וַיֶּחֱרַד יִצְחָק חֲרָדָה גְּדוֹלָה עַד־מְאֹד . . . וַיֹּאמֶר הֲלֹא אָצַלְתָּ לִּי בְּרָכָה.

**"And Isaac trembled very greatly.... And he (Esau) said: 'Have
you not reserved a blessing for me?'"**   *(Gen. 27:33,36)*

Many of our great Commentators ask why Isaac should have
wanted to give the full blessing, for which both of his sons were vy-
ing, to one son alone, and to Esau at that? True, Isaac might not
have considered Esau an out-and-out evildoer, but by that time he
must have known that Jacob was the better of the two young men.
Nevertheless, it would appear that he intended to bless Esau only.

Here is the *Moshol* with the aid of which Rabbi Yaakov Mi-Dubno sought to explain this strange paradox.

In a certain town there lived a wealthy man who had a large estate, a great fortune, and also the only tavern in the town. This man had two sons; the one was upright and wise, but the other was a glutton, a drunkard and an incorrigible spendthrift. When the father wrote his will, it was to the latter that he bequeathed his entire estate with all his assets, while to the good son he left the tavern only. When asked the reason for this seemingly most unfair procedure, the old man sighed and said, "Is not my disobedient son also the flesh of my flesh? And is it not my duty, therefore, to provide for him also? To this end I have given him all of my fortune. But I fear that he will not be able to keep it long, for, being what he is, he will spend all the money in the tavern so that, eventually, it all will go to his brother."

This *Moshol* can be applied also to Jacob and Esau. We are told of Jacob and Esau, *"and the one people shall be stronger than the other people"* (Gen. 25:23). In other words, the one brother will be strong and mighty only at the expense of the other. They will never be equally great and important at the same time. If the one brother should forfeit his blessing by his bad conduct, God will give supremacy to the better of the two.

That is why it had been Isaac's original intention that Esau should be blessed with all the riches and advantages of this world (Gen. 27:28 ff) while Jacob would be told *"And it shall come to pass when you will break loose that you will shake his yoke off your neck"* (Gen. 27:40); that is, "If at any time, Jacob will have cause to complain about Esau, he will be able to rid himself of his first-born brother's tyranny." For Isaac knew that, eventually, Esau would be led to sin grievously, and thus, in accordance with the promise given Jacob, all the blessings bestowed upon Esau would go to Jacob instead.

But when Isaac noticed that Jacob had seized the entire blessing for himself at the very beginning, he "trembled greatly" because he now knew that the only blessing he could leave to his other son, Esau, was the assurance of just retribution if his brother should sin, which had originally been intended for Jacob. And as far as Esau was concerned, this was as good as no blessing at all, because even Balaam, the enemy of Israel, was forced to admit that God *"had not seen evil in Jacob"* (Num. 23:21). Therefore Esau, and the nations which were descended from him, persistently strove to take away the blessing which had been given to Jacob. Hence the promise which Isaac gave to Esau became a weapon for Esau and his descendants and a challenge to Jacob. Therefore the children of Edom have never ceased to pounce upon any wrong of which the off-spring of Jacob might be guilty

□ 8 — ESAU AND HIS BIRTHRIGHT

וְיַעֲקֹב נָתַן לְעֵשָׂו לֶחֶם וּנְזִיד עֲדָשִׁים וַיֹּאכַל וַיֵּשְׁתְּ וַיָּקָם וַיֵּלַךְ וַיִּבֶז עֵשָׂו אֶת הַבְּכֹרָה.
(תולדות)

"And Jacob gave Esau bread and a pottage of lentils; and he ate and drank, and rose up, and went his way. So Esau despised his birthright."   *(Gen. 25:34)*

Thus does the Bible tell us how lightly Esau esteemed his birthright. But we ask why the Scriptural account should go into so much detail, stating that Esau ate, and drank, and rose and went on his way. Is not all this superfluous and irrelevant?

Not at all, said the Maggid of Dubno, and proceeded to explain his answer by means of a pithy *Moshol*. A person who owns an article of great value, such as, let us say, a diamond, and gives it away for no more than a few pieces of silver, may have been prompted to do so by either one of two considerations. He may need the money badly and therefore will sell the stone for whatever money it may bring him. Or perhaps he may not realize the dia-mond's intrinsic value and is therefore entirely satisfied with the small amount he receives for it. Now if a person throws a diamond away for a pittance because his need for money is desperate, he may regret his rash descision at some later date. But if he never had any conception of the value of the diamond, he will never wish that he had asked for more money.

The Torah means to stress that Esau, too, had no conception of the spiritual value inherent in the birthright that he sold for the bowl of lentils. Therefore we are explicitly told that he ate and drank to his heart's content, which must have taken some time to do, and finally went away, still without even giving a thought to what it was that he had so lightly cast away. Thus it is clear that he sold his birthright not out of hunger, but out of utter contempt and disdain for the spiritual gifts and responsibilities that the birthright carried with it.

□ 9 — JACOB AND ESAU

הֲכִי קָרָא שְׁמוֹ יַעֲקֹב.   (תולדות)

"And Esau said: "Did he call his name Jacob* in that he has supplanted me these two times? He took away my birthright, and behold, now he has taken away my blessing."   *(Gen. 27:36)*

"Did he call his name Jacob?" This question is difficult to understand. Jacob certainly did not call his own name Jacob. His father, Isaac, did that. Therefore we might rather have expected that Esau would ask Isaac: "Did *you* not call him Jacob with good cause?" ("Jacob" being the synonym for deceit), but we would certainly not expect that he would ask concerning his brother "Was it for nothing that he called himself Jacob?"

---

* This is the literal translation for what is usually rendered *"Is he not rightly named Jacob..."*

The Maggid of Dubno cites the following *Moshol* to resolve this question:

A man of noble descent lost his fortune and decided to visit his prominent relatives abroad who, he felt sure, would help him. The alderman of his town gave him a letter attesting to the fact that he was indeed a member of the eminent family to which he claimed to be related and, thus armed, he set out on his journey.

When evening came, he decided to stop over at an inn, where he was given a room together with another poor man. The latter, who soon found out about the family connections of the newcomer, stole the passport and credentials and, early in the morning, went into the city to visit the wealthy man named in the letter of recommendation, and posed as the impoverished cousin from abroad. The credentials were accepted and he was given a large sum of money. As he was about to pass through the gate of the estate onto the public highway, he was stopped by the true owner of the documents who berated him for stealing the papers. The imposter, suddenly afraid, returned the documents and then tried to escape. In the end, however, he was arrested and brought to court. There he refused to plead guilty, pointing out that he had returned all the documents to their rightful owner. But his accuser arose and said to the judge, "Certainly, if he had visited my relatives and managed to get money from them under his own name, which his father had given him, I would not be standing here. His crime was that he used *my* name, and now I shall never be able to get the gifts which were intended for me."

Such too, was the reproach which Esau leveled at Jacob after the latter had taken away the blessing intended for him. Esau went to Isaac and said to him. "Had my brother called himself Jacob and asked for the blessing I would have had no objections. But *did he call his name Jacob* when he asked for your blessing? Not at all; the impostor used my name, Esau (Gen. 27:32), and by this deceit he managed to get the blessing which was intended for me."

□ 10 — JACOB AND LABAN

וַיֹּאמֶר אֵלָיו לָבָן אִם־נָא מָצָאתִי חֵן בְּעֵינֶיךָ נִחַשְׁתִּי וַיְבָרֲכֵנִי ה' בִּגְלָלֶךָ. וַיֹּאמַר נָקְבָה
שְׂכָרְךָ עָלַי וְאֶתֵּנָה. וַיֹּאמֶר אֵלָיו אַתָּה יָדַעְתָּ אֵת אֲשֶׁר עֲבַדְתִּיךָ.   (ויצא)

**"And Laban said to him: 'If now I have found favor in your
eyes — I have divined that the Lord has blessed me for your
sake.' And he said, 'Specify your wages to me, and I will give it.'
And he (Jacob) said to him, 'You know how I have served you,
and how your cattle have fared with me.' "**   *(Gen. 30:27-29)*

Laban knows full well that whatever blessings God has sent him
have come to him on Jacob's account, and he asks Jacob how he
should reward him for it. In view of Laban's willingness to reward
him, Jacob's answer appears strange. Why did Jacob have to call
special attention to the credit due him for the prospering of the cattle which Laban had entrusted to his care? Laban had never denied
that Jacob had taken excellent care of his sheep.

Said Rabbi Yaakov of Dubno: Jacob had a good reason for
answering his kinsman as he did, as is illustrated in the following
Moshol. A prosperous merchant had a large and well-trained staff
in his employment. They were a happy group, apparently well-
satisfied with working conditions, and, under the supervision of
reliable foremen, they kept the firm functioning quite well. Hence
the merchant did not have to concern himself at all with the
numerous details usually involved in even the routine operation of a
corporation such as his plant was. Being a man of great piety, he
spent most of his days in his private office, studying the Law with a
group of ten pious men who did nothing but pray and study with
him and who received regular payments for the service they
rendered the merchant by their presence and participation every
day.

The business continued to flourish. Secure in this knowledge, the
employees decided to request a wage increase. When their plea was
ignored, they submitted the request once again. When once more

they received no answer from their employer, they decided to go on strike. It was only then that, fearful for the future welfare of his concern, the merchant called them into his office for a conference and granted them a salary increase so that the firm could continue to function and prosper.

Now the ten pious men who spent all their days in prayer and study with the merchant said among themselves, "If our excellent patron has the means to raise the wages of the men who run his business, why should we not be entitled to the same treatment?" And they employed the same strategy as the workmen had used with such great success; they "went on strike" and no longer came to their patron's office to study and to pray with him.

When he heard this, the merchant laughed aloud. "What fools you are!" he said to them. "What are you trying to achieve by this game? When my workers asked for an increase, I had no other choice but to grant it, for skilled workers are hard to find. But if you go on strike, all that will happen is that you will lose your meager earnings. Remember, you may not be able to get along without me and my bounty, but I don't need *you* for the prosperity of my business, and I can easily find others to study with me."

Now, said the Maggid, we should be able to understand the answer Jacob gave Laban. Laban wanted to pay Jacob as little as possible. Hence Laban tried to minimize Jacob's real contributions and pretended that God had blessed him merely because he had been willing to keep in his house a pious and scholarly young man who could devote much of his time to the study of the Law. Laban therefore said to Jacob: "I know full well that God blessed me because I supported you so that you could devote all your days to scholarly pursuits. For this you must have some reward. Name it and I shall give it to you." But Jacob replied: "Ah, Laban, you are quite wrong. God did not bless you simply because I lived in your house, spending my days in study and prayer at your expense. The Lord has blessed you because of the actual work I did at your home. You know how well I have served you, and what good care I have taken of your sheep. It is in this light that you must value the blessing God has given you ever since I have come into your home. I have not been just a pious student living on your bounty. I have become a most proficient shepherd and much of the prosperity of your enterprise is due to my actual hard work. I have therefore made a genuine and tangible contribution to your wealth. Consider these things when you give me whatever reward you feel I may deserve."

□ 11 — Joseph — On the Interpretation of Dreams

וַיֹּאמֶר לוֹ יוֹסֵף זֶה פִּתְרֹנוֹ, שְׁלֹשֶׁת הַשָּׂרִגִים שְׁלֹשֶׁת יָמִים הֵם. בְּעוֹד שְׁלֹשֶׁת יָמִים יִשָּׂא פַרְעֹה אֶת־רֹאשֶׁךָ וַהֲשִׁיבְךָ עַל־כַּנֶּךָ וְנָתַתָּ כוֹס־פַּרְעֹה בְּיָדוֹ כַּמִּשְׁפָּט הָרִאשׁוֹן אֲשֶׁר הָיִיתָ מַשְׁקֵהוּ . . . וַיַּעַן יוֹסֵף וַיֹּאמֶר זֶה פִּתְרֹנוֹ שְׁלֹשֶׁת הַסַּלִּים שְׁלֹשֶׁת יָמִים הֵם. בְּעוֹד שְׁלֹשֶׁת יָמִים יִשָּׂא פַרְעֹה אֶת־רֹאשְׁךָ מֵעָלֶיךָ וְתָלָה אוֹתְךָ עַל עֵץ וְאָכַל הָעוֹף אֶת בְּשָׂרְךָ מֵעָלֶיךָ.   (וישב)

While Joseph was in prison, his cellmates were the chief butler and the chief baker of the king of Egypt. One morning both of them came to Joseph and asked him to interpret for them the dreams which they had had during that night. Joseph replied that only God could interpret a dream, but it might be that God would reveal the true meaning of their dreams through him, and therefore he agreed to listen to their story. The chief butler then said that he had dreamed of a vine which had three branches laden with ripe grapes, and he had pressed out the juice of the grapes into the cup of Pharaoh, and he had given the cup into Pharaoh's hand.

"And Joseph said to him, 'This is the interpretation of it: The three branches are three days; in another three days, Pharaoh shall lift up your head, and restore you to your office; and you shall give Pharaoh's cup into his hand, as you did formerly, when you were his butler!' "   *(Gen. 40:12-13)*

Then the Chief Baker told of his dream. He had carried three baskets of white bread on his head; in the uppermost basket there had been bread and pastry for Pharaoh, and the birds had eaten it all out of the basket on his head.

"And Joseph answered and said:'This is its interpretation: The three baskets are three days; in another three days, Pharaoh shall lift up your head from off you, and shall hang you on a tree; and the birds shall eat your flesh from off you.' "

(Gen. 40:18-19)

And this is exactly what happened.

Now we might well ask ourselves: how was it evident from the dreams that the butler would be reinstated while the baker would be hanged?

The Maggid of Dubno answers our question with a *Moshol.*

An artist once painted a beautiful picture in which a handsome young man was seen carrying a basketful of rolls on his head. He displayed the painting in the market place in order to sell it. Soon some birds alighted on the picture and pecked with their beaks at the canvas where the rolls were painted. A passer-by who saw this said to a companion, "What a genius the painter must be; why, the rolls look so real that even the birds were fooled." Whereupon the other man replied, "I'm afraid I can't agree with you. If the birds settle on the painting it shows that they are not fooled at all. For if the entire picture would look real to them, they would have been afraid of the man in it and they would never have dared peck at the rolls on his head."

In the baker's dream, too, the birds ignored the man beneath the baskets when they lighted on the rolls he carried. If birds thus ignore the presence of a man, thought Joseph, it is obvious that the man is either dead, or about to die. Therefore Joseph knew that the chief baker at the court of Pharaoh would not live much longer.

The butler's dream had been quite different. There the only active person was the butler himself, discharging the duties of his high office even then. It was obvious, therefore, that the butler would very soon be freed and restored to his old place at the court of his king.

□ 12 — JOSEPH AND HIS BROTHERS

וַיִּרְאוּ אֲחֵי יוֹסֵף כִּי מֵת אֲבִיהֶם וַיֹּאמְרוּ: לוּ יִשְׂטְמֵנוּ יוֹסֵף וְהָשֵׁב יָשִׁיב לָנוּ אֵת כָּל
הָרָעָה אֲשֶׁר גָּמַלְנוּ אֹתוֹ ... וַיֹּאמֶר אֲלֵהֶם יוֹסֵף ... הֲתַחַת אֱ-לֹהִים אָנִי ?   (ויחי)

"...And when Joseph's brothers saw that their father was dead, they said: 'It may be that Joseph will hate us, and will fully repay us for all the evil which we did to him.'...and Joseph said to them...'Am I in the place of God?'"   *(Gen. 50:15,19)*

Rashi remarks that the Hebrew word *loo* which is translated here as "it may be" (or "perhaps") actually may have two different meanings. It may be rendered as "it may be," as it is here, implying the fear of the brothers that Joseph might take revenge now that their father was dead. But in that case this would be the only verse in the Scriptures where the word *loo* is so rendered. Therefore Rashi recalls that it may also imply a wish, in which case we would translate it as *"Would that* Joseph will hate us." The *Baal Haturim* accepts this latter interpretation. To us, however, this rendering seems very strange and quite out of context with the rest of the passage.

The Maggid of Dubno reconciled the rendering with the text by means of an ingenious *Moshol*.

A rich man had a poor brother who always came to him when he needed money or food. Eventually the wealthy brother lost his patience and one day, while the two were walking together on the seashore, he pushed his brother into the water so that he would be rid of what he considered to be a constant source of irritation. But a miracle came to pass, and the poor man did not drown. Instead, he drifted until he was cast ashore at an island where he found a great treasure and became wealthy himself. When, years later, he returned to his home town with his riches, he found that his brother, who had supported him in the olden days, had lost his fortune and was now earning a scant living for himself and his family.

The impoverished man gaped in amazement at the brother who

he thought had drowned long ago, and he said to him: "My brother, push *me* into the sea now," for he hoped that an accident of this sort might bring him the same good fortune that had come to his brother. But the other man replied, "No, this I will not do. You pushed me into the sea to get rid of me, and it was only through a kind Providence that I was rescued and raised on high. But if I were to throw you into the water, I am not so sure that you would be as lucky. I cannot force the hand of Providence, you know."

This *Moshol* holds true for the story of Joseph and his brothers as well. When Jacob had died, and the brothers looked at Joseph seated in splendor upon his throne, they said, "Joseph sits on high only because we threw him into the pit that time in the land of Canaan. *Would that* Joseph will hate us and repay us in kind for what we did to him. Perhaps we shall then be as fortunate as he was and come to the same high honors."

But Joseph, hearing this, said to them: "No, this I will not do. In my case, God intervened and turned the evil into good. But if I were to do to you what you did to me then, who can tell whether this would be for your good? Am I in the place of God?" (Gen. 50:19).

□ 13—BENJAMIN AND COMMON SENSE

וַיִּגַּשׁ אֵלָיו יְהוּדָה וַיֹּאמֶר בִּי אֲדֹנִי . . . אר"ס בְּנִימוּסוֹת שֶׁלָּנוּ (בְּתוֹרָתֵנוּ) כָּתוּב (שמות כ"ב ב') אִם אֵין לוֹ וְנִמְכַּר בִּגְנֵבָתוֹ, וְזֶה יֵשׁ לוֹ לְשַׁלֵּם. (ויגש)

"...And Judah came near to him (Joseph) and said: 'Let your servant, I pray thee, speak a word in my lord's ear...'" (Gen. 44:18). To this Rabbi Simon says: What Judah said to Joseph was: "In our Law it is written. 'If he (a thief) has nothing, then he shall be sold (as a slave) to make restitution for his theft' (Exod. 22:2), but this one, Benjamin, does have some possessions and can afford to make restitution."   (*Midrash Vayigash*)

In one of the communities where he had been invited to be a guest preacher, the Dubnoer received an unusual request: "Rabbi, could you give us an explanation on a difficult Midrash on any verse from the Bible, at a moment's notice, in plain language and without using any of your parables?"

The Maggid agreed, and they chose as their text the above passage from Genesis 44:18.

The question now arises: At that time, Judah and the other sons of Jacob were still under the impression that they were speaking not to Joseph their brother, but to an Egyptian Viceroy. Why, then, should they have attempted to explain to him what is written in "*our*" Law? The Egyptians were surely guided by their own laws!

The Dubnoer replied forthwith: "The Torah teaches us that a thief must make restitution for what he has stolen, and if he is not able to do so, he must be sold as a slave. But who'd buy a slave with a criminal record? He will stand a chance only if the prospective master is told that the thief has no means of his own and stole only because of pressing need. Certainly no man in his right mind would take into his house a 'professional' criminal who steals even though he has means of his own. Therefore, when Joseph sought to keep Benjamin as a slave, Judah said to him: "Now if our brother Benjamin is a thief, he did not steal your cup because of pressing need. He *has* sufficient means to make restitution. If you know this and you still wish to keep him as a slave, you would be acting counter to all reason. Our Law prohibits us from taking such a thief as a slave, but this can be understood, too, from common sense. For is it not obvious to you that a professional thief would not make a trustworthy slave?' "

□ 14 — MOSES' REWARD

לָמָה הֲרֵעֹתָה לָעָם הַזֶּה וכו' . . . עַתָּה תִרְאֶה אֲשֶׁר אֶעֱשֶׂה לְפַרְעֹה. ‎(שמות)

"And Moses returned to the Lord and said: 'Lord, why have You worsened the plight of this people? Why is it that You sent me?

**For since I came to Pharaoh to speak in Your name he has
worsened the plight of this people; and You have not delivered
Your people at all.' And the Lord said to Moses: 'Now you will
see what I shall do to Pharaoh.' "**   *(Exod. 5:22-23; 6:1)*

The Midrash comments as follows on this last verse: *"You will see
what I shall do to Pharaoh* — but you will not see what I shall do to
the thirty-one kings of Eretz Canaan. It will be Joshua, your disciple, who will take revenge upon them. From this one statement of
God as recorded in the Scriptures, Moses understood that he would
not be permitted to enter the Holy Land" *(Midrash Sh'moth)*.

The foregoing would imply that Moses would not be allowed to
enter the Holy Land *as a punishment* for having been so
presumptuous as to complain to God: "Lord, why have You
worsened the plight of this people" and thus question the wisdom of
His Almighty Providence. From another Midrash *(Va'ethchanan)*,
however, we must infer that Moses was buried outside of the Holy
Land not in punishment, but *as a reward,* so that when the dead
would rise again, he would have a share in the resurrection of millions of his brothers who would also be buried not in the Holy Land
but in cemeteries the world over. The role which Moses was meant
to play in this connection is explained in the Midrash by a parable
as follows:

A man lost some small coins of great sentimental value in a dark
cave and could not find them because there was not enough light.
Finally, he stopped the search and wondered what to do next. Soon
he arrived at a solution for his problem. He dropped a small gold
coin some distance away and let it be known in the nearby town that
whoever would find that one gold piece would be welcome to keep it.
Naturally, this brought out all the people, and each one carried a
torch or candle the better to be able to see, so that the cave was
soon brilliantly lit by hundreds of lights and our friend could find
the other coins with ease.

All our dead, says the Midrash, that are buried in the wilderness
(*i.e.* outside Eretz Yisrael) during the Galuth, might easily go
unnoticed at the time of resurrection. But it would be impossible

that as great a man as Moses would be forgotten. Therefore Moses was buried not in the Holy Land but in the midst of his brothers, "in the wilderness," so that the others, too, would be remembered on that day when Moses will be recalled to life.

Nevertheless, it still remains for us to establish whether Moses' death and burial in the wilderness were meant to be accepted by him as a punishment or welcomed as a reward. Said the Maggid of Dubno: Let me tell you a *Moshol.*

Two poor people came to a town, one old and one young, and they spent the night at an inn. An argument arose between them and the older struck the younger one, and injured him. The youth took him to court. "Why did you do this?" the judge asked the old man. And the latter replied, "I am his uncle and since his father is dead, I feel responsible for him. Therefore, when he misbehaved, I struck him."

"That is a lie," shouted the young man indignantly. "He is not my uncle. I met him for the first time in my life last night, when we shared a room at the inn. He attacked me and tore my clothes; I demand that he make restitution at once."

The judge was silent for a moment. Then he turned to the old man and said, "You must go out and buy new clothes for this boy. This is my sentence. Whether you will view it as a reward or as a punishment depends upon where the truth lies. If he is really your nephew, then you will surely want to see him look his best and you will be glad of this opportunity to do something for him. But if your testimony here was false and the lad is a stranger who can be of no interest to you, then take the expense of the purchase as a fine, imposed as punishment for the injury you have done him."

This sentence may well be compared to that pronounced on Moses by the Divine Judge in Heaven. As we have already explained above, the Jewish people were in need of the help of a great personality like Moses. Moses had been arraigned before the Heavenly Court, as it were, for having questioned God's wisdom, having cried out: "Why have You worsened the plight of this people?" And the Heavenly sentence was that Moses would die and be buried not in the Promised Land but in the wilderness. Now had

Moses not been filled with anxious concern for the welfare of his people, this would have been a harsh punishment. But from his very question, God had seen that Moses was a part of the people of Israel with all his heart and soul. And the same sentence which would have been grievous punishment indeed for any other person was accepted by Moses as a reward, for while it meant that he could never enter the Holy Land, it also enabled him to assure the future life and welfare of his people. Thus Moses may well have felt amply rewarded for the services which he rendered to the people of Israel.

□ 15 — MOSES AND THE ANGELS

וּמֹשֶׁה עָלָה אֶל הָאֱלֹהִים. (יתרו)

"And Moses went up unto God."   *(Exod. 19:3)*

The Midrash tells us that when Moses entered into the celestial spheres to receive the Torah directly from God, the angels were disgruntled, saying: "What does this mortal want in our midst?" for they thought that Moses, mere man that he was, was much lower than they. Thereupon the Lord said to Moses: "Take hold of the Throne of My Glory," a unique honor of which even the angels of heaven had never been deemed worthy. Now it occurred to the heavenly hosts that indeed Moses must be a great personality to be accorded such distinction. And after Moses had assured them that the laws of the Torah had never been meant for the angels, but for human beings only, to govern human lives under human conditions on earth, the angels realized that Moses was truly not an intruder attempting to steal a heavenly treasure but a messenger of God sent to take back with him to earth a sacred code of laws made to guide the earthly activities of mankind. Therefore the angels heartily repented of their unkindness to Moses and sought ways to make amends to him. They decided that they would reveal to him heavenly mysteries which they had never disclosed before to any mortal being. The Angel of Death, for instance, told him that a certain type of incense, *K'toreth*, was an antidote against death; the Angel of Poverty said that he thrived only in the midst of filth and that, therefore, cleanliness would drive him away, while the Angel of Good Sustenance confided to him that cleanliness alone could keep him on earth. Thus did the angels seek to make good for the insolent manner in which they had received Moses.

Now we may say: Our Rabbis tell us (*Rosh Hashanah* 21) that there are fifty Gates of Insight in the Universe and that all but one had been open to Moses. For Moses, like no other human being, was a disciple of God and hence all the mysteries of heaven and earth were well known to him. Why, then, did he accept these tokens of homage and good will from the angels without telling them that he had no need of them?

The Maggid of Dubno answered this question with a *Moshol*. A wealthy man had an only daughter for whom he wanted to select a good husband. His choice fell upon a young man who was of fine character and well-versed in the Torah. It seemed that this would be an excellent match. Then, suddenly, on the day before the wedding, someone came to the bride's father and told him that the young man was suffering from a loathsome skin disease. Not wishing to postpone the marriage at this late date, the worried father decided to go through with the wedding, but before the ceremony he sent for the best and most expensive medicines for the treatment of the ailment with which he had been told that his future son-in-law was afflicted. After the wedding, however, the young bride delightedly told her father that whoever had said her husband was ill must either have spread an evil rumor or told a deliberate lie. The bridegroom had been examined by a physician and pronounced in perfect health. So pleased was the father with the good news that he made another banquet for the newlyweds and, in order to make amends to his son-in-law for the suspicion, he begged him to choose as a gift whatever he would like best from among the heirlooms of the family. Now the bridegroom had learned of the medicines which his wife's father had procured at so great an expense for his benefit, and he wanted to show the older man that he bore him no ill will for believing the rumor that had been spread about him. Therefore he said that, as his gift, he would choose the medicines. "I don't need them for myself," he explained to his father-in-law, "I am quite well. But you were good enough to buy them for me, and therefore I will take them as my gift. Perhaps I can pass them on to some poor people who have the disease and could not possibly afford to buy such costly lotions."

Moses, our great leader, was just as considerate as the young bridegroom in our story. Anxious to demonstrate to the angels that he bore them no ill will for their unkind behavior, he accepted their conciliatory overtures with thanks. And when he returned to earth, he utilized for the benefit of Israel the wisdom which the angels had sought to reveal to him.

☐ 16 — Z'CHUTH AVOTH — THE MERITS OF OUR FOREFATHERS

וְהָיָה עֵקֶב תִּשְׁמְעוּן אֵת הַמִּשְׁפָּטִים הָאֵלֶּה וּשְׁמַרְתֶּם וַעֲשִׂיתֶם אוֹתָם וְשָׁמַר ה' ... אֶת
הַבְּרִית ... אֲשֶׁר נִשְׁבַּע לַאֲבֹתֶיךָ. (עקב)

"...And it shall come to pass, as a consequence, if you will listen to these ordinances, and keep them, and do them, that the Lord your God shall keep with you the covenant and the loving-kindness which He swore to your fathers." *(Deut. 7:12)*

Asks the Maggid of Dubno: Why does the Torah imply that the merits of our forefathers will stand by us if we obey the commandments of God? We have been taught that the merit of our fathers is the one thing that may save us from dire punishment for sin. But as long as we lead lives of righteousness and observe the *Mitzvoth* in their entirety, it would seem that we can stand on our merits and do not need to recall those of our ancestors when we pray to God for our needs such as wisdom, repentance, good health, happiness and prosperity. Why then, this strange association in the Torah?

And once again, Rabbi Yaakov answers this question with a *Moshol:*

An old man had stored away a thousand pieces of gold for his young son. Before he died, he authorized a friend to assume all responsibility for the education and training of the child and to see to it that he would receive adequate training for some gainful calling. The friend was also to keep the pieces of gold in trust for the boy and to turn them over to the young man once, in his judgment, the latter would have reached maturity. Not long after he had made these arrangements, the old man passed away.

The boy grew up under the care of his guardian and eventually was taken into his foster-father's store as a regular employee. The years passed quickly. One day the young man learned of the money that was being held in trust for him, and he went to his guardian and said, "Please give me my money so that I need no longer work for others but can have my fortune work for me instead." But the older man replied: "Are you quite sure that you really want it right now? If so, I will not withhold your money from you. But take a wise man's counsel. You are still young and capable of making a living by the work of your hands, and your work has been most satisfactory. I would suggest that you leave your little fortune untouched and keep it against that time when you will be old and dependent on your savings."

Said Rabbi Yaakov Mi-Dubno: Our forefathers brought their *Z'chuth*, their merits, to their Father in Heaven Who held these eternal values in trust for their descendants. But our Torah is quick to point out that this should not lead us to ignore God's commandments, secure in the assumption that the credit left us by our ancestors will redeem us from all trouble and sorrow. For if we should follow this course our credit in heaven would be squandered before we knew it. Therefore we are told that "If you will obey these ordinances...*v'shomar*, then the Lord will continue to keep the *Z'chuth Avoth*, the guarding merits of our Patriarchs, in trust for you. You will have merits of your own and will not be dependent upon those of your ancestors, which will then be saved for you against that day when you will be in dire need of more help from Above than you could obtain on the strength of your own record of goodness and righteousness."

CHAPTER EIGHT

☐ THE TORAH AND ITS COMMANDMENTS

☐ 1 — WHY ISRAEL WAS CHOSEN TO RECEIVE THE TORAH

מַגִּיד דְּבָרָו לְיַעֲקֹב, חֻקָּיו וּמִשְׁפָּטָיו לְיִשְׂרָאֵל. לֹא עָשָׂה כֵן לְכָל גּוֹי וּמִשְׁפָּטִים בַּל
יְדָעוּם.   (תהלים קמ"ז)

"He declares His word to Jacob, His statutes and His ordinances to Israel. He has not done this with any nation, and as for His ordinances, they have not known them."   *(Psalms 147:19-20)*

We are told in the Midrash and in the Gemara that, before finally giving His Holy Law to Israel, God offered it to every other nation. But every other nation rejected the Torah, for none was willing to be burdened by regulations that would restrict one's choice of whatever way of life would seem easiest and most pleasant. It was only the people of Israel who accepted the Torah freely and unconditionally.

Asks the Maggid of Dubno: How did God go about presenting His Law to one nation after the other, offering it for unconditional acceptance? And he proceeds to illustrate his account with a *Moshol:*

116

A tradesman once went to a wholesale store to buy wearing apparel on credit terms. The storekeeper was rather reserved and showed him some of the articles he carried, but he did not bring out staple commodities, and quoted high prices for everything he had on display. In the end the tradesman left the store without having purchased anything. A little later another customer entered and said that he was willing to pay cash. This time the storekeeper brought out the best and most marketable of his stock and quoted reasonable wholesale prices. Soon a sale was made and the customer left, well satisfied. After the door of the shop had closed, an apprentice, who had been watching the proceedings, asked his employer why he had so obviously discriminated against the customer who had wanted to make purchases on credit terms. Answered the storekeeper, "Did you see that first man? I could tell at once that he was not dependable and would never have paid his debts. I had to be courteous to him, but I was not anxious to have his trade, and I acted accordingly. Now the other man, who always pays cash for what he buys, is an old customer, a trustworthy gentleman to whom, in fact, I would have extended unlimited credit if he had requested it. Naturally, I am pleased to do business with a person like that and I did my best to accommodate him."

The One Above, said Rabbi Yaakov, had the most precious merchandise of all to offer — the Holy Torah. Now He knew in advance what the attitude of the other nations would be. They were anxious to enjoy the pleasures of this world to the full, and therefore they could hardly have been relied upon to keep the Law. Hence God was not anxious that they should have it. Nevertheless, He did not wish to be unkind, and so He offered His Torah to one heathen nation after the other. However, in each case, He emphasized that aspect of the Torah which would be the most difficult for that nation to accept. Thus, for example, when He presented it to the Edomites, He told them, first of all, of the Sixth Commandment, which prohibits murder, for the Children of Esau had made murder a part of their way of life. The Ammonites and the Moabites, who were notorious for their harems, were shown, first of all, the Seventh Commandment, which forbids adultery. All these nations

had demonstrated throughout their previous history that they would
be unable to observe a Code of Law such as the Torah contained,
and God preferred not to give it to them, for the laws of the Torah
are meant to be kept, not violated. The Children of Israel, however,
had proven from the very beginning their constancy and their
readiness to do whatever would be God's will. Therefore God, anxious that they should have His Torah, revealed to them all the
profound wisdom that is contained in His Eternal Law.

□ 2 — THE ETERNAL VALUES OF TORAH AND MITZVOTH

לֹא יָמוּשׁ סֵפֶר הַתּוֹרָה הַזֶּה מִפִּיךְ וְהָגִיתָ בּוֹ יוֹמָם וָלַיְלָה . . . כִּי אָז תַּצְלִיחַ אֶת דְּרָכֶךְ
וְאָז תַּשְׂכִּיל.   (יהושע א')

**"The Book of this Law shall not depart from your mouth, but you
shall study it day and night, so that you will be careful to do according to all that is written in it, for then you will make your
ways prosper, and then you will have success."** *(Joshua 1:8)*

The Torah, when diligently studied and strictly observed, can help
us overcome the hurdles of daily life. The eternal values it contains
remain constant for all times to come. Other ideas may come and
go, but the lofty ideals of the Torah will abide forever.

The Dubnoer Maggid would illustrate this important lesson with
a simple *Moshol*, as follows:

A man who, through the force of circumstances, was reduced to
poverty, finally left his native land to make a new start elsewhere.
The ship on which he sailed landed at an island which was almost
entirely untouched by modern civilization. It was there that our
friend decided to settle.

Conditions on the island were the most primitive imaginable.
The dark natives knew only the bare rudiments of agriculture and
had only a few species of fruit and grain, so that they eagerly
crowded around the newcomer when he let it be known that he had

brought with him a great variety of fruits and vegetables. The white man was amazed when the islanders paid him with precious stones. It seemed that a treasure chest had been washed ashore from a shipwreck, and its contents had little value for the natives, who regarded them as nothing but colored pebbles. Our friend built himself a home, tilled the soil around it and eventually became famous for the golden grain and the luscious fruits he had been able to grow. Gradually he came to forget his native land and even the wife and son he had left behind him there. He married one of the native women, who bore him several children. Before he died, he called his sons and daughters together and told them that he had another son, by a previous marriage, living in a country beyond the seas. "He is a very learned and clever young man," he said to them, "and I want you to invite him here after I am gone. Show him my fruit, my grain and my seeds, and my precious stones, too, and tell him that he may take as his inheritance whatever he may choose, for, in fact, he is my firstborn son."

After the death of their father, the children did as he had requested and called their foreign half-brother to come to them. Of course the young man, coming from a civilized country, immediately chose as his inheritance the diamonds, emeralds and rubies which his father had left and hardly even glanced at the barns and storehouses which his father's children showed him. It seemed quite ridiculous to the islanders that the foreigner should spurn the precious fruit and grain and content himself with the bright pebbles which were on the island in great abundance. And his young half-brothers simply could not understand why their father should have thought him so clever.

The foreigner liked the island so well that he decided to stay there. Soon he began a large-scale project of teaching modern agricultural methods to all the natives so that they, too, could achieve the abundant harvests for which his father had been famous. He was more than successful, and after a few years the entire island had been turned into one vast tract of fertile fields and gardens.

What with the overabundance of fruits and vegetables, the

natives' sense of value underwent a gradual change. Fruit and corn, which seemed to be everywhere and lay rotting in the streets, were held in low esteem, while jewels, of which few were left on the island, rose amazingly in value. Now the white man, with his treasure-chest full of precious stones, was regarded as fabulously wealthy, and his half-brothers said: "He was clever, after all! He looked ahead; he saw what the future would bring and made sure that he would have plenty of what would be of value the world over, while we were stupid and thought only of the present time and place."

Said Rabbi Yaakov: Most of us, too, are inclined to be like the natives of that far-off island. We adopt whatever sense of values is current in the society in which we happen to live and give little thought to the future. But, as our Prophets have never ceased to warn us, the day will come when the eternal, immutable values will be established once more, when the world will forsake the fancies that have proven transient and perishable and return to the eternal ideals set forth in the Torah and the *Mitzvoth* that were given by God to the people of Israel on Mount Sinai.

"Then the eyes of the blind shall be opened, and the ears of the deaf shall be unstopped" (Isaiah 35:5). *"And the glory of the Lord shall be revealed, and all flesh shall see it together, for the mouth of the Lord has spoken it"* (Isaiah 40:5). *"And the word of our God shall stand forever"* (Isaiah 40:8)

□ 3 — No Omissions, No Additions

אֶת כָּל הַדָּבָר אֲשֶׁר אָנֹכִי מְצַוֶּה אֶתְכֶם אֹתוֹ תִשְׁמְרוּ לַעֲשׂוֹת לֹא תֹסֵף עָלָיו וְלֹא תִגְרַע מִמֶּנּוּ. (ראה)

"All this matter which I command you, be careful to do it; do not add to it, nor diminish from it." *(Deut. 13:1)*

Over and over again, our Torah tells us that its commandments represent the will of God, which we must obey faithfully and implicitly if we are to meet with the approval of our Heavenly Father. The laws of the Torah are not man-made, but Divinely-given; hence we must not deviate from them, either to the left or to the right. Any change that we might make in the Law, whether it be in the form of abridgement or by means of additional legislation, will serve only to deprive the commandments of their Divine character and value.

Most of us have come to understand that we dare not drop or even abrogate any of these laws, but we may very well ask why it should also be forbidden to make new, additional laws, or to add to the existing ones, which would only serve to increase the power and scope of the God-given Torah.

Said Rabbi Yaakov Mi-Dubno: "I shall answer with a *Moshol.* Reuben once lent a plate to his friend and neighbor Simon. After some time Simon returned the plate, but also gave Reuben a saucer, remarking that the plate had had offspring which he was herewith turning over to its rightful owner. Reuben accepted the gift un-questioningly. A few weeks later, Simon borrowed a pitcher from Reuben, and when he brought it back he also brought a smaller pitcher, explaining that the pitcher, too, had had offspring. Again Reuben did not protest. A few months passed. Then Reuben lent Simon a silver candlestick, but this time Simon did not return it. When Reuben asked Simon to give it back to him, Simon sadly reported that the candlestick had died. "What do you take me for?" Reuben shouted angrily, "You know as well as I do that a candlestick cannot die." Replied Simon calmly, "When I told you that your plate and your pitcher had had offspring, you believed it without question. Well, if plates and pitchers can reproduce, then candlesticks can also die!"

This amusing little story, said Rabbi Yaakov, should help us understand the attitude we should have to the Law of God. If we would permit ourselves to add to it new laws of our own making, we will gradually forget that our Law is God-given, and without even realiz-ing it we will cease to regard it as inviolate and abrogate those laws that seem to us too difficult or inconvenient to keep. Therefore the Torah would have us know: "Not only are you not permitted to diminish from the Law, but you are enjoined just as strictly from adding to it. For whoever tampers in any way with the Law of God will soon cease to believe in its Divine nature, and then the Torah and its commandments will not be strengthened but only weakened by his actions."

□ 4 — Laws and Statutes

זֹאת חֻקַּת הַתּוֹרָה אֲשֶׁר צִוָּה ה׳   לֵאמֹר דַּבֵּר אֶל בְּנֵי יִשְׂרָאֵל וְיִקְחוּ אֵלֶיךָ פָרָה אֲדֻמָּה תְּמִימָה.   (חקת)

"This is the statute of the Law which the Lord had commanded, saying: 'Speak to the Children of Israel, that they bring you a red heifer, without blemish....' "   (Num. 19:2)

If we study the Mitzvoth of our Torah from a solely human point of view, we can divide them into two distinct categories: First there are the *Mitzvoth Sichliyoth,* those universally accepted moral laws which are easily acceptable to any intelligent human being, such as the commandment not to steal, which is entirely in keeping with our natural sense of justice and equity, or not to murder, which has become part of almost every civilized man-made code of laws as well.

Then, however, we have the *Mitzvoth Chukioth,* the so-called "statutes" for which finite human intellect may know no complete explanation, but which we must accept and observe nevertheless because they have been given to us by God, Who knows what is best for us and to Whom we owe absolute and unquestioning obedience. Perhaps the most puzzling of all of these statutes is the law we have quoted at the beginning of this chapter — the Biblical precept relating to the laws of purification connected with the red heifer, which even Solomon, the wisest of all men, could not explain. Among other such statutes, which are known as *Chukim,* are the laws of *Shaatnez,* the prohibition against the wearing of mixtures of wool and linen (Deut. 22:11); *Kilayim,* the prohibition against the planting and cultivation of certain mixtures of plants and the cross-breeding or harnessing together of various kinds of animals (Lev. 19:19); the ban against shaving with a razor (Lev. 19:27); and that against the eating of blood (Gen. 9:4). These laws may seem strange to the modern student, but it must be remembered at all times that, like the so-called moral and civil laws of the Torah, these precepts, too, are God-given and therefore must have our welfare as their purpose.

Now we may ask ourselves: If these statutes truly are intended for the welfare of our people, why were they given only on Mount Sinai, and not centuries earlier to Abraham, Isaac and Jacob, who had also been Jews in the fullest sense of the word?

Said Rabbi Yaakov of Dubno: God originally endowed man with the natural physical instinct to select for himself only those foods that are conducive to his survival and good health and to cultivate only such habits as would further his well-being. This same instinct, if allowed free rein, will impel him to shun all those foods and habits that might endanger life and health. Our patriarchs, Abraham, Isaac and Jacob, lived lives of such pristine purity that they knew at all times what was good and evil not only in human society, but also for their own physical and spiritual welfare. All these things stood clearly revealed before them, so that they needed no special Revelation to learn of them. But our forefathers died, and the men and women who came after them were no longer so close to God as their ancestors had been. Their pure, God-given instincts had gradually been buried beneath the amenities and artificialities that had come to be considered essential aspects of everyday living. They were no longer sure of what was good and what was evil, and therefore God had to proclaim His Law for all to hear, so that if instinct could no longer lead them, the Word of God would be their guide.

This Law, which we know as our sacred Torah, was divided into two parts. First, the civil and criminal codes, laws conducive to social welfare, which pure reason would dictate us to observe even if we did not know that they are Divine in origin. And secondly, the *Chukim,* the statutes which man no longer has the gift to understand but which are essential, nevertheless, to the good health and happiness of every individual. That which, in better days long since gone, had been part and parcel of life, and had come as naturally to our ancestors as their very breathing, now had to be set forth in an explicit legal code lest man come to disregard it and suffer thereby. "This is the enactment of the Torah," we are told of these statutes. Each of them is a *Chukah* proclaimed by the Divine Lawgiver and must be strictly observed, though we may be incapable of fathoming its meaning, even as we read in the Book of Job, *"Behold, the fear of the Lord is wisdom; and to depart from evil is understanding"* (Job 28:28).

Moreover, we must not view any of God's laws as arbitrary, as the whims and caprices of some unreasoning power. We must know and remember at all times that they were prompted by infinite Wisdom, too profound for our limited intellect to grasp.

We are told: *"And these words, which I command you today, shall be upon your heart"* (Deut. 6:6). Note that we are not told, *"in* your heart" but *"upon* and *over* your heart." The commandments of God are to be over our hearts, binding upon us and not subject to the emotions that we harbor deep within. Therefore, do not say, "I cannot keep the *Mitzvoth,* for I do not understand them." Regardless of whether or not your intellect can grasp the *Mitzvoth,* it is your duty to keep them *"over and above"* the emotions and desires of your heart.

In view of what we have just learned, it would seem obvious that the purpose of the giving of the Torah on Mount Sinai was not so much the promulgation of the moral laws that all civilized nations now observe, but much more specifically the proclamation of the *Chukim,* those statutes which man would no longer keep were he not commanded by an explicit directive from God Himself to obey them for his own happiness and welfare.

□ 5 — THE LANGUAGE OF THE TORAH

מִכֹּל הַבְּהֵמָה הַטְּהוֹרָה תִּקַּח לְךָ שִׁבְעָה שִׁבְעָה . . . וּמִן הַבְּהֵמָה אֲשֶׁר לֹא טְהֹרָה הִיא
שְׁנַיִם . . . (נח)

In the Book of Genesis we read that before Noah entered the Ark, the Lord spoke to him as follows:

"Of every pure beast take to yourself seven and seven, each with his mate; and of the beast that is not pure, two and two, each with his mate." *(Gen. 7:2)*

It is noteworthy that the Torah says not simply *b'hemah t'me'ah,* "and of the *impure* beast" but *b'hemah asher lo t'horah hee,* "and of the beast *that is not pure."* The Talmud notes (Pesachim 3) that our sacred Books are replete with such euphemisms. For example, when reference is made to the blind, the Talmud speaks not of the "blind" but of persons who are *sagi nahor* "rich in light." On the other hand, in the dietary laws, the Torah does not hesitate to use the term *tamei,* "impure," over and over again with reference to the animals which are forbidden as food.

Why does the Torah in the above cited verse use apparently superfluous letters for euphemistic reasons, but not in the dietary laws?

This is the *Moshol* of the Dubnoer to answer our question:

There were two rich men living in one town, and they were both named Yossel. Now, the one Yossel was a wise and learned man, but the other man, though just as wealthy, was an ignoramus, generally known as "Yossel the Boor" to distinguish him from his learned and cultured namesake.

It happened that one day a stranger came to the house of Yossel the Scholar and asked the servant, who opened the door, where the other Yossel could be found. "You mean Yossel the Boor, don't you?" the servant responded. When his master heard the servant speaking thus of the man, he took him to task, saying: "You must not refer to any man as a boor. The others say they must call my namesake 'The Boor' to distinguish him from me. But in this house there can be no such excuse, for I will not have strangers think that I look down on any of my neighbors."

Soon thereafter, a marriage broker came to the house of the learned Yossel and proposed a match between the daughter of the latter and the son of his ignorant namesake. Yossel was furious that anyone should presume to suggest such a marital alliance, and cried out, "My daughter — married to the son of Yossel the Boor! Never! Not while I am alive!"

After the marriage broker had left, the servant came to his master and asked him why he had spoken of his neighbor in such uncomplimentary terms when, only a few days before, he, the servant, had been reprimanded for using the same term in connection with the ignoramus.

Said the learned Yossel, "Don't you understand? If you are asked for information as to where a certain man resides, you are not asked to give an account of his character. All you need tell is his address; if you refer to him by an uncomplimentary name such as the "Boor" you are guilty of *lashon hara,* of gossip, vile and uncalled-for. But when I receive a proposal of marriage for my daughter, I must be blunt and straightforward in explaining the reason why I must object to an alliance such as this. It was my duty as a father to make it plain to the marriage broker that I will not have my daughter marry the son of a man who is well known as an ignoramus and a boor."

So, too, it is with the language of the Torah. When, in the Book of Genesis, the Scriptures enumerated the species of animals and birds that entered the Ark, the classifications "pure" and "not pure" were used only for the sake of information, to identify, but not to brand the animals. Therefore the Torah uses a *lashon nekiyah,* a euphemism: "beasts that are not pure." In the dietary laws of the Books of Leviticus and Deuteronomy, on the other hand, it is the aim of the Torah explicitly to draw the boundary line between food in general and the food allowed to Israel. Israel is bidden to strive after holiness, and must not eat the same food as the other peoples of the earth (Lev. 11:44). Here the Torah mentions the non-pure animals not simply for the sake of giving interesting data, but in order to make a clear distinction between those animals that we may eat and those which we must shun as impure. Here the Torah cannot afford to mince words, but must tell us quite bluntly *"These are impure to you"* (Deut. 14:7 and 10; Lev. 11:8 *et al.*).

If we are to attain holiness, it is absolutely essential that we observe these Divine laws of purity. Hence they had to be set forth in clear and definite terms *"that you may differentiate between the holy and the profane, and between the impure and the pure"* (Lev. 10:10 and 11:47).

□ 6 — HELP YOUR NEEDY BROTHER

הִשָּׁמֶר לְךָ פֶּן יִהְיֶה דָבָר . . . קָרְבָה . . . שְׁנַת הַשְּׁמִטָּה וְרָעָה עֵינְךָ בְּאָחִיךָ הָאֶבְיוֹן וְלֹא תִתֵּן לוֹ וְקָרָא עָלֶיךָ אֶל ה' וְהָיָה בְךָ חֵטְא. (ראה)

"Beware lest there be an evil thought in thy heart, saying: 'The seventh year, the Year of Release, is at hand,' and your eye will be evil against your needy brother, and you will give him nothing; and he will cry to the Lord against you, and it will be a sin for you."
(Deut. 15:9)

This Biblical passage is a blunt warning to the wealthy not to use the financial problems presented by the *Shemitah* year, the Year of Release, as an excuse not to give charity or to grant loans to the needy, saying: "For one whole year now, I will not be permitted to till the soil or to sow, and to harvest the fruits of my field and so I must be very careful with what I have." Charity to the poor, motivated by brotherly love for our fellow-men, is one of the basic traits of the truly Jewish personality. As the Talmud puts it, "Israel is known by three characteristics: mercy, chastity and charity" (Yebamoth 79a). If you close your ears to the cry of your needy brother, the Scriptures tell us "it will be counted against you as a sin."

Said the Maggid of Dubno in a *Moshol* to make this clear:

A great ship was proudly sailing on the high seas. She carried aboard many important merchants bringing huge quantities of merchandise abroad. One day, there arose a violent storm and it became obvious that the ship was in danger of sinking. The captain called his passengers together and asked them to throw overboard whatever heavy merchandise they carried with them, lest they all be drowned. The merchants, anxious to save their lives, immediately began to bring out their precious cargo and to ditch it as quickly as they could. One of them, however, who was known to have with him a considerable load of valuable goods, was about to ditch not his well-sealed crates, but his *Tallith* and *Tefillin* and the holy books he had carried with him to help him do his duty to his Father in Heaven. But his companions stopped him, saying: "Foolish man! Throw into the ocean your crates of precious stones; you can do without them! But are you insane, to throw away the holy symbols and utensils of your religion? These are *our life*, the very things that we need if we want God's protection!"

When people are in stress and fear for their survival, they hasten to throw overboard not their luxuries and excess finery, but the laws of mercy and charity on which, in fact, their very life ultimately depends. As our Sages have stated in the Talmud: "If a man sees that his own means of support are growing scanty, he should increase his contributions to charity" (Gittin 7a).

Thus the Word of God warns us never to forsake the needy, not even when the Year of Release draws near and we are tempted to be careful with our resources. If we will try to economize with our own possessions at the expense of the poor man, "he will cry to the Lord against you, and it will be a sin for you." Rabbi Yaakov translates the Hebrew word *chet*, which is usually rendered as "sin", by the term "lack." In other words, if the poor man must complain to Heaven about your callous disregard of his needs, it is not he, but you, who will suffer loss thereby. It is therefore within your own power to avoid such loss by showing kindness and consideration to the needy even if you think that you yourself are in financial straits.

□ 7 — THE MITZVOTH AS PREVENTIVE MEDICINE

שׁוֹמֵר מִצְוָה לֹא יֵדַע דָּבָר רָע.   (קהלת ח׳ ה׳)

"Whoever keeps the commandment shall know no evil thing...."
(Ecclesiastes 8:5)

The commandments of the Torah are not simply "ritual laws" but rules essential for the soundness of body and soul. Whoever will consider them binding on himself and observe them faithfully "will know no evil thing." As long as we obey the Law of God we will remain sound of mind and spirit, but if we should ever come to disregard it, we run the risk of physical and spiritual disaster.

A sick man must have implicit confidence in his doctor and obey his orders diligently and accurately, if he is to be cured. No patient would dare argue with his doctor, or insist that he can take the prescribed medicine only if the reason for doing so could be adequately explained to him. He must be convinced that whatever his physician has ordered him to do is essential for his well-being. If he refuses to listen to his doctor's advice, he cannot expect to be cured.

So, too, the Torah tells us: *"If you will diligently hearken to the voice of the Lord your God, and do what is right in His eyes, and will listen to His commandments, and keep all His statutes, I will put none of the diseases on you which I have put upon the Egyptians, for I am the Lord your Healer"* (Exod. 15:26).

According to this Scriptural verse we are actually in the position of patients to our Heavenly Physician, to Whose regimen we must adhere implicitly and without question if we are to remain alive and sound in body and mind.

Thus the Book of Ecclesiastes teaches us as follows: *Whoever keeps the commandment,* unconditionally, unquestioningly, as an emanation of God's will and wisdom, *shall know no evil thing.* He will be safe from all harm, for *"the heart of the Wise One* (meaning God) *discerns time and judgment"* (Ecclesiastes 8:5). God, as the Source of all wisdom, knows the right time and place for action. He alone knows what the future will bring and His Laws are designed solely to help us live through that future and to ensure our welfare for all times to come. It therefore behooves us to be obedient to the Law for our own welfare.

□ 8 — THE MITZVOTH AND THE PLEASURES OF THIS WORLD

לֹא נִתְּנוּ הַמִּצְוֹת אֶלָּא לְצָרֵף בָּהֶם אֶת הַבְּרִיּוֹת.   (בראשית רבה)

"The Laws have been given for the purpose of refining man through them."   *(B'reshith Rabbah 44)*

If we study Prophetic literature, we will find that our Prophets do not attach great importance to the pleasures of this world. In fact, there is a strong tendency in the Holy Writings to label all the joys of this life as transient and trivial, rather than praiseworthy. The Book of Ecclesiastes, for example, considers that feasting and drinking, riches and honor are of little importance and may actually have a detrimental effect on man's character.

Now we may ask: But is it not a fact that some of the most important *Mitzvoth* of our Torah could not be fulfilled if it were not for these very joys of this world? How could we give charity if we had no wealth? How could we share our possessions with our fellow-men if we had none of our own? And why should theft and robbery be such a great sin if wealth and property are not considered fundamental? If all earthly riches are truly "vanity of vanities," as we read in the Book of Ecclesiastes (1:2), why should a thief be branded a criminal?

There is an answer to our question. Wealth and luxury are not evil in themselves, but they serve a worthwhile purpose only if they are used as means to purify and refine our own personality. What matters is not what wealth we possess, but what *Mitzvoth* we perform with it, for it is only by fulfilling the commandments of God that we can come nearer to Him. If we will adopt this attitude to material wealth and to the performance of all *Mitzvoth*, we will eventually find that we will come to observe God's Laws as a matter of course, spontaneously and out of love and affection for Him Who ordained them.

This is what the Rabbis mean when they say that "the Laws (of the Torah) have been given for the purpose of refining man through them." Hence, when a man gives up part of his wealth for charity he will become a better person for what he has done, and thus fulfill the purpose for which that *Mitzvah* was originally given. Man is easily influenced by his environment, but his personality is affected even more by his actions. Every good deed a man performs will encourage the other good traits in his basic character to unfold, while any evil that he may do will bring out even more of the evil that may dwell hidden deep in his soul. Therefore God has commanded us to be merciful, to strive for goodness in all earthly affairs and not to covet evil things. Covetousness hurts us more than it harms our neighbors, for it makes our soul turn to evil rather than to good. It is the Torah's aim to uproot every bit of selfishness from our hearts.

When a theft has been committed, God is not angry because some person has been deprived of a cherished possession, for wealth has little worth in His sight. He is angry only that a creature of His should have so degraded himself as to resort to such self-destructive conduct. *"So are the ways of every one that is greedy for gain; it takes away the life of its owners"* (Prov. 1:19). He who does good to others helps himself thereby; he who does wrong only harms himself.

God has created for us a world full of things to be desired and coveted, and has handed them over to us. But they were given to us not for our selfish enjoyment, but only in order that we may employ them to do good. Wealth was not meant to be the be-all and end-all of human endeavor; it has value only if it is used to do good.

Said the Maggid of Dubno in a simple *Moshol:*

A father once said to his son, "My son, I will give you an inn, fully stocked with delicious food and with drinks that gladden the heart. The inn will afford you a good living, but remember always that the food and drink are not for you but only for your customers. Use the food to satisfy the hunger and thirst of the rich and the frivolous, but be abstemious yourself, if you wish to prosper."

So it is with the blessings of this world. The Creator put wealth upon this earth, but it was not His intention that the people of

Israel should revel in luxury. God is good to every living thing and therefore seeks to provide for all of mankind. Israel, as His chosen people, is charged with the duty of helping to provide for those in need. The unbridled enjoyments of this world are not for the faithful believer, but only for those who have not yet attained the spiritual plane at which a human mind can understand such things. The Bible tells us, *"And you shall be to Me My own treasure among all peoples; for all the earth is Mine"* (Exod. 19:5).

The Lord has said to Israel: "Here is all the wealth of the world, placed before you. But remember, you are not to partake of it limitlessly for your own advantage. If you wish to prosper, you must use this wealth as My representatives on earth, to provide for the needs of others. For you, as My own chosen nation, are set apart from the rest of mankind, and the only way in which you can demonstrate your chosenness is by the superiority of your conduct and by the refinement of your character."

□ 9 — THE EVIL IMPULSE — AN ARTFUL DODGER

אָמַר ר׳ יוֹחָנָן מִשׁוּם ר׳ בְּנָאָה: אַשְׁרֵיהֶם יִשְׂרָאֵל, שֶׁבִּזְמַן שֶׁהֵם עוֹסְקִים בַּתּוֹרָה וּבִגְמִילוּת חֲסָדִים יִצְרָם מָסוּר בְּיָדָם, וְאֵין הֵם מְסוּרִים בְּיַד יִצְרָם.
(עבודה זרה ה׳)

"Rabbi Yochanan said in the name of Rabbi B'na'ah: 'Happy is Israel, for during the time that they are occupied with the study of the Torah and with lovingkindness, the Tempter is delivered into their hands, but they are not delivered into the hands of the Tempter.' " *(Avodah Zarah 5b)*

The Psalms, too, tell us: *"Depart from evil and do good"* (Psalms 34:15). But there are many people who deliberately ignore the good and prefer to do evil. To them the Psalmist says: "God will likewise break you forever; He will take you up and pluck you out of your tent, *v'sheresh'cha,* and He will root you out of the land of the living. Selah" (Psalms 52:7).

It is interesting to note that, in the Hebrew language, the verbal root *sharash* can be employed to form either of two verb structures that denote the extreme opposites of one another. In the *Pi-el* inflection, as it was used in the verse from Psalm 52, it means "to uproot" or "to extirpate." But in the ordinary inflection, the *Kal,* it means just the opposite; namely "to take root." This contrast is highly significant, as explained by Rabbi Yaakov in an ingenious *Moshol:*

A thief, bent on no good, saw a bank messenger carrying large bags of money from a large business house to a nearby bank. The thief pondered how he could gain possession of the money. After several more trips from the store to the bank, the bank messenger stopped to inspect the show-windows of a large clothing store. The thief, noticing this, himself entered that store and told the salesman that he wanted to order a very expensive suit, of the best quality, for his master. "Money is no object to my master," he explained, "but he insists that the suit must fit perfectly."

"How can I be sure that it will fit?" asked the salesman. "I do not know your master's measurements."

"Easily," replied the thief. "Come to the door with me, and I'll pick out a person outside with the same figure that my master has, and you can use that man as a model for taking the measurements." The salesman agreed to the suggestion, and the two stood in the entrance of the store, looking out into the street. After a few moments they both noticed the bank messenger, whose jacket was crammed with bags filled with bank notes. The thief pointed to the man and said to the salesman, "This man has exactly my master's build." Thereupon the salesman called the stranger in and offered to pay him if he would remain for five minutes to serve as a model for a customer. The messenger had hardly taken off his jacket and hung it over the back of a chair in the fitting room, when the thief pounced upon it, emptied its pockets and silently stole away with his loot. Meanwhile the sumptuous silken material was being fitted on the messenger's body, and the fitter was busy basting the material to measure. Suddenly, the messenger became aware that he had been robbed, and attempted to get free in order to catch the thief. But the fitter held him back and said, "I am sorry, but you cannot leave. I have not completed the fitting for the suit." And when the messenger became insistent, the fitter replied, "Well, if you must go, then first take off my silken garments because I will not let you run away wearing my unsold merchandise." And so the messenger had to remove the fitted garment before he could rush out and try to locate his money.

This parable, said Rabbi Yaakov, can be applied most appropriately to man. Man consists of two parts, the body, *Guf,* which is earthly, and the soul, *Neshamah,* which is an emanation of God. It is that heavenly spark within us that uplifts us to greater heights while we live on earth, and which never ceases yearning for the moment of release from earthly life, when it will be able to return to God in perfect purity. But then the Tempter comes in the guise of a thief, and attempts to rob man of his heavenly riches by making him covet the silken luxuries of wealth and revelry on earth, so that he will be reluctant to discard them. And as long as man cannot free himself from the wrappings of earthly pleasures, his soul cannot obtain the yearned-for release.

Hence, by having become so firmly *rooted* in the earth, in the antithesis of Heaven, man has become *uprooted* and cut off from the life of Heaven, the "land of the living." This is what the dual connotation of the verbal root *sharash* implies. By allowing the wicked man to strike firm roots in this world, God uproots him from the healthier soil of the World-to-Come. The Tempter, the evil impulse, is only a tool, performing God's will upon the wicked. But the same God Who made the impulse of evil also established firm bulwarks against it in the form of the Torah and the *Mitzvoth.* The only way in which we can foil the Tempter is to spend all our lives in the performance of the duties enjoined upon us by that Law of God.

While the pleasures of this world tempt man to become too firmly rooted in earth and thus threaten to cut him off from the higher spheres of the spirit, the study of Torah and the practice of loving-kindness will help him overcome these temptations so that he will readily divest himself of the fleeting luxuries of earthly living and become rooted for all eternity in the *Olam Ha-emeth* and rise to the lofty heights of heavenly holiness and happiness.

☐ 1 — ISRAEL'S TRUE HOLINESS

קְדֹשִׁים תִּהְיוּ כִּי קָדוֹשׁ אֲנִי ה' אֱ־לֹהֵיכֶם.   (קדושים)

אָמַר הַקָּדוֹשׁ בָּרוּךְ הוּא לְיִשְׂרָאֵל הוֹאִיל וְהִקְדַּשְׁתִּי אֶתְכֶם לִשְׁמִי עַד שֶׁלֹּא בָּרָאתִי
הָעוֹלָם לְפִיכָךְ הֱיוּ קְדוֹשִׁים כְּשֵׁם שֶׁאֲנִי קָדוֹשׁ.   (ילקוט)

"You shall be holy; for I, the Lord, your God, am holy" (Lev.
19:2). To this, our Sages comment as follows: "Said the Holy
One, blessed be He, to Israel, 'Because I sanctified you for My
Name, even before I had created the world, for that very reason
shall you be holy, even as I am holy.' "   (Yalkut)

We may ask what difference it makes whether Israel was sanctified
before the Creation of the World or after it.

   Said the Maggid of Dubno: It should be easy to understand why
God hallowed the people of Israel long before the world was created.
And he made the reason quite clear with the help of a Moshol:

135

A wealthy man of a small town had an only daughter for whom he was seeking a husband. As was the custom then, he went to one of the great yeshivoth and asked the head of the academy to give him as a son-in-law that student who had shown the greatest piety and the greatest erudition and eagerness for study in the entire institution. "If you will find me such a young man for my daughter," the father promised, "I will donate a large sum of money for any good cause you may choose." The head of the academy excused himself and a few minutes later returned with a student whom he praised highly as a most pious and clever young man. "His zeal for study is so great," said the learned Rabbi, "that he turns night into day in order to miss no opportunity for study." The wealthy man was duly impressed, took the youth with him to his home town and married his daughter to him in a most elaborate wedding.

Some time later the father-in-law noticed that the young husband was spending less and less time on his studies, and called him to account for his laziness. The son-in-law looked at the older man with ill-concealed contempt. "You may ask the beadle of the house of study here," he asserted, "whether I am not the most regular and industrious scholar in the entire town. Even if I don't study all day long, I'm still better than most of the other men. Why, they often let a whole week pass without even looking at a holy book, while I still spend at least two hours each day at study. In fact, even if I should stop studying altogether I would still know much, much more than all the others put together."

But his father-in-law replied sternly, "Have I brought you here just to be able to say that you're the best student in my little town? Remember, I picked you from among all the students of a great yeshivah because they told me you were the most outstanding and the most zealous student in the entire institution. It was because of your great potential as a scholar that I wanted you as a husband for my daughter. It is not enough for me that you simply are content to know more than all the other young men in this town. I am not asking you to compare yourself to the others here; what I want is to have you continue studying so that you may realize all the potential that your Rabbi assured me you possess."

We may well compare the people of Israel to that conceited yeshivah student. Had the people of Israel been chosen from among all the nations after the Creation of the world, Israel might easily have fallen prey to the delusion that, whatever it may do or fail to do, it would still be better than any other nation on earth, for had not God looked at them all, and found them wanting in comparison to the Jewish people? But this is not what God desires. What He requires of Israel is that Israel realize the unique potential for holiness with which it has been divinely endowed. Therefore He says to the people of Israel: "Remember, I sanctified you for My Name long before I made the world and all the peoples that dwell upon it. I did it then, and not later, lest you be led to evaluate your spiritual growth in terms of that of the other nations and be lulled into complacency by the knowledge that you surpass them still. No, *you shall be holy even as I, the Lord your God, am holy*, unique and beyond all comparison."

□ 2 — HOW TO LOVE GOD

שְׁמַע יִשְׂרָאֵל ה' אֱ־לֹהֵינוּ ה' אֶחָד. וְאָהַבְתָּ אֵת ה' אֱ־לֹהֶיךָ בְּכָל לְבָבְךָ וּבְכָל נַפְשְׁךָ וּבְכָל מְאֹדֶךָ. וְהָיוּ הַדְּבָרִים הָאֵלֶּה אֲשֶׁר אָנֹכִי מְצַוְּךָ הַיּוֹם עַל לְבָבֶךָ.   (ואתחנן)

"Hear, O Israel, the Lord our God, the Lord is One. And love the Lord your God with all your heart, and with all your soul, and with all your might. And these words which I command you today, shall be upon your heart."   *(Deut. 6:4-6)*

In the great anthology of Midrashic literature known as the *Yalkut*, we are told: "If you do not know how to fulfill the command to '*love the Lord your God with all your heart* ...,' you can learn how this may be done by reading on: *'And these words which I command you today, shall be upon your heart...'*"

The Maggid of Dubno comments: "If you wish to release a bird from a trap, all you need do is open the trap and the bird will fly out of his own volition. It is not necessary for you to lift out the bird with your hands and help it spread its wings. The bird can do that by itself.

"Our soul, like the bird, is entrapped, caught in the snare of the evil inclination of our heart. If this trap is sprung by the mighty effort of our willpower, the soul will need no help in breaking free and finding its connection with its Heavenly home."

And he would cite the *Moshol* about the peasant from a small village who went to the city to buy a fine coat for himself. "This one will surely fit you," said the dealer. But the peasant could not get into the coat which the dealer had brought out; it seemed to be too tight.

The dealer laughed. "If this coat is to fit you, you must first take off your old sheepskin jacket and all your other rags. If you don't, it's quite obvious that you'll never be able to get into this fine garment. Besides, those rags certainly don't go well with such a coat."

Most men are like that peasant. They seek to clothe themselves in the attire of the love of God, but they find, to their dismay, that they cannot ever get into this new garment until they have cast off the ragged remnants of their evil impulses and the slovenly habits which have become their second nature. If men could readily discard the evil that is in them they would not find any difficulty in knowing how to love God.

Now what must we do if we are to love God in all truth and sincerity? The Torah itself gives us the answer: *"And these words...shall be upon your heart..."* The sacred teachings of God must be directly next to your heart, with no barriers in between. You must remove from your heart all its wrappings of smugness and sophistication so that the word of God may rest directly upon it, inscribed upon your heart to remain there forever. It is only in this manner that you can love your God as He wishes to be loved.

☐ 3 — LEST WE FORGET

צוּר יְלָדְךָ תֶּשִׁי וַתִּשְׁכַּח אֵ־ל מְחֹלֲלֶךָ.   (האזינו)

"The Rock fathered in you the ability to forget, and you forgot God Who bore you."   *(Deut. 32:18)*

This is the literal translation given by the Maggid of Dubno for the verse that is usually rendered as *"Of the Rock that fathered you, you were unmindful, and you forgot God Who bore you."*

Before you pass judgment on the Dubnoer's unique translation, let the maggid himself explain his rendering with one of his clever *Mesholim:*

A man was once arrested and hauled into court under a false accusation. All the evidence was against him and he did not know how he could escape the unfortunate miscarriage of justice that seemed inevitable. In his despair he went to a renowned lawyer who said to him, "Pretend you are insane. Then perhaps they will not find you guilty." The man followed his counselor's advice, and was cleared. When the lawyer called on him to collect his well-earned fee, he found his client talking gibberish and grimacing for all the world like a real lunatic. Said the counselor: "You cannot make me believe that you are mad enough not to know what I want, for it was I myself who taught you how to act the madman. Come, come, young man, do not attempt to use against me the very thing I taught you to do to save your own life."

God, our wise Father in heaven, has the same complaint to make of us here below. God gave man the special faculty of being able to forget, lest he grow too weary from all the troubles and miseries of a lifetime on earth. But instead of putting this blessing only to that use for which it had originally been intended, man has turned the ability to forget against Him Who graciously gave it to man, for man has come to neglect God's holy commandments and thus forgotten his Heavenly Benefactor.

□ 4 — ON THE FEAR OF GOD

וַיֹּאמֶר מֹשֶׁה אֶל יְהוֹשֻׁעַ בְּחַר־לָנוּ אֲנָשִׁים וְצֵא הִלָּחֵם בַּעֲמָלֵק. (בשלח)
לָמָה יְהוֹשֻׁעַ? אָמַר לוֹ: זְקֵנְךָ אָמַר, "אֶת הָאֱ־לֹהִים אֲנִי יָרֵא" (מקץ). וּבָזֶה כְּתִיב
"וְלֹא יָרֵא אֱ־לֹהִים" (פ' זכור, כי תצא). יָבוֹא בֶּן בְּנוֹ שֶׁאָמַר "אֶת הָאֱ־לֹהִים אֲנִי
יָרֵא" וְיִפָּרַע מִמִּי שֶׁנֶּאֱמַר עָלָיו וְלֹא יָרֵא אֱ־לֹהִים".   (מדרש)

**"And Moses said to Joshua: 'Choose us men, and go out to fight
with Amalek.' "**   *(Exod. 17:9)*

Asks the Midrash: "Why was it Joshua of all people who was
chosen to fight the Amalekites?" It was because his ancestor,
Joseph,* said of himself *"I fear God"* (Gen. 42:18) as opposed to
Amalek, of whom the Bible tells us explicitly that *'he did not fear
God'* (Deut. 25:18). This is the reason why Joshua was destined by
Providence to wage this war that was to be so important for Israel's
survival.

But the Maggid of Dubno says: This is an oversimplification.
First of all, there were many other great men in the olden days who
genuinely feared the Lord. Why, then, is so much credit given to
Joseph in particular for having proclaimed *"I fear God"*? Besides,
why should a nation like Amalek, that was a heathen nation, have
been expected to "fear God"?

And Rabbi Yaakov proceeds to answer his own question with a
simple *Moshol:*

There were once two brothers in a town, the elder rich, and the
younger poor. The rich brother supported the poor one with money
and food, and gave him all of his worn clothing which he had put
aside. But unfortunately the younger man could not keep them for
long; after he had worn the garments for only a few weeks they
would be so shabby and dirty that he had to go to his brother to ask
for others. Eventually the older man grew impatient and attempted
to teach his brother how to care for the clothes so that he might be

---

* Joshua was of the tribe descended from Ephraim, a son of Joseph.

able to keep them for at least another year. Said the younger brother, "It is all very well for you to talk. When you get the clothes, the material is still brand new, but by the time they come to me they are practically worn out and I cannot make them last any longer."

Thereupon the wealthy man took him to his tailor, and ordered two suits, each of the same quality and make, one for himself and one for his brother, and he said, "Now let us see whose suit will last longer—yours or mine."

The outcome was quite as the older of the two had expected. While his garments were still intact a few weeks later, his brother's suit was nearly worn out. But when he questioned the young man, the latter only replied, "Do you really think you can change the laws of nature? A poor fellow simply cannot go about in clothes that look brand-new; it is a law of life that garments of the poor are tatters and there is nothing that you can possibly do about it."

Several weeks later, both brothers attended a wedding banquet where a *Badchan*, a professional buffoon, amused the audience by mimicking a poor man. But while his voice and his mannerisms were quite in keeping with the role he played, his clothes were tidy and well kept.

"Look at this man," said the older brother to the younger. "He is being paid to give a true-to-life imitation of a beggar, but see, he looks quite presentable. This should teach you that it is not necessary for poor people to go about in rags. Even the poor can at least look tidy and neat at all times. Tatters are not necessarily part of a life of poverty; in fact, they are an absolute disgrace for the poor."

Said the Maggid of Dubno: This should help us understand the Midrash, too. The Torah specifically says of Amalek, "He did not fear God," for even as rags are not an essential ingredient of poverty, so, too, blatant disrespect of the One God is not a basic tenet of the Gentile. The best proof of this may be found in the story of Joseph. Just as the buffoon at the wedding gave a perfect imitation of a poor man, so Joseph in Egypt felt compelled to pretend to his brothers that he was not Joseph the Israelite, but the ruler of Egypt. Naturally, he took great care not to make the slightest blunder, for he was not yet ready to make himself known to his brothers. Yet he said to them quite openly, "I fear God." Had he thought for even one moment that an Egyptian was exempt from the duty to fear the One God, he would certainly never have made this utterance. Thus we learn that if even an Egyptian was duty-bound to fear the Lord, it was certainly incumbent upon Amalek as well to fear Him. And if Amalek did not show the proper respect for the One God, then he was truly deserving of the extreme penalty. It is for this reason that the Torah puts special emphasis on the fact that Amalek did not fear Him. And since it was Joseph, and none other, who thus taught us that even the heathen nations are obliged to respect our God, he is given particular credit in the Torah, and it was Joshua, the most prominent personality among his descendants, who was chosen to lead Israel in battle against that nation of whom the Torah explicitly states that it *"did not fear God."*

□ 5 — HIS WAYS ARE UNSEARCHABLE

וְעַתָּה אַל־תֵּעָצְבוּ וְאַל־יִחַר בְּעֵינֵיכֶם כִּי־מְכַרְתֶּם אֹתִי הֵנָּה כִּי לְמִחְיָה שְׁלָחַנִי אֱ-לֹהִים לִפְנֵיכֶם. (ויגש)

"And now do not grieve, nor be angry with yourselves that you sold me here; for God sent me before you to preserve life."
(Gen. 45:5)

Joseph takes great pains to reassure his brothers that he not only forgives them for their wicked deed, but actually sees in it the fulfillment of God's will. For it was only due to his enforced stay in Egypt that he could save his own family and the entire people of Egypt from sure starvation.

Rabbi Yaakov of Dubno uses these verses as a text to illustrate that there is good even in what may seem to us to be the greatest calamity. And he proceeds to explain his thesis with a beautiful *Moshol:*

A king once had a precious ring the like of which did not exist anywhere else in the world. One day he was most distressed to find an ugly scratch on the smooth surface of the jewel set into the golden band. The experts whom he called in to look at the stone did not know how to go about removing the blemish without doing irreparable damage to the rare and beautiful jewel.

Finally, the king summoned a jeweler from a far-off country, who looked admiringly at the ring and then said with a sigh, "What a pity that a fine ring such as this should not be perfect!"

The others present thought, naturally, that he was referring to the scratch. But he continued. "There is something missing. Such a magnificent treasure ought to bear the coat of arms of its owner. Look here!" he suddenly exclaimed with delight. "This scratch, I think, is a perfect beginning for the design, and from here I will continue it until the jewel has a perfect likeness of your coat of arms engraved upon it. Only then will the ring become what it really should be."

Thus, said the Dubnoer, adversity is often nothing but the scratch in the ring of life from which the triumph of perfection can and must be wrought. We may not always understand the ways of God, but we know that He sends us no misfortune that does not carry good in its wake. Therefore do not grieve but put your trust and faith in His infinite wisdom.

□ 6 — WE NEED HIS GUIDANCE

וַיֹּאמֶר אִם־נָא מָצָאתִי חֵן בְּעֵינֶיךָ ה' יֵלֶךְ־נָא ה' בְּקִרְבֵּנוּ כִּי עַם־קְשֵׁה עֹרֶף הוּא.
(כי תשא)

"And he (Moses) said: 'If now I have found favor in Your eyes, O Lord, let the Lord, please, go among us, for it is a stiffnecked people.'" *(Exod. 34:9)*

In Exodus 33:3, however, we read that God Himself had said that "I *will not* go up among you, for you are a stiff-necked people." How, then, could Moses, but a short time later, ask God to enter into the midst of Israel for the very reason that it is a stiff-necked people?

Said the Maggid of Dubno: Let me reconcile what seems a contradiction with a little *Moshol:*

A trader once tried to sell earthen pitchers and wooden spoons in an elegant neighborhood of his city but found that no one there would buy his wares. One of the passersby smiled at him and said, "The people on this avenue do not fancy this type of merchandise — plain pitchers and crude wooden spoons. Why not go to the slums where the poor live; there you ought to get rid of your stuff much more easily, for those people are in need of what you have to sell."

To apply our *Moshol* to the history of our people, we must remember, at the outset, that Moses was under the erroneous impression that the Torah had been written not only for men, but for the angels as well. Therefore he said to God: "You and Your Torah are in Heaven. But obviously the angels, pure and lofty beings that they are, have no need for this Law. It is mankind, poor and weak, that needs Your direct guidance. My people are not perfect like the angels, *they are a stiff-necked people,* therefore let Your glory and Your Law descend into their midst to guide them so that they may conduct their lives in accordance with Your will."

□ 7 — HIS LAW DEMANDS STRICT OBEDIENCE

וַיֹּאמֶר מֹשֶׁה אֶל אַהֲרֹן הוּא אֲשֶׁר דִּבֶּר ה' לֵאמֹר בִּקְרֹבַי אֶקָּדֵשׁ וְעַל־פְּנֵי כָל־הָעָם
אֶכָּבֵד וַיִּדֹּם אַהֲרֹן. (שמיני)

"And Moses said to Aaron: 'This is what the Lord spoke, saying: Through them that are near unto Me I will be sanctified, and before all the people I will be glorified.' And Aaron held his peace."   *(Lev. 10:3)*

With these words of God, Moses attempted to console his brother Aaron after the death of Nadab and Abihu, two of Aaron's sons. This double tragedy had occurred shortly after Aaron had been installed as the High Priest in the new Sanctuary. The two young men, Nadab and Abihu, either motivated by unseemly zeal or perhaps under the influence of intoxicating drink, rushed into the Sanctuary and offered before the Lord a fire in a manner not in accordance with His command. As a result they perished instantly, on the very day that the Sanctuary was dedicated.

We read in the Midrash (Chapter 12) that Moses, attempting to console his brother, said to him, "O my brother, it was revealed to me on Mount Sinai that the Sanctuary was to be sanctified by the sacrifice of those who are especially dear to the Omnipotent. I had thought, therefore, that the one to offer his life to God would be either you or I. But, instead, it was your sons who had to perish. Therefore, take comfort in the thought that they must have been greater than either you or I, for otherwise they would not have been the ones chosen to lay down their lives before the Altar of the Lord."

Now we know that the death of a human being has never been pleasing in the sight of God. What, then was His purpose in having these two promising young men die—human sacrifices, as it were, before the fire of His Altar?

The Maggid of Dubno, when asked this question, would counter with a most ingenious *Moshol:*

A great king was about to build a city which he desired to make a model community. He invited traders, merchants, artists and artisans to settle there. He encouraged the building of factories, recreation grounds, schools, houses of worship and theatres. When the city was completed, the king had every reason to be pleased with his work, for it was indeed a place of great beauty and culture. In order to make quite sure that nothing had been forgotten in the planning of the community, the king called in a wise man and asked him to investigate and then report to him. When the expert had completed his study, he went to the king and said, "Your town, O King, is wonderful indeed. But you have forgotten to import physicians. No one should live in a town where there is no physician."

The king, anxious to remedy this situation, sent letters to prominent medical institutions throughout the world, asking them to recommend one of their most competent doctors to take charge of the health needs of his model community. From all the names submitted to him, the king finally chose a physician who enjoyed worldwide renown and who had the reputation of being able to cure any ailment that could possibly strike a human being. When the great doctor finally arrived, the entire city turned out to do him honor. To test his knowledge, the people began to look around for someone to bring to him as his first patient. They did not have to search for long, for in the crush of the welcoming crowd a man was taken ill and fainted. He was at once brought to the doctor, and all the people who had gathered at the scene thought the man most fortunate to be the first to be treated by a physician such as this. After examining him, the physician asked that the patient be brought to his home so that he might be able to observe him for several days. He spared no effort in attempting to cure the man, and he issued regular bulletins to keep the public informed of his progress in dealing with what turned out to be a lengthy illness. In the end, the patient died. Because of the violent reaction of the public to these tidings, the king felt it wise to summon the doctor and question him as to why the patient should have died of an illness which might have been unpleasant but seemed so simple a thing to treat.

Said the doctor: "According to the best of my knowledge, nothing further could be done for the patient. Why he died is beyond my power to explain. However unfortunate, it may be well that this should have happened to my very first patient here, when all of your subjects expected me to be able to work miracles. Probably they all had thought that, with a great physician such as I in their midst, they could throw all caution and all their health rules to the winds because I would be able to cure them if they should become ill. Now let this be a lesson to you and to them: No physician, however great, is a magician. A doctor cannot always bring about a cure, and then only if the patient cooperates and abides by the rules the doctor has given him to preserve his good health. Failing that, even the most outstanding of physicians cannot help his patient."

This *Moshol,* said Rabbi Yaakov, should answer our question.

After God had given the Law to His people Israel and erected His Sanctuary on earth, He wanted to give them a wise physician to heal them of all their ills. For this purpose He had the Sanctuary provided with an Altar, through which it was possible to help cure the people of any illness of mind or spirit. Of course, the Altar was not a magic instrument; it had no curative powers unless it was properly employed in the worship of God in accordance with the rules which He Himself had set forth.

But the people labored under a misconception; they thought that the Altar was a cure-all. And even Nadab and Abihu, the sons of the High Priest, who surely might have been expected to know better, did not follow the rules of the Law, but hastened to the Altar and offered a foreign sacrifice upon it. But, you may ask, why should they have had to die because of this small transgression? Are there no worse crimes than this? Know, then, that the Lord intended this to be a lesson to His people. The sacrifice to be offered in the Sanctuary was not meant to be a magic formula. The Sanctuary and its Altar can do nothing for Israel if Israel does not abide by the rules and regulations set down by God for its conduct. The Sanctuary must not be taken lightly or treated in accordance with human whim and caprice. It must be accorded the respect properly due it as a holy place. This is the fact that God sought to impress upon the Jewish people by the sudden death of Nadab and Abihu in the presence of all the people gathered to celebrate the dedication of the Sanctuary.

Therefore, the Talmud tells us that Moses said to his brother Aaron: *"Your sons died only to give you an opportunity to sanctify the Name of the Holy One, blessed be He"* (*Zevachim* 115b). Your sons, O Aaron, were chosen to serve as instruments to impress upon all of Israel the fact that God and His Sanctuary must not be taken lightly. Let this thought, that the Name of God will henceforth be accorded the honor rightly due it, be your consolation.

□ 8 — HE RENDERS ISRAEL IMMUNE TO ANY EVIL SPELL

כִּי לֹא נַחַשׁ בְּיַעֲקֹב וְלֹא־קֶסֶם בְּיִשְׂרָאֵל כָּעֵת יֵאָמֵר לְיַעֲקֹב וּלְיִשְׂרָאֵל מַה־פָּעַל אֵ-ל.
(בלק)

"For there is no (evil) spell with Jacob, neither is there any magic with Israel; in due time it shall be said to Jacob and to Israel: What has God wrought!"   *(Num. 23:23)*

What connection does the first part of the verse have with the second? The Maggid of Dubno explains it with the following *Moshol*:

A nobleman heard that a man in a far-off country had discovered an ointment which, if applied to the body, would render a person invulnerable. As he frequently had to travel through dark forests and lonely places in connection with his affairs, he gladly underwent the trouble and expense of travelling to the famed inventor and procuring the miraculous lotion. Before leaving for home, he liberally applied the ointment to every part of his body.

The way home led through a dark and lonely place, and the nobleman was suddenly attacked by a gang of highwaymen. They tried to beat him, and then to shoot him, but found that he remained unhurt through it all. Thinking that there must be some sort of magic at work protecting their victim they turned tail and fled, terror-stricken.

But imagine their surprise when their victim called them back and offered them some brandy to drink. They looked at him full of distrust and asked him why he should be so kind to them when they had just sought to rob and kill him. Replied the nobleman: "I am really grateful to you for giving me this opportunity to prove something of which I could never have been sure otherwise. I have just gone through great trouble and expense to secure a miraculous ointment which I was told would make me immune to physical attack. And it took your vain efforts to kill me to convince me that I have not been cheated. I could never have worked up the courage to find out through deliberate action on my own whether the ointment was really effective."

The people of Israel, like the nobleman, presumed that they were immune to all black magic and evil spells, for tradition had taught them that *"there is no (evil) spell with Jacob, neither is there any magic with Israel."* Their ancestor Jacob had served Laban for twenty years, and during all that time Laban had constantly been at work concocting evil spells to bring about Jacob's downfall, but to no avail. Jacob repelled them all, unhurt. The people of Israel, as the heirs of their patriarch, assumed that they had inherited this immunity as well. But they had no way of definitely ascertaining whether they were truly invulnerable.

The Biblical verse which we are here explaining deals with the vain attempts of Balaam to curse the people of Israel by means of crafty and evil spells. It was only then, *ka-eth,* when they saw that even the curses of Balaam had turned into blessings by the power of God's constant protection, that the Children of Israel knew that the tradition which had been handed down to them from the days of Jacob had indeed retained its validity. God, in His Providence, had proven to them that which, before, they had only been able to presume. Then Israel gave thanks to the Lord and exclaimed: *"What has God wrought!"*

□ 9 — HE GIVES GREAT REWARD

פִּינְחָס בֶּן־אֶלְעָזָר בֶּן־אַהֲרֹן הַכֹּהֵן הֵשִׁיב אֶת־חֲמָתִי מֵעַל בְּנֵי־יִשְׂרָאֵל . . . לָכֵן אֱמֹר
הִנְנִי נֹתֵן לוֹ אֶת־בְּרִיתִי שָׁלוֹם. (פינחס)

(The Lord said) **"Phinehas, the son of Eleazar, the son of Aaron the Priest, has turned My wrath away from the children of Isael, in that he was very jealous for My sake among them so that I did not consume the children of Israel in My jealousy. Therefore say: Behold, I give unto him My covenant of peace..."**

(Num. 25:11-13)

The Scriptures and, in fact, all of our sacred literature are unstinting in their praise for Phinehas, scion of a priestly family whose zeal for God and His Law was so great that he did not hesitate to act when prompt and drastic action was sorely needed. Israel was stricken by a plague because of its immorality and idol worship. When Phinehas saw the Israelite sinning with the

Midianite woman he became filled with divine wrath and rushed up and killed them both, whereupon the plague ceased and Israel was saved.

Yet we are at a loss to understand why God should have made a promise of a covenant of peace to Phinehas that was even greater than any vow He had ever made to either Moses or Aaron. The Midrash says that Phinehas was greatly blessed by God and that, "it is by right that he shall reap his reward." Why should so much stress be put on the fact that he was rewarded?

"Let me illustrate what I mean," says the Maggid of Dubno, and he proceeds with a simple *Moshol:*

A young man was hired out as an apprentice to a wealthy merchant. He had to work very hard, and he zealously applied himself to his tasks. In return, he received free room and board. One Purim day the merchant, together with his family and friends, was enjoying a sumptuous *Purim S'udoh,* to which the apprentice, as a member of the household, had also been invited. In the midst of the dinner, a stranger arrived and asked to see the master of the house, for he wanted to place a large order with his business concern. The merchant, however, refused to be disturbed at his dinner, but the young apprentice rose without a word, asked his employer for the keys to the warehouse and went out to help the customer. The transaction took several hours. After the stranger had left, the apprentice returned to his master and told him of the great profit which he had been able to obtain for the firm. The next morning, the merchant asked the boy what compensation he owed him for his extraordinary service of the day before.

"Nothing," replied the apprentice. "The agreement was that I was to receive free room and board from you for whatever service I might render."

Said the merchant: "Until now I thought that you liked the food that I gave you, and that you considered this as your pay. But now I have seen how zealous you are in your work. You were even prepared to miss a good dinner for the sake of my business, and I feel that what I have given you thus far is not sufficient compensation for such devotion."

Thus spoke the merchant. The apprentice, however, would have had no right to claim a reward on his own initiative, for he was still deeply in debt to his master, who had treated him like a son throughout the months of his service.

Now the same holds true, under ordinary circumstances, in the case of God and man. God, our heavenly Master, has given us life and health, and supplied us with food and with all the other things we need to remain alive. Therefore we shall remain forever in His debt, and whatever good we may do on this earth is still not nearly sufficient to repay Him for His kindness. How, then, could any man, Phinehas included, stand up and lay claim to a special reward for what he might have done in the Service of God?

In the Ethics of the Fathers, we read "But keep in mind that the *grant of reward* for the righteous is reserved for the Hereafter" (Avoth 2:21). Note that the word used here in connection with the reward of the righteous is *matan*, "a grant," as distinguished from compensation payable on demand. Not even the most righteous among men can ever presume to ask God for a reward.

But Phinehas had dedicated his whole life to the worship of the Lord. The Talmud tells us that in his zeal to fight for the cause of God, heedless of the consequences, Phinehas had put his own life in such jeopardy that it took ten miracles to save him from death. He thus demonstrated that life and health were not as dear to him as they were to others. It is for this reason that the Torah stresses that he, like the devoted apprentice, was truly deserving of a special reward from the Master Whom he had served so well. Of course Phinehas could and would never have asked for it on his own initiative, but God was determined to render His faithful servant some recompense for the devotion he had shown beyond the call of duty.

Since an earthly reward such as health and long life would not have been sufficient for Phinehas, his wages were to be paid in the currency of eternal values: *"Behold, I give to Him My covenant of peace."*

Thus we now more readily understand the statement in the Midrash concerning this zealous servant of God: "It is by right that he shall reap his reward."

☐ 10 — OUR GUIDES TO TRUE REVERENCE

אֶת ה' אֱ־לֹהֶיךָ תִּירָא. (עקב)

"The Lord your God you shall fear." *(Deut. 10:20)*

In the Hebrew language, the accusative may or may not be preceded
by the particle *eth*. In certain instances this particle may also
connote the preposition "with."

It is generally accepted as a principle of Biblical interpretation
that the particle *eth* in the Torah, particularly in connection with
actual law, always connotes additional implications which are not
expressly mentioned in the text, and must therefore be ascertained
by the diligent student. Simon the Amsonite categorically stated
that *eth* when found in the Torah always implies the inclusion in the
object of something else not expressly set down in the text. But
when, in his studies, he came to the passage we are now consider-
ing, he stopped short. For if he were to apply this principle here, it
might be easy to come to the conclusion that, in addition to the
Lord, we must fear also some other power not named in the verse.
Rabbi Akiva, however, explained that the principle was valid even
in this case. The particle *eth* in the above Biblical verse simply
implies that, next to God Himself, we owe respect and reverence to
the Sages and the holy men who expound His law on earth:
Eth — l'rabboth Talmidey Chachamim (Bava Kamma 41b).

Yet, we may well ask ourselves, why did Rabbi Akiva think it
proper to place a human authority, however great and wise, side by
side with the name of God, and how did he come to derive this great
teaching from the particle *eth* of this one particular Biblical verse?

And here is the *Moshol* of the Maggid of Dubno to answer our
inquiry:

There was once a blind man who had to travel about constantly
in order to earn his living. In order to be able to get about, he
always had with him a friend who acted as his guide. Whenever his
travels took him beyond the borders of his country, he would carry
with him a safe-conduct pass attesting to the fact that he was per-

mitted to leave his country and return to it whenever he so desired.

One day, when returning from such a journey abroad, the blind man and his guide were stopped at the frontier and questioned by officials who demanded to see their papers. The blind man promptly took out his safe-conduct pass. The officials looked at the document and then asked to see the passport of the guide.

"My guide does not need a passport," said the blind man, "for he is included in my own safe-conduct pass." The officials then re-read his document but could not find the guide's name anywhere.

"Read aloud for me what is written on my passport," retorted the sightless traveller. And the border official slowly read, "This certifies that the bearer of this document, who is blind, is permitted to travel about both in this country and abroad in pursuit of his livelihood."

"Do you understand now?" exclaimed the blind traveler triumphantly, "How could a blind man travel without a guide? Naturally, in any passport like this, a guide is included by implication."

Said the Maggid of Dubno: Let this apply also to our verse from the Bible, "The Lord your God you shall fear." Ordinary men cannot know the path to true reverence; like the blind, we feel and grope for the right way that might lead to the fear of the Lord. Therefore if we are to be able to find the way, we need guides who possess the sense of direction we lack. These guides are our Sages and Rabbis, our *Talmidey Chachamim*. They are the guides included by implication as denoted by the particle *eth* in this Biblical verse. Proper respect for them is an essential part of the fear of the Lord, for if we do not take these wise men "with" us as our guides, we can never hope to live such a life as would find favor in the eyes of God.

□ 11 — ISRAEL VS. IDOLATRY

כִּי כָּל־הָעַמִּים יֵלְכוּ אִישׁ בְּשֵׁם אֱ־לֹהָיו וַאֲנַחְנוּ נֵלֵךְ בְּשֵׁם ה' אֱ־לֹהֵינוּ לְעוֹלָם וָעֶד.
(מיכה ד' ה')

"For let all the peoples walk each one in the name of its god, but as for us, we will walk in the Name of the Lord our God forever and ever."   *(Michah 4:5)*

When Hananiah, Mishael and Azariah refused to bow down to his idol, Nebuchadnezzar, King of Babylonia, said derisively: "Why do you think you are better than the others who worship gods other than the God of Israel? Look into your own sacred books, read your Book of Judges, and you will find that many times in its history Israel, too, has favored other gods."

How, indeed, are we to answer this question? Rabbi Yaakov helps out with the aid of a *Moshol*.

A man once married a wicked widow who always found an excuse to pick a quarrel with him. She had a number of children of her own, and while she was a shrew to her husband, she lavished all her love on the children from her first marriage. The husband decided that, in order to preserve peace, he would put up with his wife's indifference to him and treat her children as kindly as possible. He showered them with gifts and fine clothes, so that everyone thought that he must love his stepchildren as much as if they had been his own. In the end, however, his wife's constant quarrelling became too much for him and he informed her that he had decided to obtain a divorce from her. The distraught woman ran about among her neighbors, asking them to prevail upon her husband to keep her. Finally, one friend agreed to help her and said to her husband, "Why should you want to divorce your wife? She's a shrew? Let me tell you; my own wife's much worse than yours, but she is still with me."

Replied our friend: "Your case is different from mine; you have children whom you both love, and that is why you stay together. You could not manage without her."

Said the neighbor: "But you have children too, and you apparently love them very much, for why else would you give them such expensive gifts and such beautiful clothes?"

"Don't talk so foolishly," answered the irate husband. "Do you really believe that I can truly love those children who are not even my own? Whatever I did for them was to make their mother happy. But it was all to no avail and now that I am divorcing her, I no longer have any interest in her children."

This analogy may be applied also to the difference between Israel and the idolators among the other nations. The heathens loved their idols by instinct, as a father loves his children, for idolatry was their second nature. Any heathen with even a semblance of intelligence must have realized that the idols he worshipped were nothing but wood or stone and could have done nothing for him, but instinct has always been stronger than all knowledge. They went on worshipping the work of their own hands. It must be admitted that Israel, too, frequently succumbed to paganism, but to the Jew idolatry has always been a foreign element, and if he embraced it he did so only in an attempt born of temptation or fear, to appease the rest of the world, to be like them, so that he might not suffer persecution or hardship for his basic belief in the One God.

But the day will come when Israel will secure a divorce from unreasoning fear and temptation; once that divorce will have come about, the *yetzer hara* will be dead and then paganism, the foreign creature which Israel took into its household as a stepfather would a stepchild, will hold no more interest or attraction for the Jewish people.

It is only while wed to the temptations of the material riches of this world that Israel has in some instances succumbed to idolatry, that child of temptation. This acceptance, however, has never been wholehearted, so that, once freed from the bondage of earthly temptations and pressures, the spirit of Israel readily forsakes the idols and finds its way back to the true God.

□ CHAPTER TEN

□ "THE GOOD LIFE"

□ 1—WHAT IS "THE GOOD LIFE"?

דִּבְרֵי קֹהֶלֶת . . . מַה־יִּתְרוֹן לָאָדָם בְּכָל עֲמָלוֹ שֶׁיַּעֲמֹל תַּחַת הַשָּׁמֶשׁ. (קהלת א' ג')

"The words of Koheleth...What profit has man from all his labor in which he labors under the sun?"   *(Ecclesiastes 1:3)*

No two men have ever quite agreed on what really constitutes "the good life."

A playboy who has frittered away his life in idle pleasures may say on his deathbed: "What have I gained by all my selfish pleasures? Was it a good life? If I had my life to live over again, I should act quite differently."

Another man, who lived solely for wealth, may die regretting that he devoted all his days to the accumulation of the silver and gold which, after all, he cannot take with him to the grave.

And still another, who acquired fame as a warrior, may cry out before he dies, "What a fool I was to waste my strength on as useless a pursuit as warfare and bloodshed!"

156

All success is relative. A tailor who had hoped to turn over his workshop to his son might lament because the boy had chosen to become a physician instead; the learned schoolmaster, on the other hand, might fervently hope that his son might not follow in his footsteps, but become a businessman instead so as to earn a better living.

Our neighbor's pastures often seem greener to us than our own. Most of us fail to appreciate what we possess, while our brother's good fortune grows large in our eyes and stirs our envy. We only know the futility of our own endeavors but fail to consider our neighbor, who also may well have suffered frustration and disappointment at some time during his life.

King Solomon, the wisest of all men, saw all the values of this world for what they really were. "Vanity of vanities," he exclaimed, "all is vanity!"

Actually, the Hebrew verb *Sheyaamol,* in the verse from Ecclesiastes quoted above, is in the future tense, and therefore the literal translation should be not "...in which labors," but "...in which he *will labor* under the sun...." In other words, if a man should be given a second life on earth in which to labor, he may engage in a new pursuit, but once again it will be a wasted life no less than the first.

The pen-name used by King Solomon, the author of the Book of Ecclesiastes, is *"Koheleth,"* "a reservoir" or treasury of all human wisdom and experience, of hopes and disillusionments. And in this summary of his life's wisdom, the wise man who wrote it was fully entitled to make the sweeping general statement that *Hakol Hevel,* "all is vanity."

What, then, is the "good life"?

Said the Maggid of Dubno in a classic *Moshol:*

A group of blind men were walking along a street when they lost their guide. A callous stranger, wanting to have some sport at their expense, turned to one of them and said, "Here's a bagful of gold coins. Divide them among yourselves." But in fact, he had not given anything to any of them. As soon as he had left, each of the blind men asked the others for his share, thinking that the others had cheated him and were withholding from him his share of the money. And soon they all set to quarrelling bitterly with one another, each thinking that he had been the only one cheated of his rightful due.

It is the same with life. Each one of us is all too ready to believe that all the others have been favored while he has been singled out for misfortune and disillusionment.

Therefore King Solomon tells us, at the very end of his great book: *"The final summing up, after everything has been heard, is: Fear God and keep His commandments, for that is what constitutes the perfect man"* (Eccl. 12:13).

Since all of life is vain and fleeting, our lives have some value only if we devote them to the fear of God and to the keeping of His commandments. This, and none other, is the "good life."

□ 2 — THE HIDDEN TREASURE

Asked the Maggid of Dubno: Why should man constantly seek to grasp the Infinite in wisdom and in the fear of heaven, when it is obvious that he will never attain it? Why, then, should this divine aspiration be so deeply rooted within his heart that he will never entirely give it up?

And the Maggid, as he did so often, answered his own question with a wonderful *Moshol,* as follows:

A wealthy man, afraid that he might be robbed of his possessions in the turmoil of war, hid everything in various secret places throughout his house.

Unfortunately he died quite suddenly and his son did not know where he could find his inheritance. As he sat gloomily in his room, counting his own last few silver pieces, one of the coins dropped from his hand to the floor and rolled away before he could reach it. Since he had so little money, he desperately searched for the coin, high and low. Finally, at his wits' end, he tore out the floor boards and — lo and behold! — beneath the planks he discovered a chest full of ducats which he had never expected to find. Naturally this happy discovery impelled him to go on searching. He never found his own piece of silver that he had lost, but wherever he looked, he came upon new treasures of golden coins.

True, his silver coin was lost forever, but can we say that his efforts to find it therefore were nothing but a waste of time? No, indeed, for it was during this search that he discovered other unexpected wealth and treasure.

The same is true also of our own striving after the Infinite. We may not find the thing we have set out to seek, but on the way we may well come upon magnificent treasures of mind and spirit which, had we sat idle, we would never have discovered.

□ 3—OUR SAFEGUARD AGAINST SIN

רָצָה הַקָּדוֹשׁ בָּרוּךְ הוּא לְזַכּוֹת אֶת־יִשְׂרָאֵל לְפִיכָךְ הִרְבָּה לָהֶם תּוֹרָה וּמִצְוֹת.
(מכות ג' ט"ז)

"The Holy One, blessed be He, desired to grant merit to Israel; therefore He multiplied for them Torah and Mitzvoth."

(Makkoth 3:16)

At times it may seem difficult to understand why God had to give Israel such an abundance of commandments in order to hallow it. Would not a less complex Torah have sufficed? In fact, if there were fewer commandments, would this not mean that there would actually be also fewer chances for Israel to be guilty of sin by omission?

Said Rabbi Yaakov of Dubno: Not at all, and I will tell you a *Moshol* that should prove my point.

A young man from the country went to the city to buy goods for his father's store. There he met an uncle of his whom he exuberantly told that he fully intended to make short order of his business engagements so that he might have sufficient time to enjoy the pleasures and entertainments of the city which he had never visited before. He then merrily bade his uncle farewell and went off to his lodgings.

In the meantime the wise uncle pondered on what he could do to see to it that his gay young nephew would spend most of his time on business and would have little free time to get into trouble. Finally, he visited all the various business connections of his nephew's father and told them to go and see the young man who would have good business for them. And so the visitor was kept constantly busy receiving the merchants who passed in and out of his room at the hotel, so that he had no time at all to go out and see the sights of the city. When he had bought all the merchandise he could possibly buy with the money he had brought with him, he made ready for the homeward journey. Before leaving the city, he paid a call on his uncle to take his leave. There he complained bitterly that he had been so busy that he hardly had a moment for rest and recreation or to partake of the excitements of the big city.

The uncle nodded knowingly. "My dear boy," he said with an affectionate smile: "You may blame it all on me. You see, I was afraid that you might have spent your free time exploring the city and that, young and inexperienced as you are, you might have neglected the business and might have been robbed of your money or come into bad company. So I simply sent you all these merchants so that you would have no free time for mischief!"

And so it is also with God and man. The Almighty sends man into the great city, the world, in order that he may acquire the treasures of Torah and Mitzvoth which he can acquire only on earth. And in order to prevent man from succumbing to the temptations that are so much a part of life here below, God gave him so many commandments that he would have no spare time to lose himself in the transient pleasures and enticements of this world.

This is what the Mishnah we have quoted above means: The Holy One, blessed be He, desired to have Israel acquire merit, and so He gave them a copious Torah and many commandments, as it is said: *"It pleased the Lord, for His righteousness' sake, to magnify the Law and to make it honorable"* (Isaiah 42:21). The greater the number of commandments to be observed, the greater the opportunities to acquire merit and the less the chances of falling victim to sin.

□ 4 — MAN IS FULLY RESPONSIBLE FOR HIS ACTIONS

וְאַל־יַבְטִיחֲךָ יִצְרְךָ שֶׁהַשְּׁאוֹל בֵּית מָנוֹס לָךְ שֶׁעַל כָּרְחֲךָ אַתָּה נוֹצָר וְעַל כָּרְחֲךָ אַתָּה
נוֹלָד וְעַל כָּרְחֲךָ אַתָּה חַי וְעַל כָּרְחֲךָ אַתָּה מֵת וְעַל כָּרְחֲךָ אַתָּה עָתִיד לִתֵּן דִּין וְחֶשְׁבּוֹן
לִפְנֵי מֶלֶךְ מַלְכֵי הַמְּלָכִים הַקָּדוֹשׁ בָּרוּךְ הוּא.   (פרקי אבות ד' כ"ט)

"...and let not your imagination give you hope that the grave
will be a place of refuge for you; for you were formed against
your will, and you were born against your will, and you live
against your will, and you will die against your will, and against
your will you will in the future have to give account and reckon-
ing before the Supreme King of kings, the Holy One, blessed be
He."   *(Avoth 4:29)*

Men often argue that they cannot be held responsible for their
actions because, after all, they came into this world without their
consent. Had they been given a choice, they say they would have
preferred to renounce the pleasure of living rather than undertake
the onerous duties that living entails.

The Dubnoer Maggid, however, points out that this argument is
fallacious, as demonstrated by this pertinent *Moshol:*

There was once a couple who had lived in peace and harmony for
a good many years. The husband was ugly and had always been
deaf; the wife was a shrew and had been blind from childhood. Being blind, the wife never knew how ugly her husband really was,
while her husband, being deaf, was not troubled at all by his wife's
sharp tongue.

One day they learned of a physician of whom it was said that he
could work miraculous cures, and they decided to go and see
whether he could heal them of their handicaps. They agreed in advance to pay whatever amount of money the physician might charge
them.

And it happened that the physician was successful, so that the
wife was blind no more and the husband was no longer deaf. But,
unfortunately, this amazing cure also spelled the end of the couple's
domestic felicity. The husband now heard his wife's constant

scolding and soon lost his patience with her, while his wife, clearly seeing his ugly features for the first time, could not bear to look at him. Therefore, when the physician presented them with his bill, they refused to pay. In fact, they told him, it was he who owed them some compensation for having ruined their happy marriage. When he saw that he could not prevail upon his two patients to pay for his services, he sighed and said:

"If it is really true that I have made you unhappy by my cure, I will attempt to restore your happiness to you. If you wish, Sir, I can make you deaf again, and you, Madam, can easily be returned to your former state of blindness, and then your life will be as happy and peaceful as it was before you met me."

To this, however, both the man and his wife objected most strenuously.

"Well," replied the physician, "if you are unwilling to return to your former state, then it is obvious that my skill must have made you happier than you were before. Hence it is only fair that you pay me for my services."

Let this be a lesson for those who refuse to accept responsibility for their own actions because, as they view it, they were put into the world without their consent. Quite true; man has no choice in the matter of being conceived and born. But it is equally true that, once he is in the world, he obviously likes to live, for no normal person wishes to be deprived of the gift of life once he has it. Hence, if life, once given him, is so dear to man that he will not relinquish it voluntarily, it stands to reason that he must pay for the privilege of living. And what form must this payment take? In return for the Divine boon of life, man must consider himself responsible to His Maker for whatever he does on earth, ready to render account to God for what he has done with the privilege so graciously accorded him.

□ 5 — "... THE BLESSING GOD HAS GIVEN YOU..."

אִישׁ כְּמַתְּנַת יָדוֹ כְּבִרְכַּת ה' אֱ-לֹהֶיךָ אֲשֶׁר נָתַן־לָךְ.　(ראה)

(When coming to the Temple on the Festivals) "...every man shall bring according to the ability of his hand to give, according to the blessing of the Lord your God which He has given you."

(Deut. 16:17)

The Maggid of Dubno comments that he had pondered long and diligently on the wording of the Blessings set down by our Sages. We will find for example that, in the blessing over bread, one thanks God not "for the bread which He has *given* to me" but for "having brought forth bread from the earth." When we put on a new garment, too, we do not bless the Lord for having *given us* clothing, but simply for "clothing the naked." Indeed, the term *"Who has given to us"* is not used in any of the Blessings except in one, and that is the Benediction recited over the Torah, where we give thanks to God for *"having given us the Law of Truth and having planted life eternal in our midst."* This is the only benediction of all the common blessings that is specific rather than objective.

Why should this be so? Perhaps, in order to understand the significance of this difference and thus its meaning in the above-quoted verse, we should first determine what the Jewish concept of "giving" is; namely, what "giving" implies to the Jewish mind.

We are told, for example, that if we see a king of a non-Jewish state, we are to recite a blessing as follows: "Blessed be He Who has *given* of His glory to flesh and blood." But if ever we should be privileged to see a Jewish king, the blessing we say is: "Blessed be He Who has *imparted* of his glory to them that fear Him."

In other words, the non-Jewish king is permitted to consider his position as his own. He may amass riches and glory for himself, and for his own use. Therefore our blessing when we behold such a ruler also recalls the non-Jewish concept of "giving" and we praise God for *"giving of His glory"* to the Gentile king.

The Jewish kings, however, were told over and over again that true kingship belongs to the Lord alone and that they, the kings of the Jewish people, were only trustees, delegated by the King of kings to execute His Law of truth and justice on earth. It was the task of every such king to see to it *"that his heart not be lifted up above his brothers and that he turn not aside from the command-ment to the right or to the left"* (Deut. 17:20). And to recall both to him and to ourselves that our king is only a representative on earth of a Higher Authority, the blessing which we will recite on beholding him will read "Blessed be He Who has *imparted* of His glory to them that fear Him."

Whatever the Jew receives he regards as being entrusted to him by God, a loan which he must employ to help him do the will of God and for which he is accountable to God in the end.

For example, the food eaten by a wicked man is nothing more than fuel that is wasted on crime, while the food eaten by the righteous man is used by him to the best possible advantage; that is, to enable him to work constructively on earth for the Holy One, blessed be He.

Now if, on eating bread, we would thank God for having *"given us"* bread, we would imply that we take this staple food as our rightful due, "given us" to do with whatever we wish. Therefore we bless Him, instead, for having *"brought forth"* the bread, to show that we are fully aware that this nourishment was turned over to us to be used not simply as we see fit but for a specific purpose—to give us the strength to do the will of Him Who has supplied it. In other words, the bread is not an end in itself, but only a means to a higher goal.

The Torah, on the other hand, is not a means at all. It is the ultimate goal which should be the be-all and end-all of our whole life. Therefore, in the case of the Torah, a blessing is recited in which we render thanks to God for having *"given"* us the Torah, to love and to cherish and to study thoroughly until we have made it our very own and it has actually become part of our very being.

Now when the Scriptural verse we have quoted at the outset of this chapter employs the expression *"which He has given thee,"* we are thereby taught a lesson of profound significance. We are told that, actually, we are entitled to use the blessings of God for our own benefit, provided that we discipline ourselves so that we do not squander these blessings on things that would not meet with God's approval. Therefore we do not ordinarily employ the term "Who has given" in a benediction, for if we believe that any blessing entrusted to us by God was "given to us" to do with whatever we please it is no blessing at all.

Whenever we are given the opportunity to partake of the blessings of this world, we must remember that all things of this world are given to us only so that we may fulfill the purposes of God.

□ 6 — STUDY VS. WEALTH

כָּךְ הִיא דַּרְכָּהּ שֶׁל־תּוֹרָה, פַּת בְּמֶלַח תֹּאכֵל. . . וְחַיֵּי צַעַר תִּחְיֶה וּבַתּוֹרָה אַתָּה עָמֵל.
אִם־אַתָּה עוֹשֶׂה כֵּן אַשְׁרֶיךָ וְטוֹב לָךְ אַשְׁרֶיךָ בָּעוֹלָם הַזֶּה וְטוֹב לָךְ לָעוֹלָם הַבָּא.
(פרקי אבות ו, ד)

"This is the way of the Torah: Eat a morsel of bread with salt, drink water by measure, sleep upon the ground and live a life of trouble, and let your toil be directed to the Torah; if you do this you will be happy, and it will be well with you; happy you will be in this world and it will be well with you in the world to come."

(Avoth 6:4)

The Torah has the marvelous power not only to afford ample compensation for his hardships to him who must live on salt and bread alone, but, in fact, so to ennoble a poor man's life that he will not even consider his poverty a hardship at all. One draught from the eternal wellsprings of the Torah will fully satisfy him who cannot afford even the water from the public well to quench his thirst.

What is the lesson inherent in the words *"if you do this?"* Rabbi Yaakov helps out by means of a *Moshol* as follows:

Two young men studied together at a Yeshiva, sharing the joys as well as the hardships which such a student life entailed. Eventually, one of them left the academy and bent all his efforts to the task of amassing wealth and climbing the rungs of the social ladder of the city. The other young man, however, had no other ambition but to continue to explore the Word of God, and so became an outstanding, if not wealthy, scholar. One day he received an announcement to the effect that his former classmate had just bought one of the largest business concerns in the city. He therefore decided to visit the new office of his wealthy friend.

When he arrived, he was most impressed with the multitude of workers, clerks, salesmen and customers who went in and out of the reception room, all anxious to gain admittance to have a word with the prominent man of affairs in the inner office. Suddenly the door of that office opened and the man for whom they all had been waiting appeared. He bade his former classmate a most cordial welcome and invited him into his office where they spent a few moments reminiscing about the days long past. All too soon the wealthy merchant rose. "I want you to come to my house for dinner today to meet my wife and we can have a long chat then. But now I must beg you to excuse me, for you can see for yourself how many people there are outside all waiting to see me. I shall see you later, then. Agreed?" he asked with a smile.

The guest arrived at his friend's house at the appointed hour, but to his amazement he found that his host had not yet come home from his office. One hour passed, then two hours and he had still not returned. The hostess, greatly distressed, complained to the scholar that her husband's business was taking up even the time that he should be devoting to his home and his family. At long last the merchant arrived, weary and hungry, with profound apologies for his failure to come home in time.

After dinner, when the two men were able to retire to the drawing room and chat, the scholar said, "It is truly splendid to see how God has blessed you and what you have been able to achieve. But can you truly say that you are happier now than you were when we were both young and lived together in an attic on bread and onions, and studied the Torah day and night? Are you surprised at my question? True, your life is much more comfortable now, but have you not paid heavily for these luxuries? What good is all your money to you if you cannot find the time to enjoy it? Why, you hardly have the time to eat a proper meal in peace!"

But his friend replied, "Then, I suppose, your concept of happiness differs from mine. You are distressed that my business affairs keep me from eating my meals on time. But, believe me, it is the ambition of every businessman to be so greatly occupied like this that he has no time to eat. I see in your face that you cannot believe me, but if you were a merchant like me you would agree."

Answered the scholar: "Truly, we differ greatly on what true happiness means. Had you remained a student instead of leaving the Yeshiva for the marketplace, you, in turn, would understand how blessed is he who spends his life studying the Word of God even at the expense of luxurious living. But since you have left study far behind, you can no longer even imagine it, even as I cannot see happiness in your present hectic life."

This is the lesson taught us by the *Beraitha* quoted in this chapter. If you tell a person who lives a life of privation, on water and bread and without proper rest and shelter, that the diligent study of the Torah will assure him happiness in this world and eternal blessings in the world to come, he will readily believe you. But most people will only smile when you tell them that such a life of hardship, disdaining all ease and comfort for the sake of studying the Word of the Lord, will assure happiness right now, in this world here below. Yet it is worthwhile to make the experiment, even in a limited measure.* For only *"if you will do so"* will you be happy even now in this world, in addition to securing the full benefits of the world to come.

□ 7 — TWO WAYS OF LIVING

וַיֹּאמְרוּ כֹּל אֲשֶׁר־דִּבֶּר ה' נַעֲשֶׂה וְנִשְׁמָע.   (משפטים)

"And they said: 'All that the Lord has spoken we will do, and listen.' "   *(Exod. 24:7)*

It may seem somewhat surprising that, in this Scriptural verse, the

---

* It should be recorded here that the many young men, learning day and night, in the Yeshivoth of this country give proof of this.

"doing" is mentioned before the "listening." However, this is only in keeping with the Jewish concept of "the good life." In order to lead a life that is good in the eyes of God, we must "do" first; the understanding of *why* we must do it is not a primary requirement.

Thus we read in the Talmud that a Sadducee, protesting that the people of Israel at the foot of Mount Sinai had been much too impulsive in accepting the Torah, remarked to Raba: "On that day at the foot of Mount Sinai, you did not consider what it was that you had engaged yourselves to keep. You should first have listened in order to learn whether you could indeed accept and observe all those commandments."

Replied Raba: "It is said of us, who walk in sincerity, *'The upright are guided by their integrity'* but of those who walk in deceit, it is said *'but the perverseness of the faithless shall destroy them'* " (Prov. 11:3).

Indeed, we Jews are an impulsive people, and this is quite as it should be when it comes to matters such as the voluntary acceptance of a Divinely ordained way of life.

Why were the heathen nations averse to the Torah, whereas Israel was so quick to accept it? Said the Maggid of Dubno: "He who is good in his heart can easily overcome evil, but he who is entangled in licentiousness is not as free to do so and ultimately may be ruined by his vices." And he continued with a *Moshol:*

There were once two blind men who wandered from town to town and from house to house soliciting alms. One of them, a man of good character, was ashamed of having to go about and having to live off the bounty of others. His companion, however, was a born tramp who quite frankly said, "I enjoy going from place to place, meeting all kinds of people and taking from them whatever good things they might want to offer me. Why not?"

One day the two came to a city where they met a famous physician whom they promptly accosted for alms. He gave them some money, but then said, "I may be able to give you some permanent help, for I can cure you so that you will be able to see again and you will no longer be forced to resort to begging for a living."

Now the first blind man readily accepted the offer and faithfully followed the regimen which the physician prescribed for him. Not long thereafter the physician was able to say to him: "If you continue faithfully in my charge, I can promise that you will soon have full vision and then your life will be happier than it could ever have been otherwise."

But the other blind man was steadfast in his refusal to take advantage of the great doctor's willingness to help him, and he said, "Begging has become my profession. As long as I am blind, everyone will be willing to help me, but if I should cease being blind I will simultaneously lose my livelihood." And so he was not helped.

So, too, Raba said to the Sadducee, "Those of us who believe in the continuity of our tradition have always sought to lead lives of uprightness and moral integrity. As long as we had no Torah to guide us to these ends we felt as though we were blind, and our blindness troubled us greatly so that when the Divine Healer offered us a cure in the form of His Law we accepted it without a moment's hesitation. But you, who disavow the tradition of our people, are like the blind man who cherishes his handicap because life is so much easier for him when he cannot see. Therefore it is better that you go on living in blindness and ignorance as you have until now. You are in love with your irresponsible way of life and would not change it; therefore, leave the Torah alone and do as you see fit."

To those who were content to live in depravity, the Commandments of God were nothing but a burden. But those who were truly anxious to leave lawlessness behind were so glad to receive a Law to guide them that they cried out *"Naaseh venishma.* We are determined to do what is required of us, without reasoning why. Later on we shall study the Law in detail so that we may better understand it."

□ 8 — AVOID PERVERSE CONDUCT

כִּי דוֹר תַּהְפֻּכֹת הֵמָּה.   (האזינו)

"For they are a generation given to perverseness." *(Deut. 32:20)*

The Maggid explains this biblical statement with an apt *Moshol.*

A rabbi's daughter was about to wed the son of a simple coachman. As the wedding day drew near, it occurred to the rabbi that his daughter's new father-in-law would probably come dressed in a coachman's suit, and might suffer embarrassment when the two fathers would stand together at the wedding ceremony. In order to avoid this, he decided not to wear his silken rabbinical garments but to don coachman's livery for that one occasion.

In the meantime the coachman had made plans of his own. He said, "I am a poor working man, and if I also dress the part, all the people at the wedding will look down on me as unfit to associate with these great and learned men in the bride's family." Therefore he bought a black hat with a wide brim, and a silken caftan such as rabbis would wear, and completed the disguise by putting on a false gray beard. Thus attired, he set forth for the wedding.

Imagine the confusion when the two fathers, the coachman in the rabbinic robes and the rabbi in coachman's gear, stood together near the marriage canopy. Naturally, all the guests mistook the coachman for the rabbi and the rabbi for the coachman.

So, said Rabbi Yaakov, it is also with the Jews and the Gentiles. The non-Jews, among whom we live, have come to emulate us in many ways; they give their children names from the Bible, they practice charity and adopt other Jewish ways as outlined in the Torah. In many instances this tendency among the Gentiles is very strong. But what about the Jews themselves? They strive to imitate Gentile clothing, habits, and behavior and often call themselves by Gentile names. This is what the Torah means when it says, "For they are a very perverted generation, children in whom there is no faithfulness," for they do just the opposite of what would be expected of them.

At the end of the Biblical portion from which our title verse is quoted, Moses admonishes his people as follows: *"Set your heart to all the words which I enjoin upon you today... because it is your life and through this thing you will prolong your days upon the land, to which you are going over the Jordan, to possess it"* (Deut. 32:46-47).

A life led in accordance with the laws of the Torah will prolong man's days and establish him securely on his soil; it is a life of health, happiness and holiness.

□ 9 — STEADINESS, BUT MODERATION

אֵין־טוֹב בָּאָדָם שֶׁיֹּאכַל וְשָׁתָה וְהֶרְאָה אֶת־נַפְשׁוֹ טוֹב בַּעֲמָלוֹ, גַּם־זֹה רָאִיתִי אָנִי כִּי
מִיַּד הָאֱ־לֹהִים הִיא. (קהלת ב', כ"ד)

"There is nothing better for a man than that he eats and drinks and makes his soul enjoy pleasure for his labor; this also I have seen, that it is from the hand of God." *(Ecclesiastes 2:24)*

This verse is hard to understand. Is there really nothing better than to eat and drink, and to make one's soul enjoy pleasure for his labor?

Certainly not. The Maggid of Dubno clarifies the meaning of the verse by means of a *Moshol:*

A poor wanderer came to a village one afternoon, tired and hungry.

Now in this village there were two inns. The proprietor of the one was an honest man, always ready to do a good deed, while the owner of the other was a miser and a swindler to boot.

It so happened that our hungry friend first came upon the miser's inn, and asked whether he could have a meal and lodging for the night. Replied the host, "Here is some work that you can do for me, and when you are done, you may claim a meal in payment for your pains."

Thus the poor man, tired though he was, had no choice but to do the work, which was difficult and strenuous.

When he had finally finished, the host came to him, smiling, and said, "Good work! Now I will see to it that you get the meal I promised you." He pointed across the street. "See that inn over there?" he asked. "They will give you all the food you want."

Near exhaustion, the man dragged himself to the other inn,

where he was given a warm welcome, good food and a comfortable room in which to spend the night. He felt richly rewarded for his toil.

A few days later he told his friends of the generous reward he had been given for an hour's work in that village. But they laughed at him and said: "Fool! You worked for nothing! The inn where they gave you food and lodging is a shelter for poor travelers like you. They would have accorded you the same generosity at any time. They have nothing to do with the owner of the other inn. That miser used you for his own ends to get some work done free of charge."

Therefore Ecclesiastes asks: *"What profit has man of all his labor in which he labors under the sun?"* (Eccl. 1:3).

But by this he does not mean that all endeavors for sustenance are in vain. He seeks to teach us by this statement that while it is God's will that we work each at our own vocation, *labor* in excess will not yield a greater profit. For whether we achieve much or little, so long as our work is faithful and steady, God will supply us with food and shelter and with whatever else we need to live on His earth. Therefore, we should work, by all means, but not engage in *amal*, hard labor, to irrational excess.

In this vein Rabbi Yaakov interprets the initial verse thus: *"It is not good for man that he should eat and drink and make his soul enjoy pleasure thinking that this is due to his labor."* Man should *not* think that whatever blessings he may receive in this world are his only as a result of his own strenuous efforts. He must always remember that God, Who provides for all living things, will see to it that his wants, also, are supplied. True, God will not help him who sits idle, but by the same token, overwork, to the exclusion of other things that life is for, is neither healthy nor praiseworthy, nor wise.

□ 10 — HUMAN STANDARDS AND HEAVENLY SCALE

אַל־תְּבַהֵל עַל־פִּיךָ וְלִבְּךָ אַל־יְמַהֵר לְהוֹצִיא דָבָר לִפְנֵי הָאֱ־לֹהִים כִּי הָאֱ־לֹהִים בַּשָּׁמַיִם
וְאַתָּה עַל־הָאָרֶץ עַל־כֵּן יִהְיוּ דְבָרֶיךָ מְעַטִּים. (קהלת ה׳, א׳)

"Be not rash with your mouth, and let not your heart be hasty to utter a word before God; for God is in Heaven, and you are upon earth; therefore let your words be few." *(Ecclesiastes 5:1)*

Why did Ecclesiastes insert the statement that "God is in heaven and you are upon earth?" Might this not defeat the purpose of the entire admonition? For it might easily lead us to believe that there is no reason, after all, to watch one's speech and conduct, since God is, in fact, so very far away. Would it not have been better to make it clear instead that the Lord is everywhere, in heaven above as well as on earth below, and that none can hide from His all-seeing eye?

What, then, is the purpose of this statement? We shall soon see.

Man cannot imagine that, one in millions that he is, his words or deeds might have any significance in the world in which he lives. But the Talmud tells us, "One who indulges in idle talk transgresses the Law, for it is said *'And you shall speak of them'* (Deut. 6:7); that is, of the words of the Torah and not other words" (Yoma 19b). This teaches us that what man says and does on earth is very important indeed.

The Maggid of Dubno made this clear by means of one of his famous *Mesholim*.

An architect once received from abroad a detailed blueprint of the plans for a splendid palace, drawn on a greatly reduced scale on a tiny sheet of parchment.

The master told his assistant to make an accurate copy of this blueprint so that it might be readily available when it would be needed. The assistant went to work and took great pains to reproduce the plan most faithfully. When he had finished the drawing he proudly showed it to his employer, expecting great praise for his neatness and accuracy.

The architect silently looked at the boy's work for a few minutes, and then snapped impatiently: "Disgraceful! You forgot to put in the dot that is on the original. How careless of you! Why did you leave out this dot?"

The young man, greatly upset, asked why his employer should have become so angry on account of one tiny dot.

Replied the architect: "Do you not understand that this blueprint is drawn to a greatly reduced scale? That little dot that you didn't copy represents one of the pillars which is to support the entire upper floor. If this pillar is forgotten, the whole building will collapse! It may look like a mere dot, but actually it represents a vital part of the building and you were very wrong to think it unimportant!"

The moral of this story? Man was made in the image of God; *"in the image of God He created him"* (Gen. 1:27). Every man and woman is a small-scale representation of a pillar of the Universe, and if he were to be omitted from the Divine scheme of things, the equilibrium of the Divinely built structure of the entire universe would cease to exist. Therefore man is much more important than he may think. He may not realize the importance of his words or deeds here on earth for, measured by human standards, what he says or does may indeed hardly be of consequence.

But, as Ecclesiastes so wisely tells us, "God is in Heaven and you are upon earth"—there is a vast difference between man's standards, which are small and narrow, and the Heavenly scale, which is vast, far beyond our power of comprehension. Therefore what seems so small and unimportant by our own standards, will appear in its proper dimensions when projected onto the clear and infinitely larger scale of Heavenly wisdom. We will then see the consequences of our long-forgotten acts of thoughtlessness in all their far-reaching implications. By the same token, our good deeds and our words of wisdom and prudence, often brushed aside as utterly insignificant by human shortsightedness, will also be shown on the Heavenly scale, in full and proper perspective.

□ 11 — MORE EFFECTIVE CRITICISM

לֹא תִשְׂנָא אֶת־אָחִיךָ בִּלְבָבֶךָ הוֹכֵחַ תּוֹכִיחַ אֶת־עֲמִיתֶךָ וְלֹא־תִשָּׂא עָלָיו חֵטְא.
(קדושים)

"Do not hate your brother in your heart; you must rebuke your neighbor and not bear sin because of him."   *(Lev. 19:17)*

We will gain a better understanding of this verse if we open the Book of Proverbs to Chapter 27, Verse 22, where we read the following wise statement: *"Although you may pound a fool in a mortar with a pestle among groats, yet his foolishness will not depart from him."*

This is to teach us that even the most trenchant criticism cannot make a wise man out of a fool. Folly is an incurable condition.

But what is the significance of the groats mentioned here in connection with the pestle? Would the presence or absence of the groats make a difference in the behavior of the fool who, by way of simile, is pounded with the pestle?

The *Moshol* which Rabbi Yaakov would cite to explain this point is in a humorous vein.

It once happened, in a small town, that a gang of rascals looking for some amusement lured the village idiot into a big wooden mortar which was used for the pounding of stale bread and for the grinding of corn and groats. They then covered up the mortar and went to work unmercifully with the pestle until the fool inside was beaten black and blue.

When the unfortunate man finally emerged, covered with bruises, the boys fully expected him to shower them with curses. To their amazement, he said nothing at all.

When they asked him whether he was not badly hurt, he meekly replied, "I suppose it couldn't be helped. Nobody meant to beat me up. They must have mistaken me for the groats!"

Similar situations occur over and over again not only with village idiots, but also with people of normal intellect. Often, a good preacher will come to town and people will throng to hear him. But his admonitions will not always have the effect they might have had, because each listener will think that they apply to everyone else in the room except himself. In the words of the *Moshol*, everyone present is like the fool in that he thinks that the preacher did not mean him, but must have mistaken him for the groats.

Nor should any preacher think that admonitions of this nature are intended only for his students. Let him remember always that once he admits that he himself is not perfect, others will also be more likely to profit by what he preaches.

This then, is the explanation for the Biblical verse quoted in the beginning of the chapter. *"Do not hate your brother in your heart, and if you are compelled to admonish him, do it as a friend, for then you will achieve the best results, as the verse continues: rebuke him as your neighbor.* You will remember that you yourself are not immune to the errors for which you rebuke him, *and you will not be guilty of the sin* of blaming only him and not mending your own ways."

You will find that criticism given in this spirit will yield the best results in terms of the betterment of both our fellowmen and ourselves.

□ 12 — EXILE IS NO FIRM FOUNDATION

אִם־לֹא אַעֲלֶה אֶת־יְרוּשָׁלַיִם עַל רֹאשׁ שִׂמְחָתִי.   (תהלים קל"ז, ו')

"...if I do not set Jerusalem above my greatest joy."
(Psalms 137:6)

Al rosh simchathi—"...*above my greatest joy."* Our Maggid begins the discussion of this statement with a *Moshol:*

The favorite of a baron decided to settle in the town which the baron governed. His protector patronized him, but the man made no effort to make friends of the common folk in the town. The citizens therefore boycotted him, and when he sought to buy a site for a home no one came forward to offer him land or material. In the end he appealed to the baron, and was given permission to buy any lot that might be available in the town. Armed with this baronial writ, he acquired a spacious piece of land near a river. The winter

---

* In fact, as we have already mentioned in a previous chapter, the particle *eth*, as such, implies an object in addition to that explicitly written in the text, and may be taken here, too, in conjunction with the neighbor, to imply that we ourselves should be the second object of the rebuke.

was drawing to a close, but it was still bitter cold and the ground was as hard as stone. He began building a large house with ample storage rooms, working at top speed in order to be able to move in as soon as possible. To his bewilderment, everyone who passed by either giggled or laughed at him outright, but when he inquired to the reason, he received no answer. "Is my mansion not properly built?" he asked. "Does it not fit in well with the landscape or is it not in harmony with the style of the buildings round about? What, then, is wrong with my house? There must be some reason why people look at it so strangely as they pass by." But again, he received only smirks for an answer.

Finally he discussed the situation with an expert. This master architect assured him that the building itself was well-planned and handsome in every respect. However, he felt compelled to tell him that he should never have attempted to build at this particular spot, on the banks of the river. "You will have no solid foundation here for a home," he told our friend. "When spring will come, the heat of the sun will melt the ice on the ground, and since the ground is not solid here, your house will sink in."

Our friend stared at the expert in amazement. It had never occurred to him that the rays of the sun would be able to undermine the stability of a house built as solidly and firmly as the one he was erecting.

But this is an everyday occurrence in human life. Over and over again we hear of men who, disregarding all prudent and well-intentioned advice, set up business concerns and sign contracts which later prove unsound.

Nor are we Jews immune to such mistakes. As long as we lived in the land of Israel, our lives were on solid ground, and the generations that followed benefited from the fruits of the labors of their fathers.

But now, alas, we are in exile. Whatever wealth we may acquire in the countries in which we live is as if it were built on sand, for history has shown that once those who hate us see that we have done well, their jealousy and anger is kindled against us and often that for which we have labored is buried as if by quicksand. To know this is not a happy feeling, and it is brought home to us all the more forcibly, at the time of our greatest joy, when we look down from the pinnacle of success and happiness and wistfully contemplate how wonderful it would have been if our joy would have come to us not in exile but in our own Holy Land, where we would have had no cause to fear the hatred of jealous foes. It is at moments such as these that we can truly understand what the Psalmist meant when he called out, *"How shall we sing the song of the Lord in an alien land?"* (Psalms 137:4)? For the "song of the Lord" to which the Psalmist refers was a hymn of thanksgiving to God for all His favors, which was sung in the Temple. In exile, and without the Temple, it is obviously out of place.

Thus, it is especially at the time of our "greatest joy" that we remember Jerusalem and its past glory; it is at such moments that we are most painfully aware of our present exile.

As long as we are in exile, wealth and success may be but transient glory. Therefore, while we must still live on alien soil, let us rather aspire to the higher aspects of living; let us direct all our efforts to that good life which is characterized not by pleasures and luxuries but by the term, the "life of the world to come."

Jerusalem is still in ruins and has not yet risen "above our greatest joy"; therefore, whenever some unexpected happiness comes our way, let us remember her, and find comfort and joy in doing so. And until Jerusalem is rebuilt with the Messiah, let us devote our energies not so much to the amassing of worldly goods but to the cultivation of spiritual values so that we may be better prepared for the days to come when Jerusalem will rise again in all her ancient splendor.

□ 13 — Israel's Public Wedding

Many a time the question is asked why *Shavuoth*, the Festival which marks the Giving of the Law on Mount Sinai, is not also the Feast of Rejoicing in our Law. Why should the Feast of Rejoicing, which we know as *Simchath Torah*, be celebrated not together with *Shavuoth* but only several months thereafter?

The Maggid of Dubno answers this question with a very ingenious *Moshol*.

Once there was a great and mighty king who possessed vast treasures and much gold and silver. But his happiness was not complete, for he had no children and he feared that once he died, only strangers would enjoy all his wealth.

He and his queen had consulted the greatest medical authorities to help them, but to no avail.

One day a friend told the king that there might be hope for him, after all. "In a forest," he said, "there dwells a hermit, of the Jewish faith, a most saintly man. He is neither greedy for gain nor covetous of glory for himself, but his prayers in behalf of others have always been answered most speedily. Therefore let the king himself go to the forest immediately to ask this wonder-working rabbi to pray for you."

The king followed his friend's advice without delay and unburdened his troubled heart to the pious Jew. After a brief period of prayer and meditation, the hermit turned to the king and promised him that his prayers would be answered and that, within the year, his queen would bear him a daughter. However, this would come to pass only if the king would promise in advance that no man must ever see or speak to the child before she would be married. If any man, including her own father, were to look upon her before that time, she would die forthwith.

The king was somewhat taken aback, of course, for he had looked forward to watching his daughter grow from infancy to childhood and then blossom into womanhood, but, since he had no choice in the matter, he reluctantly agreed to the stipulation set by the man of God.

The king immediately began preparations for the little princess. He chose a remote but beautiful island on which he built a palace surrounded by a great wall so that no man would be able to enter it. When the time for the birth approached, the queen took up residence there, together with a staff of servants, nurses, physicians and teachers, all women, in accordance with the rigid specifications excluding all males from the entire island. In due time the baby was born. She was a beautiful child, and as the years went by it was obvious that she would also be a beautiful woman, of truly regal bearing. She studied music and languages, dancing and art, and also such serious subjects as history, literature and science. The king, who had remained in his capital, never attempted to see his child and contented himself with the reports which the queen gave him once each month when she would come alone to the city to visit him.

When the princess reached her eighteenth birthday, her father sent messengers to the kings of all the surrounding countries, announcing that he was now ready to give his daughter in marriage, and he invited all eligible princes of royal blood to present themselves as candidates for her hand. Naturally, a great assembly of young royalty gathered at the palace. But when they were told that they could not meet the young lady until the wedding day, they became suspicious that something might not be quite right with her, and they all left to return to their homes. All, that is, except for one whose father was a vassal of the king. This man could not very well humiliate his royal host as the others had done. He therefore decided to become engaged to the princess whom he had never even seen. But he could not conceal from himself the secret fear in his heart that his wife-to-be might be crippled or insane, or perhaps ugly or stupid, for he could not imagine why he should have been betrothed to her without ever having had the opportunity to meet her.

The wedding too, was strange, at least for a royal marriage, for there was no man present at the beginning of the ceremony.

We will therefore readily understand the young bridegroom's immense relief and delight when, after the ceremony, he found that the bride was the most beautiful maiden he had ever seen. But after the first joy of what was truly love at first sight, he began to worry all over again. True, his young wife was beautiful, but why had she been hidden from men until this very day? Was she dull or perhaps even feeble-minded? And even if she were not, might her personality not have been adversely affected by the abnormally sheltered life she had been forced to lead? During the weeks of the honeymoon he tested her intelligence by seeking to converse with her on subjects such as art, science, literature and philosophy. And he found, to his amazement, that her wit and learning were at least as great as his own, and he was a highly cultured young man indeed.

When the couple returned to the capital from their honeymoon, the young husband immediately went to his new father-in-law and confessed to him the misgivings with which he had first become engaged to his daughter. But he hastened to add, all his fears had proved totally unfounded, for even if he had had completely free choice in the matter, he could hardly have chosen a wife of more grace, beauty, dignity, goodness and intelligence than his own princess. He therefore asked the king whether he could not now make arrangements for a great public festival to celebrate the marriage, for he felt that the quiet wedding ceremony had not done justice to the lovely bride at all. To this the king readily agreed and the nuptials were now celebrated with all the pomp and splendor worthy of the occasion and of the charming bride.

Said Rabbi Yaakov: This *Moshol* should help explain what happened when Israel received the Torah. The Torah, like the beautiful princess for whom a suitable mate had to be found, was offered to all the nations, but they refused to accept the Law, because they did not know it and feared the hardships which its whole-hearted observance might entail. But, like the vassal prince, Israel, which had been the loyal servant of the King of kings from the very beginning, did not hesitate to accept the Torah unconditionally, sight unseen.

Now, of course, it remained for Israel to find out the true nature of the Teaching which it had espoused for all times to come. It was a most difficult task for Israel to study all the numerous details and ramifications of the Torah, in addition to the precepts of the Oral Law, and to readjust its way of life so as to be in conformity with the newly-given Word of God. But if Israel was truly to accept the Torah, it was imperative that all this be done.

Hence it is obvious that when the Law was first given to the Jewish people on *Shavuoth*, Israel was not yet ready to rejoice in it.

It was only after months of study that Israel could presume to state that it had come to know at least a little of its Torah and to love it in truth. Only then was it fitting, nay, even mandatory, that there be a "public wedding feast" of Israel and the Torah, a festival which we know today as *Simchath Torah,* The Rejoicing in the Law. And the joy and delight with which we celebrate this gladsome feast should last us throughout the year to come; in fact, it should endure through all the generations until the time which will usher in the glorious days of the Messiah.

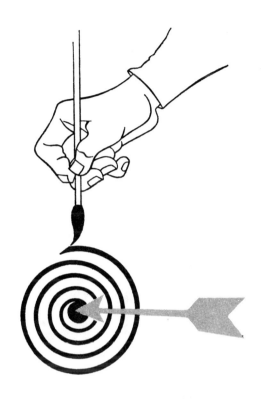

Part Two

THE MAGGID'S WIT AND HUMOR
HIS SOCIAL AND
INTELLECTUAL WORLD

☐ INTRODUCTION

גַּם הָאִישׁ מֹשֶׁה גָּדוֹל מְאֹד.   (בא)

"Moreover the Man Moses was very great in the land of Egypt, in the sight of Pharaoh's servants and in the sight of the People."
(Exod. 11:3)

Why *"the man* Moses?" One of our wise commentators explains this statement as follows: It stands to reason that Moses, who had wrought so many miracles on behalf of his people and who had been able to deal so successfully with the Pharaoh of Egypt, would command much respect because of his proven talents of leadership and diplomacy. But it is often forgotten that Moses was great also as a human being, as "a man." His character and personality were such that all those who met him not only honored the leader but also came to love the man. This the Torah would have us remember always.

The same may also be said of Rabbi Yaakov of Dubno. He was known far and wide for his wisdom and his eloquent sermons which appealed to the learned and the simple alike. But even more than that, he was loved by all for his simple piety, goodness, and modesty, which remained with him all his life.

185

The Gemara teaches us that *"even the everyday conversation of Torah scholars merits study"* (Sukkah 21b).

Accordingly, we shall learn of some of the things the Maggid of Dubno had to say outside the synagogue and the house of learning. The parables and anecdotes that follow will shed an interesting light on the personality of this revered teacher. We shall listen to him set-tling arguments with quick and ready wit combined with a thorough knowledge of even the minutest details of the Holy Writ. We shall hear him chide misers and remonstrate with those who took the Torah lightly and broke with its sacred traditions. We shall also watch him hold his own against other *Maggidim* and against the *Hassidim*, who challenged him on numerous occasions.

And we shall see that, despite his great modesty, the Maggid of Dubno could cope with all these problems and master every situa-tion with his calm assurance and sparkling wit. In time the style and tenor of his parables and sermons became well known in the Jewish world. Today, when the parables of the Maggid of Dubno are told and retold in circles that are familiar with Jewish learning, there is no necessity to make a point of mentioning the author's name, for the listeners are bound to exclaim with pleasure and delight: *"Hakol Kol Yaakov!* This is indeed the voice of Jacob! This could be from no one else but from Rabbi Yaakov of Dubno."

CHAPTER ELEVEN

□ THE MAGGID OF DUBNO AND THE GAON OF VILNA

□ 1 — FIRST MEETING

Rabbi Elijah, know as the Gaon of Vilna, who lived in the eighteenth century (1720-1797), was one of the greatest rabbis and one of the most eminent spiritual leaders of Jewry in recent centuries. An uncompromising opponent of Hassidism, he was known and revered not only in his native Poland but throughout the Jewish world as the outstanding spokesman of Jewry and the uncontested Torah authority of his time.

Eventually, the fame of the Maggid of Dubno as the "Prince of Maggidim" had reached even the study of this famous Gaon, who lived in strict seclusion, devoting all his days and nights without respite to the diligent study and teaching of the Torah, in keeping with the words of the Holy Scriptures *"and thou shalt meditate in them day and night"* (Joshua 1:8).

By the time Rabbi Elijah had reached his seventy-first year his physical strength was on the wane and he began to feel the burden of old age weighing heavily upon him. He did not, however, consult a physician. In his judgment there was only one man who might be able to alleviate his sufferings—the Maggid of Dubno, whose fame as a preacher and deviser of ingenious parables had not failed to come to his attention. He therefore wrote the Maggid a letter, begging him to come to him and to refresh his mind and spirit with his wise words spiced with some of his famous *Mesholim*. The Maggid of Dubno gladly accepted the invitation and travelled to Vilna to be at the Gaon's side.

□ 2—BE OUTSTANDING, BUT DO NOT STAND APART

The Maggid of Dubno was a little overawed at the thought of visiting the great Rabbi of Vilna, whom Jews throughout the world honored as the Rabbinic genius of the age. He became even more frightened when the Gaon welcomed him with a hearty handclasp and said to him: "I am told that you are a famous Maggid who can speak to the very hearts of those who listen. Now from time to time, like anyone else, I am in need of admonition. Therefore, I beg of you, give me a lesson in *Mussar* (ethics), for I need it badly."

Dumbfounded, the Maggid asked for a few minutes' grace. How could he, the country preacher from Dubno, presume to lecture the most eminent scholar of the age? Was it his place to attempt to move the heart of so great a man?

In the end he gathered his courage and began:

"In this week's portion of the Torah—it was *Vayera*— we read that God said to Abraham: 'If there are only fifty righteous men in the midst of the city of Sodom, I will save her.' Now what does the Torah mean by explicitly mentioning '*in the midst of the city*' (Genesis 18:26)? The Lord says: 'It is not pleasing to Me to see righteous men living in seclusion, and poring over My sacred teachings in the privacy of their homes without taking any notice of the troubles and sorrows of their neighbors. I need men who are outstanding, but who will not stand apart from their neighbors. I need men who will live in the *very midst of the city* not only in body but also in spirit, who will devote their energies to being a good influence on their fellow-men and who will work to the end that the entire community should live in keeping with My commandments.' "

The Gaon sadly nodded his head for the reprimand and found its mark. He knew that he did not readily mix with others and had taken little interest in the affairs of the community. This was part of his greatness, but it was also a grave weakness for a man of his stature. And the venerable Gaon of Vilna bowed his head and shed tears of genuine repentance.*

□ 3 — A KIND WELCOME YIELDS GOOD RESULTS

On another occasion, the Maggid of Dubno again paid a visit to the Gaon. Though the Maggid was a little weary from his travels, the Gaon greeted him with: "You are the famous Maggid of Dubno, who has delighted the whole world with his wonderful parables. Please do let me hear a *Moshol* of yours."

The Maggid gladly granted this request, and began forthwith:

There was once a couple who lived in dire poverty. They went to the Rabbi to ask his advice on how to make a decent living. Said the Rabbi: "You have one single asset of value, a precious ring. Go and sell it and buy yourselves a cow with the money. If you will milk the cow each day you will have milk and butter and cheese aplenty to sell, and you will make a fine living."

The couple hastened at once to the neighboring town, sold their ring and, with the money they received for it, bought a fine and healthy-looking cow. Delighted with their good fortune, they led their new bread-winner into their hovel, and at once set about to

---

* Other authorities have it that the Gaon of Vilna had known the Maggid of Dubno for a long time before then and, in fact, had even attended the latter's Bar Mitzvah festivities. It seems that while the Bar Mitzvah boy was reciting his learned Bar Mitzvah discourse some of the people present paid little heed to him but centered their attention upon the delicious food that had been prepared in honor of the occasion. After young Yaakov had finished his speech, the Gaon of Vilna arose and said, "Gentlemen, it seems that you prefer the *Shulchan Aruch* ("The Prepared Table") to the *Gemara*."

milk the animal. But, to their utter dismay, the cow yielded not one drop of milk. In disgust, they rushed to the Rabbi to tell him of their misfortune to have bought a cow which yielded no milk. But the Rabbi seemed not at all upset and merely asked: "Have you given the cow a proper welcome at your home? Have you provided her with a good stable and enough food?" And when the couple admitted that they had not thought of those things, he said to them:

"Foolish people! Did you really expect the poor beast to give you milk when you did not trouble yourselves to give her what she needs in order to be comfortable?"

The Gaon of Vilna, seeing the Maggid still standing before him, at once understood the delicate hint which the latter had obviously sought to convey by means of this *Moshol*. He therefore rose, bade him a hearty welcome, had food brought in, and in general, made every effort to make his guest comfortable.

□ 4 — THE MOSHOL: HITTING THE BULL'S EYE

The Gaon of Vilna once asked his illustrious guest how he managed to find such appropriate and striking parables for almost every verse of the Holy Scriptures.

And the Maggid of Dubno replied not with a lengthy explanation but with another *Moshol*.

A prince, who was interested in archery, desired greatly to become a master in that sport himself. Unfortunately he proved to be something less than skilled and hardly ever hit the bull's eye on the target. One day, while on a journey, he came to a village where an archery contest was in progress. He stopped to watch, and soon his attention was attracted by one of the contestants whose skill seemed almost uncanny. There were a number of targets in his area, all pierced through the very center. The prince asked him how he managed to perform this feat. Replied the champion: "First I take aim at the target, and when the arrow sticks I outline the circles round that point."

Said the Maggid of Dubno: "I proceed in much the same manner as that archer did. First I hit upon an interesting story, and then I look for a Scriptural verse to which it may be applied."

The Gaon of Vilna, delighted with this clever reply, expressed his desire to become a disciple of the Master of Parables. Soon the two rabbis were united by ties of mutual respect and friendship which remained unbroken for the rest of their lives.

□ 5 — THE NIGHT OF SHAVUOTH

It is a time-honored custom to spend the eve of the Feast of Shavuoth, which marks the Giving of the Law on Mount Sinai, as a night of study. The special book which we study that night, the *Tikkun Lel Shavuoth,* is a compendium of portions from the Torah, from the *Neviim,* Prophets, and from the *Kethuvim,* the Holy Writings. Selections from the Mishnah, followed by an enumeration of the six hundred and thirteen commandments of the Torah, are also included. The cycle of study is completed with a brief selection from the Cabbalistic work known as the *Zohar.* Thus the order of study which we follow on the first night of Shavuoth is a sampling, as it were, of written and oral tradition.

One Shavuoth eve, the Maggid of Dubno happened to be at the home of the Gaon of Vilna and the two remained awake all night to study. But while the Gaon was reading the *Tikkun,* the Maggid was "learning" from the Gemara as if this were an ordinary night, and not the eve of the Feast of the Giving of the Law. After a while, the Gaon asked Rabbi Yaakov why he did not, instead, study the *Tikkun,* as would have been proper.

Replied Rabbi Yaakov of Dubno: "I am a Maggid. May I, therefore, answer your question with a *Moshol?*"

Rabbi Elijah agreed and the Maggid of Dubno began:

There was once a commercial traveller in textiles who was very successful in obtaining large orders from his customers. When calling on them he carried with him only a small book of samples, and wherever he showed them there was immediate demand for the materials.

Now this man had a neighbor, a poor man who said to himself, "If the man next door can make such a good living showing scraps of material and selling them, why can I not do the same?" And so his wife set to work and prepared for him a home-made album into which she pasted remnants of cloth. But when he made the rounds of textile dealers he found to his dismay that they would not listen to him and, in fact, even laughed in his face. Greatly discouraged, he asked his prosperous neighbor to give him the secret of his success.

The latter replied: "That should not be too difficult to explain. The book which I carry with me represents samples from huge bolts of material actually available at the warehouses of the factories which I represent. All that my customers need do, is to leaf through my sample book and select the pattern they like, and the factory will send them whatever quantity they wish. But of what good are those scraps which your wife pasted together? You have no stock in trade from which you could make the materials available to the customers. Your homemade sample book is only a collection of scraps representing nothing."

Said the Maggid of Dubno, "This *Moshol* should answer your question, O great Gaon. You, my master, have access to a vast stock of knowledge of all the holy books of our people, and the brief selections from each, which you read in your *Tikkun*, have meaning to you as exquisite samples of the spiritual treasures they represent. One section of Mishnayoth in the *Tikkun* will instantly recall to you all the laws and commentaries pertaining to that subject. But as for me," said Rabbi Yaakov modestly, "I am just a simple Maggid and have little learning. Therefore the samples contained in the *Tikkun* don't mean so much to me. I would get little more benefit from these selections than the would-be-merchant from his scraps. Hence I must go back to the original source and study the Gemara itself, even on the Eve of Shavuoth."

□ 6 — THE SOUND OF THE SHOFAR

For decades it had been the custom of the Gaon of Vilna on Rosh HaShanah to blow the Shofar himself in his *Kloiz*, his own private synagogue. But one year, when the Gaon was no longer a young man, he found that he could not get out a sound from his Shofar. The congregation therefore had to turn to another man, a simple person of little learning, who promptly strode up from his seat in the back row and managed to blow the Shofar with ease and dispatch. The Gaon was greatly distressed. "Does God no longer desire my *Tekioth?*" he asked himself. "Is this simple, uneducated man worth more to Him than I?"

The next day the Gaon sent for the Maggid of Dubno to help dispel the sadness that still lingered in his heart. And as he had done so often before, the Maggid, anxious to be of service to his great master and friend, hastened to him and consoled him with a *Moshol:*

A mighty king possessed a precious diamond which had to be cut and polished with great care, if justice was to be done to its unusual size and beauty. He summoned the most skilled and renowned diamond cutters in the land and offered a great reward to the man who would undertake the task. To his surprise, all these experts declined the invitation, pleading inability to do justice to the assignment.

And then a simple worker in the trade, who came from a small country town, and who had never heard about the stone before, happened to come to the palace and promptly offered to do the work required. When he brought back the finished stone the whole court stood astounded, for his skill had turned the rough diamond into a stone of dazzling brilliance and flawless perfection. The king thanked the artisan and wanted to give him the promised reward. But the man refused it, saying, "The reward belongs not to me but to the youngest of my apprentices. It is he who did the actual work."

The king stared at the diamond cutter in amazement. It had been difficult enough to believe that a man as simple as the one who now stood before him could accomplish this task to such perfection, but that the apprentice, who was probably even less aware of the delicate nature of the work, should have been able to do it, seemed almost inconceivable.

Then the king summoned all the diamond experts in the land to show them the stone. They gazed at it in admiration. And the king asked them, "Why is it that you, the most skilled diamond cutters in my kingdom, should have refused to perform a task which it seems that even a village jeweler's apprentice could complete with such remarkable results?"

The spokesman for the group bowed low before the king and said: "We experts know a great deal about precious stones. When we saw this rare jewel we knew at once that to bring out its true beauty and brilliance would be a most formidable task. Therefore our hands were paralyzed with fright and we did not dare touch it. Not so the plain artisan from the country and his apprentice. They neither realized the importance of the owner nor did they comprehend the true worth of the stone. To them it was just another diamond to cut and to polish. And so they set about their task without trepidation and remained at it until the work had been completed to their own satisfaction."

Said Rabbi Yaakov of Dubno to the Gaon of Vilna: "You are a man of great learning. When you put the Shofar to your lips you were overcome with awe, so that your strength failed you and you could not perform the task. Not so the plain man from the back row of the synagogue. He knew only that there was a simple piece of work to be done; namely, to blow the ram's horn in accordance with traditional law, and, knowing that his lungs were healthy and strong, he felt no fear and could sound the Shofar clearly and with ease. He did not know enough about this sacred rite to be overawed by its momentous import as was my illustrious master, the Gaon of Vilna, the most learned among our rabbis, who is fully aware of the deep meanings of the sounds of the Shofar."

□ 7 — OUR DEBT TO OUR GOD

One day the Gaon of Vilna said to the Maggid of Dubno: "Alas, it is so difficult to safeguard oneself against succumbing to pride and presumptuousness. The more knowledge God gives to a man and the more deeply he delves into the secrets of the Holy Writ, the more prone he will be to overrate himself and to become sinfully arrogant. O my great friend, I beg of you, tell me a *Moshol* that may help me overcome temptation and remember my true place in God's world!"

And the Maggid of Dubno instantly replied: "In our holy Torah there are laws specifying how a king must be chosen and what are the qualifications and the duties of a king among Jews. It is expected of him *"that his heart not be raised up above his brothers, and that he turn not aside from the commandment, neither to the right nor to the left"* (Deut. 17:20). What, you may ask, is the connection between the admonition against undue pride in the first half of this quotation, and the warning against disregard of the commandment of God?

"I might best explain it by a *Moshol*," continued Rabbi Yaakov. "It once happened that a number of merchants traveled home from the great Fair at Leipzig. One of them led a horse which pulled a carriage heavily laden with valuable merchandise. As he walked along the highway he suddenly noticed a man, one of the retailers, walking alongside him, behind a small pushcart filled with an odd assortment of cheap articles.

"The wealthy merchant turned to the small trader and asked him, 'How dare you, with your pushcart, keep company with me and walk alongside of me as if you were my equal.'

"But the other man modestly replied, 'Certainly, I know that you are a man of great wealth and well-known in the world of buying and selling, and you would indeed have cause to be proud, provided you had paid cash for all the merchandise in your carriage. But both you and I know that neither of us could advance cash and therefore we bought our wares on credit. Now I have bought little, and what I bought is cheap, but you have purchased great quantities and everything you have here is of the most expensive quality. It is obvious, then, that your debt to your creditors is much greater than my obligation to those who dealt with me. Therefore, remember:

you may be vastly richer than I, but the burden of debt you carry is correspondingly far greater than mine.'

"In the same vein the Lord our God admonishes our kings: 'Do you think that you are better than your brothers. Your position may be high and your worldly goods many, but remember that the greater the gifts you have received from God the greater your debt to Him. For this reason you must take special pains not to be overbearing *and* not to deviate from the path of My commandments either to the right or to the left.' "

So impressed was the Gaon of Vilna by these words of profound wisdom that he frequently quoted them in his subsequent works.

□ 8 — THE SHOWDOWN

... לֹא פָּחוֹת וְלֹא יוֹתֵר ...

A young rabbi who lived in a small town near Vilna was most envious of the fame of the great Gaon. Once, when talking to the Maggid of Dubno, his jealousy got the better of him and he flatly asserted: "Certainly everyone knows that this young Gaon is a great scholar, but after all, we are all learned men. Why make so much to-do about one man's scholarship?"

The Maggid was most displeased by this unseemly remark and determined to teach the impertinent young man a lesson. The Maggid concealed his annoyance and mildly began:

"You must remember that the greatness of the Gaon of Vilna lies not only in his wisdom, but in the fact that he knows in every instance how best to answer the questions put to him."

"I don't understand," replied the village rabbi. "Explain yourself."

"Certainly," said Rabbi Yaakov. "Take this one case. Let us assume someone were to ask you a question like this: Whenever the Mishnah speaks of certain ritual acts that must be performed at a specifically given time, it uses the words *Lo pachoth v'lo yother* meaning 'neither before nor after.' For example, in the first

Mishnah of Tractate *Megillah,* we read that 'The Book of Esther is to be read, depending on the circumstances, on the eleventh day of Adar, or on the twelfth, or on the thirteenth, or on the fourteenth or on the fifteenth, *lo pachoth v'lo yother,* on any one of these dates, but neither before those dates, nor thereafter.' Now in the Mishnah of Shabbath, we have a similar statement. We are told: 'A child is to be circumcised on the eighth day, or on the ninth, on the tenth, on the eleventh or on the twelfth day after birth subject to various conditions' (Sabbath 19:5). Well, master, if they asked you why in the qualifying statement *lo pachoth v'lo yother,* 'neither before those dates, nor thereafter' is missing in this one instance, how would you answer them? Let me see how well you could argue this fine point of the Law," concluded the Maggid with a smile.

The foolish rabbi meditated on the subject for a few minutes and then launched into a most long-winded and complicated argument to explain this anomaly, a most dumbfounding exhibition of casuistry and hair splitting. In the end he sat back, smiled at the Maggid and said, "Well, tell me the truth now. Could even the great Gaon of Vilna have given a better explanation?"

"Your argument was indeed most erudite," replied Rabbi Yaakov of Dubno, "but I believe the Gaon's answer would have been different."

The country rabbi was annoyed. "And, pray tell, what would he have said?" he queried.

"Why, the Gaon of Vilna would simply have answered, 'In that Mishnah of Shabbath it *also* says *lo pachoth v'lo yother,*' so there is no question at all."

□ 9— THE MAGGID AS THE BEARER OF THE GAON'S MESSAGE

When Rabbi Elijah, the famous Gaon of Vilna, passed away on the fifth day of the Festival of Sukkoth in the year 1797, the Maggid of Dubno resolved to devote himself to the dissemination of the ideals that had been so nobly advanced by his departed master and friend. Surviving the great master by seven years, Rabbi Yaakov of Dubno made it his task to render the ideas set forth by Rabbi Elijah under-standable even to the common man. Figuratively speaking, he took the gold bullion of the Gaon's wisdom, and divided it into small nuggets to distribute to Jews the world over. These nuggets he embellished with his own *Mesholim,* anecdotes and stories, so that they might prove attractive even to those who had not acquired profound learning, and the people, listening to his words were moved and inspired. The parables and tales which he employed to make his lessons clear dealt with simple things; the Maggid of Dubno did not hesitate to resort to fables and folk-tales if they would impress the audience and could be turned to serve his pur-pose, which was to give the people a better understanding of the Word of God.

Perhaps the most appealing of them all were those parables which the Maggid devised about the Days of Awe, the "High Holidays," and of which we shall present a few on the pages that follow.

Chapter Twelve

□ ON THE HIGH HOLIDAYS

□ 1 — The Fire Alarm

The Maggid of Dubno was once asked whether he believed himself to be above all sin and error, and if not, why he presumed to preach to others.

The Maggid thought for a moment, and then answered the question with a pithy *Moshol.*

In a little town a fire broke out but the people living round about the burning house did not notice it. The landlord rushed out of his burning home into the street, shouting, "Fire! Fire! Let us all save our homes!"

And there was one man who said to him, "Why are you shouting at us to safeguard our homes when it is your own house that is afire?"

Replied our friend, "Even so, my brother. If I call on you to guard your homes from fire, my house too, will be spared from destruction."

"This is also what I must do now," explained Rabbi Yaakov. "I call on you for *T'shuvah,* to repent, not despite my own shortcomings, but for the very reason that I, too, know that I have sinned. Mend your ways and thereby rescue me as well from the raging fire of evil. Let us strive together for the deliverance of our souls."

□ 2 — THE WONDROUS POWER OF CHILDREN'S PRAYERS

It is interesting to note that many of the High Holiday parables of Rabbi Yaakov of Dubno have as their subject a fire or conflagration as a simile for the evil that burns within man and which must be extinguished before atonement can be attained.

In this vein, too, the Maggid of Dubno addressed the young people, exhorting them to help their elders repent even though they, the children, might still be too young to have a full understanding of the gravity of sin. Ordinarily, he pointed out, it would be expected that the parents were duty-bound to protect the younger generation from danger, both present and future. But there are times when the young can do much to save their elders from the dire consequences of sin and error. And the Maggid would illustrate this thought by means of a moving *Moshol:*

In a clearing in a dense forest there stood a lone house where there lived a family with many children. Every evening the father would barricade the windows with shutters from the outside in order to shield the house from danger. Once, during the night, a raging fire broke out which spread quickly. Somehow a heavy stone fell down outside and sealed off the door of the house so that none of the family inside could leave. The windows were locked from the outside, and there was no way to draw the attention of others to the plight of the people within. Suddenly, one of the younger children discovered a dormer window. It proved beyond his reach, but when his big brother lifted him up on his shoulders, the little boy managed to slip through the window to the outside. The child ran quickly to the village and brought help. The villagers managed to push aside the fallen stone from the front door and the entire family was rescued from the fire, in which they would surely all have perished had it not been for the courageous work of the one small boy.

And even as this one little boy triumphantly flung open the door of his father's house, and thereby saved his family, so, too, the study, prayers and tears of our children can open the lofty gates of Heaven and thus bring about the deliverance of their elders.

□ 3 — THE FOLLY OF IDLE LIP SERVICE

Over and over again the Maggid of Dubno scolded his people for the routine manner in which they performed their devotions on the High Holidays. He never ceased to warn his listeners that the mere beating of the breast while reciting the confession of sins, mechanically performed without self-examination and without the sincere desire to mend one's ways, would never bring that Heavenly forgiveness for which we all hope in the Days of Awe.

And Rabbi Yaakov made his point by a most ingenious *Moshol.*

There was a village far off in the provinces where the people were simple and ignorant. Once one of the villagers had occasion to spend the night in the big city. Suddenly he was awakened from his sleep by the loud beating of drums. "What does this mean?" he asked in fright. In reply he was told that a fire had broken out and that the beating of drums was the city's fire alarm. Satisfied with this information, the man went back to sleep.

When he returned to his village, he excitedly reported what he had seen in the city. "They have a most marvelous arrangement!" he declared. "Whenever there is a fire in the city they beat their drums and soon the fire is all gone." The mayor of the village thought this a splendid idea and immediately bought drums for use in the event of a fire. A few days later, when a fire did break out in the village, the inhabitants quickly took up the drums and beat them loud and strong so that it was a pleasure to listen to them. In the meantime, half the houses in the village had gone up in flames. A stranger who happened to be present in the village square laughed ironically and said to the fire-brigade, who were busily beating away with the wooden drumsticks: "Why, you fools! Don't you know that you can't extinguish a fire just by beating a drum?

The drum is meant only to call out the fire brigade to come and put
out the fire; the noise of the drums won't frighten the fire away!"

This *Moshol*, said the Maggid of Dubno, may well be applied to
those of us who believe that idle lip service is sufficient to win
forgiveness from Above. However long we may beat our fists against
our hearts, it all is worthless if we regard this High Holiday ritual as
a magic formula to ward off the consequences of sin. We should instead consider it an alarm, to awaken us to true repentance and
resolute action to better ourselves and thus extinguish the searing
flame of evil that burns within our hearts.

□ 4 — THE SPARK MUST BE THERE

One day an unbeliever came to the Maggid of Dubno and taunted
him, saying, "You are the great Maggid of whom it is said that he
can change the hearts and minds of men. Would you not try your
skill on me, and transform me, wicked man that I am, into a saint?"

Rabbi Yaakov, noting the unbeliever's tone, said to him:

"Let me tell you a *Moshol*. A city man once came to a most
primitive village where he saw a crowd of men standing at a crude
forge attempting to fan the small fire into a fierce flame by blowing
at it with all the force of their lungs.

" 'Your could spare yourselves all this effort,' he said to them, 'if
you would have a pair of bellows to do the work for you.' When they
told him that they had never even heard of bellows before, he
proceeded to make them a pair and gave it to them as a gift. Then
he left to return to the city.

"When a few weeks later he came to the village again, the people
met him with derision and reproaches. 'Your bellows are not worth
a penny,' they said to him with contempt. 'We pressed them and we
pushed them with all our might but we never could get a fire.'

" 'Let me look at the bellows,' said the city man. He inspected
them most carefully. 'I can see nothing wrong with them,' he said
puzzled. 'Now let me see how you worked them. First of all, where
are your glowing coals?' he demanded.

" 'You mean we need glowing coals too?' the simple village folk asked in amazement.

"Our friend burst into loud laugher: 'Fools,' he exclaimed, 'of course you need them. The bellows alone will never give you a fire. All they can do is produce a current of air which can make a lively fire out of glowing embers. But where there is no fire to begin with even the best pair of bellows cannot make one.'

"I am a Maggid," concluded Rabbi Yaakov of Dubno, "and with my sermons I can coax the embers that glow in the hearts of men to burst into a bright and radiant flame. But, alas, once even the last glowing embers of love for God and His Law have gone from a man's spirit, I am afraid that not even the best of sermons, no matter how inspiring, will be sufficient to effect a change in him."

□ 5 — AVINU MALKENU

אָבִינוּ מַלְכֵּנוּ חָנֵנוּ וַעֲנֵנוּ כִּי אֵין בָּנוּ מַעֲשִׂים.

In many Jewish communities it is a time-honored custom to recite the moving *Avinu Malkenu* prayer responsively, by Reader and Congregation, during the Days of Awe. The name by which the prayer is known is derived from the words *"Our Father, our King,"* with which each of its verses begins. These responses are all chanted aloud and with fervor, but the last verse, which reads: *"Our Father our King! Be gracious to us and answer us, for we have no merits of our own; deal with us in charity and kindness, and save us,"* is recited quietly.

Why, of all the verses of this beautiful prayer, should this one be read in an undertone?

The Maggid of Dubno gave the reason in the following *Moshol:*

A prominent wholesaler would make all his purchases from one large factory where he would call twice each year. Whenever he came, the entire staff was waiting for him, attentive to his every wish. Then, in a booming, confident voice, the magnate would call out his orders; "Five hundred bales of this, one thousand pieces of that," and so on, and the workers would hasten to do his bidding. When the entire order had been filled, the merchant would roar,

"Now pack up the whole lot" and when he would leave, the whole factory would resound to his farewell request, "Give me my bill and I'll pay you in full immediately."

But then the time came when, due to unwise transactions, the merchant found himself short of ready cash. Naturally he wasn't anxious that the business world and, least of all, the employees of that factory should know of his financial reverses. When he came again for the first time after the catastrophe, his orders were not much different from those he had given before, except that the voice in which he gave them had become perhaps a trifle lower. But when he had completed the order he asked the manager of the factory whether he could have a word alone with him. When the two men had arrived at the manager's inner office, the merchant said to him: "You know that I have been a faithful customer for a long time now, and that I have always paid you in cash. Now, for the first time in the twenty years I have been dealing with you, I must ask you for credit terms. I have had some troubles in my business and it is just impossible for me to pay you in cash right now."

Said the Maggid of Dubno: On the High Holidays, we Jews address our God exactly as the merchant in our *Moshol* did his manufacturer. When we lustily chant the *Avinu Malkenu* we place our orders with God in a firm and self-assured voice: "Our Father, our King, let the New Year be a happy one for us! Bring to nought all the evil decrees against us! Rid us of every oppressor and adversary! Forgive and pardon all of our transgressions! Send perfect healing to the sick among Thy people! Inscribe us in the Book of Maintenance and Sustenance!" But once the order is completed, we realize how deeply we are indebted to Him Whom we expect to give us all that we have just requested. We can only manage to say to Him in a whisper: "Be gracious to us and answer us for we have no merits of our own, no means to repay You. Deal with us in charity and kindness and save us."

◻ 6 — THE CONCLUDING SERVICE OF YOM KIPPUR

It seems appropriate to conclude this chapter with a moving sermon which the Maggid once delivered at *Ne'ilah*, the Concluding Service of the Day of Atonement.

There was once a princess who married into a peasant family. They were not aware of her royal antecedents; hence to her great grief they did not treat her with the deference due her. In answer to her repeated complaints, her royal father came for a visit one day to see for himself how his daughter was faring in the peasant home. He was pleasantly surprised to see that there seemed to be no reason at all for the girl to be unhappy. Having learned that the king was coming, the family and all the others in the village outdid each other in doing honor to the princess. A few days later the King, satisfied that there really was no reason for him to be concerned about his daughter, made ready to take leave and to return to the capital. But to his dismay, the princess now gave way to utter despair and clung to her father while the tears flowed from her eyes without cease. "Why are you weeping?" asked the king. "It seems to me that you lack for nothing here. The family and all the others in the village seem to love and honor you, and I see no cause for you to be so unhappy that I am leaving."

But the princess cried even more bitterly and finally she sobbed out: "O my father, they do me this honor only as long as you are here. But as soon as you will be gone they will forget who I am and all this courtesy and deference will be a thing of the past."

The same is true also of the Divine spark which the King of kings has planted into our hearts. All year long our soul is fettered by earthly things; it suffers want and feels sorely oppressed. But when the month of Elul comes, its heavenly Father descends into our midst. During the short period that He is closer to us, things of the spirit rise high in our esteem. Hence for those few weeks the soul comes into its own, growing in stature as the Days of Awe draw near and reaching the pinnacle of honor and glory on the Day of Atonement. But at the hour of *Ne'ilah*, when God the King would ascend heavenward at the sound of the *Teruah*, the soul is filled with grief and despair. For it dreads the next day and all the days to come, when its Father will no longer be so close, in Israel's midst. How will the soul fare during the rest of the year when God is once more enthroned in His Heaven?

This is the reason for the tears we shed when the *Ne'ilah* Service heralds the conclusion of Yom Kippur. Our soul, dreading the return of man's year-round disregard of its needs, is shaken and weeps bitterly at the hour of its parting from its Heavenly Father and Protector.

CHAPTER THIRTEEN

☐ ON THE HAGGADAH OF PESACH

☐ 1 — THE BREAD OF AFFLICTION

(כְּ)הָא לַחְמָא עַנְיָא . . .

It is not generally known that there exist two versions for the statement introducing the first part of the Haggadah which is read at the Passover Seder. One version reads *Ha lachma anya, "This is the bread of affliction...;"* the other, *K'ha lachma anya, "Like this is the bread of affliction,* which our ancestors ate in the land of Egypt..." Which of these two versions, you may ask, would be the more acceptable? Said the Maggid of Dubno: Let us discuss it with the help of a *Moshol:*

A poor man, who had always had difficulty in supporting his large family, had an unexpected stroke of luck and became very wealthy. However, his good fortune did not cause him to forget his humble antecedents and he remained as modest and unassuming as he had been all his life. Every year, when the anniversary of the turning point of his life came around, he would put on his shabby garments from his days of poverty, gather his family, tell them the story of how he became prosperous, and admonish them never to become proud but to be ever grateful to God for their present wealth. The family came to look forward to the anniversary celebration when the father would show them what their days of affliction had been like long ago, for he would mark the occasion with costly gifts for them all.

Unfortunately this man's prosperity did not last. He suffered serious business reverses. First he had to sell his beautiful home. Next to go were his precious jewelry, the costly furniture, and in the end he even had no clothes left except the tatters which he had retained from the early days of his affliction. When his children saw him in these shabby garments, they shouted for joy, for they had come to associate such attire on their father with feasting, games and expensive toys.

But this time their father said to them, "I am afraid that we have very little just now to be happy about. In years gone by I would put on these rags only to show you how poor I had been long ago. But today I am wearing them simply because this is all I have left. These are the garments of poverty."

The changes in the fortunes of this family, said the Maggid of Dubno, may be compared to the state in which our people is today. When Israel prospered in its own land and sat down to celebrate its Seder, it could joyously lift up its matzoth and proclaim, "*Like this* was the bread of affliction which we were forced to eat long ago." And then Israel could give thanks to God for the many miracles which caused the present generation not to know of the misery which its ancestors had had to endure. But now that the Temple, our spiritual home, is gone, we are in exile, and many of our brethren the world over must suffer. Today the matzah is more than a symbol recalling an unhappy past. Hence, unfortunately, at our Seder service today, when we raise aloft our matzoth, we must say *Ha lachma anya*, "Verily, this *is again* the bread of affliction . . ."

Thus we understand the two readings.

□ 2 — A Difference in Attitude

חָכָם מָה הוּא אוֹמֵר: "מָה הָעֵדֹת וְהַחֻקִּים... רָשָׁע מָה הוּא אוֹמֵר: "מָה הָעֲבֹדָה הַזֹּאת לָכֶם."

"What does the wise son say? He asks: 'What is the meaning of the testimonies, and the statutes and the judgments, which the Lord our God has commanded you?' What does the wicked son say? He asks: 'What is this service to you?' "

(Deut. 6:20; Exod. 12:26)

And the Haggadah goes on to say that when the wicked son uses the expression "to *you*," he makes it quite clear that he does not include himself in the Passover ritual and thereby dissociates himself from the Jewish people. Therefore, the Haggadah urges that you *"make his teeth blunt,* that you silence his biting criticism of our tradition, and say to him curtly, 'This is done because of that which the Lord did for *me* when I came forth from Egypt' (Exod. 8:8) — for *me* and not for *him;* for had he been there, he would not have been delivered."

But, we may ask, is it not a fact that the wise son, too, does not speak of the statutes "... which the Lord our God commanded *us*" but instead, speaks of them as the laws which "the Lord our God has commanded *you?*" Why should this be less reprehensible than the way in which the wicked son expresses himself?

The answer is not so difficult as it might seem. Imagine a situation where a stranger watches some servant engaged in strenuous labor for his master. He might ask him, "Why did your master ask you to do this job? What is the purpose of this work?" This would be a courteous question, motivated by a genuine desire for information. The bystander is interested in learning more about the master and about his plans which the servant is carrying out. But if the stranger were to ask, "Why must you wear yourself out? What is this drudgery to you?" he obviously has little respect for the master's authority and implies by his question, "Why do you need to do this work? If I were you, I would just refuse to do it."

Such is the attitude of the wicked son. What he wants is not to ask for an explanation, but solely to criticize. The wise son, on the other hand, has asked a courteous, sensible question and is anxious to learn the meaning of the testimonies that the Lord our God commanded to *you*, his ancestors, when he was not yet among the living.

This is the difference in the questions asked by two of the classic figures mentioned in the Passover Haggadah.

□ 3 — THE WISE AND THE WICKED

We are told that if the wicked son, the *Rasha,* makes light of God's Law, his father must "blunt the edge of his teeth" and say to him, "It is because of what the Lord did for *me* when I went forth from Egypt."

Why is the father commanded to give so curt a reply rather than go into detailed explanations?

Replied the Maggid of Dubno in a *Moshol:*

In a small town, just before the feast of Passover, there was a fair at which tremendous bargains could be purchased. Now in this town there dwelt a Jew who was so poor that he had just barely enough money to buy wine and matzoth for the Seder. But when he heard of the bargains his friends had obtained at the fair, he hastened there to buy a small bolt of cloth, intending to have his wife make some new holiday clothes from it for the two of them. So great was his enthusiasm that he forgot his financial straits and spent almost all of his Passover money for the material.

When his wife saw the purchase, she was furious. "Fool!" she cried, "What have you done! Where will we find the money now for wine and matzoth? Go back at once to the fair and return the cloth to the people who sold it to you. If they give you trouble, tell them that the material was bad, that you don't want it and that they must give you back your money."

Our friend quickly did as his wife had asked. To his surprise the merchant did not attempt to argue with him or even to show him some of the other merchandise he had to sell. Instead, he returned the money to him without a word.

Afterwards, a customer who had heard the brief conversation, asked the shopkeeper, "Why did you give in so easily? Could you not have shown him the rest of your stock and sold him other material? Besides, you could have shown him that the cloth was perfect and not faulty as he said it was."

But the merchant replied, "That would have been of little use, for the trouble was not in the material but in the customer himself. You must have seen that he did not even try to point out the flaw he said he found in the cloth. It was quite obvious to me from his argument that, for some reason, he actually had no intention to buy this material, or any other cloth, for that matter. His complaint was nothing more than an excuse for demanding his money back. Any attempt to persuade him differently would have been a waste of time and effort."

This *Moshol* aptly illustrates the difference between the *Chacham*, the wise son, and *Rasha*, the wicked one. The wise son, believing in the Torah wholeheartedly, is more than willing to point out the places in the Law which give him difficulty, for he refuses to cast it lightly aside and is anxious for more information and knowledge. But the wicked son has no intention even to examine the Word of God. Instead, like the villager at the fair, who wanted to rid himself of the cloth, he will devise many shallow excuses for rejecting it. Therefore his questions will not be sincere and honest but malicious and impertinent, and no amount of reasoning or instruction will persuade him that he is in the wrong. Therefore, do not be troubled by his scornful arguments, but "blunt the edge of his teeth" so that he will be too stunned momentarily to corrupt others with his wicked ways. Look at him sternly and say quietly, "What I observe here is in gratitude for what the Lord did for *me*. As for you, you have rejected His Torah and therefore have no part in our inheritance. Had you been in Egypt, you would not have been saved."

□ 4 — THE GLITTERING COINS

וְאַחֲרֵי־כֵן יֵצְאוּ בִּרְכֻשׁ גָּדוֹל.   (לך לך)

"And afterwards they shall leave with great abundance."

(Gen. 15:14)

God had given Abraham a glimpse of the future of the nation which would be descended from him. He told the patriarch that the Jewish people would be enslaved and know great suffering, but that, in the end, they would "go forth with great abundance" as free men.

Now what was this great abundance? Our Sages tell us that it was the Law which the Children of Israel received in the wilderness on Mount Sinai. But if this is indeed true, why were the Hebrews, before leaving Egypt, actually commanded to ask the Egyptians for money and goods?

The Maggid of Dubno would reconcile this contradiction with one of his famous *Mesholim:*

A young man had hired himself out to a wealthy merchant to serve him for six years, for which he would be paid with a bag of silver coins. When the six years were over and the time came for the servant to leave, it occurred to the master that a bag of silver was much too small a reward for the splendid services the boy had rendered him. He therefore put the silver aside and instead wrote out a check in an amount many times that of the total value of the silver coins. But the servant, instead of thanking his master for his generosity, sullenly stuffed the piece of paper into his pocket and went home weeping.

The next day his father called at the merchant's house and said to the wealthy man, "You have been most generous to my son and I want to thank you. But the boy is still a child and does not comprehend the value of a check. All he knew was that he expected to receive a bag filled with shiny new coins and that instead he got a plain sheet of paper. I should be most grateful, therefore, if you would let him have at least part of his wages in solid silver."

In the same manner did our Father Abraham come to God, saying, "You have been generous indeed in promising the Torah to my descendants. But the nation will be young and not mature enough to understand the value of the Torah, and if they will have to leave the slavery of Egypt with empty hands they will say 'Indeed, God has fulfilled part of His promise. We did become slaves. But what about the great abundance which we were to receive at the hour of our deliverance?' "

It is for this reason, the Talmud explains, that Israel was clearly commanded to take gold and silver vessels from the Egyptians. This would be tangible wealth which they could appreciate at that time. In this manner the Children of Israel would see immediately that the promise given by God to their righteous forebear had retained its validity.

It was only as Israel grew in wisdom that it came to understand that its true wealth lay not in the coins and trinkets gathered in Egypt but in the Divine gift of the Torah, which has stood by our side to this very day.

□ CHAPTER FOURTEEN

□ THE MAGGID—RAISING MONEY FOR
CHARITY

□ 1 — THE STRANGE INVITATION

אַתָּה מְזוּמָן לְעוֹלָם הַבָּא!

"You are ready for the World to Come!"

Once the Maggid of Dubno came to a small Polish town in order to
raise money for a cause particularly dear to his heart. On this occasion he happened to come to the home of a very wealthy man of
whom it was known that he had never given even a penny of charity
to the poor. Now, too, when Rabbi Yaakov approached him, the
man bluntly refused to make a contribution. The Maggid rose
without a protest and as he left, he merely said: *"Atta Mezuman
Le'olam Habba."* Said the miser in surprise, "Why, doesn't this
mean *'You are ready for the World to Come'*? Now, Rabbi,
according to your lights, I'm a miserable tightwad, am I not? Why,
then, do you give me this great compliment?"

Said the Maggid of Dubno:

"Let me sit down once again and I will explain it all to you with a
Moshol.

"Once there was a man who possessed wealth untold, but he was a notorious miser. He kept diligent watch over his possessions and never gave anything to the needy or to the widow and the orphan. Before his death he made a will according to which all his money, all his gold, silver and diamonds, were to be buried with him in his coffin.

"When he came before the Court on High, the Angels pored over the Book of Remembrance and found that this man had never given any charity. And they asked, 'Why was it that you clung to your great wealth so zealously? Tell us, what good will all your gold and silver be to you here in the World of Truth?'

"But the man replied, 'Then you mean I should have spent my money down there, in that earthly world of falsehood and deceit? Why, down there, I am quite sure that my charity would have gone to the wrong people, to idlers and liars neither needy nor deserving of it. Hence, I was careful to leave my wealth intact to bring to the World of Everlasting Truth where it can be of profit to those who really merit it.'

"This was a strange argument. Never before had anything like it been heard in the World Above. After a few hours' deliberation, the Heavenly Tribunal handed down its decision. Said the Angel who read aloud the heavenly decree: 'You are in good company, O Earthling. There has been another who has pleaded similarly. This was none other than Korach, who was swallowed up by the earth, and arrived here with his household and all his goods (Num. 16:32). So there are two of you already...' "

Then looking sternly at the miser the Maggid concluded: "And the third of this unholy trio is none other than you yourself. Now the 'Mezuman' I mentioned is different from what you think. It's not a compliment at all. You, Korach, and the man in my story form a group of three who can 'bentch Mezuman' together in Olam Haba the 'World to Come.' But this 'World to Come,' too, is different from what you think it is, for when Korach and the skinflint in my story left the earth, you may be sure that it was not to Heaven that they went. If you continue in the way of life that you have chosen, you will have the privilege of eating together with such notorious companions, and blessing the Lord thereafter in the quorum of *Mezuman.*"

□ 2 — THE WORTHY DONOR

It once happened that the Maggid of Dubno, while collecting funds for a certain charitable cause, met a wealthy man who had the un-enviable reputation of being a great miser.

In order to induce the man to make at least a small donation, Rabbi Yaakov proceeded to enumerate some of the contributions that he had already received, not from wealthy people but from sim-ple artisans and shopkeepers.

"You know Chayim the Blacksmith" he began, "He doesn't have much money, but he gave me five thalers. Tevye the Shopkeeper donated six; and Yossel the Shoemaker, who also doesn't have too much money to give away, let me have ten whole thalers...."

"I beg your pardon," the wealthy man said, interrupting the Maggid's recital: "I would not call these people charitable. They are poor men, and when they die they won't leave anything worth men-tioning. But, Master, I shall tell you a secret; I have made my will and in it I leave most of my money to the poor after my death. You will understand, then, why I cannot give you anything today."

Replied the Maggid of Dubno: "Yes, that point is well taken and deserves a proper answer. I shall therefore tell you a *Moshol:* Do you know the difference between a hen and a pig? Never mind, I shall answer it for you. The hen is a small animal, and does not have much to give. Her eggs are small and light, and may weigh but two ounces each. And yet the farmer will coddle her like a baby. Even if she should leave her coop, walk into her master's house through the back door, and track dirt all over her mistress' newly-washed kitchen floor, not even a feather on her back would be touched. Now the pig is much larger. It weighs two hundred pounds and of this, twenty-five pounds are pure lard. You would think it's quite valuable then, would you not? And yet no one is ever nice to the pig. If it ever left its sty it would be driven back in with a broomstick, and if it ever dared enter its master's house, why, it would get a beating that it would not so soon forget."

"Come to the point, Rabbi," said the man impatiently. "What is the reason for this discrimination?"

"Be patient," retorted Rabbi Yaakov. "This is just what I want to explain. The hen may not have much, but what she does give, she gives faithfully each day as long as she lives. The pig may have much more wealth to offer, but it will give it up only after it is dead. Now tell me, which of the two is the worthier donor?"

□ 3 — THE STUBBORN MISER

וְתַלְמוּד תּוֹרָה כְּנֶגֶד כֻּלָם.

"The study of the Law outweighs all other things."

One day Rabbi Yaakov of Dubno had occasion to go to a nearby town in order to solicit donations for charity. He stopped at a gate of the home of a wealthy man who was a notorious skinflint. It was known that paupers and even collectors for the poor would not be permitted to cross the threshold of the sprawling mansion. The attendant who accompanied the Maggid refused to follow him into the house, but the Maggid insisted, saying, "Come with me and you will see that I shall win him over."

To the attendant's surprise, they were given a most courteous reception. But when Rabbi Yaakov told the man the purpose of the visit, the latter kindly but firmly replied:

"You are a rabbi of great renown and I am quite sure that you will get generous contributions wherever you go. Therefore I fear it is not much of a *Mitzvah* for me to make a donation. Now if there would be no one else to help you, that would be a different matter, but things being as they are, I am very sorry I can't oblige you."

Said the Maggid of Dubno: "May I have just a few more moments to tell you a *Moshol* that I particularly like? It seems that in a certain town a synagogue had fallen into a state of decay and the leaders of the community decided that some way would have to be found to raise money for the necessary repairs. Most of the Jews in that town dealt in wines and spirits, and therefore it was announced that every week each member of the congregation would have to bring one pint of wine or whiskey to poured into two open barrels standing in the corridor of the synagogue. The proceeds from the sale of the strong drink would then be more than ample to pay for the renovation work.

"Now there was one man who said to himself, "I will be smarter than all the other Jews in this town. I'll help fill the barrel all right, but it will be with water and not with wine. One pint of water in 100 gallons of wine! Who's to know?' And he carried out his plan the very next day. Unfortunately the same idea occurred also to another merchant, who felt that, after all, there was enough whiskey in the barrel and a little water added would only serve to improve the blend. The pity of it was that all the other congregants had also arrived at much the same conclusion, so that, when the barrel was full, it was found to contain only water and not a drop of whiskey.

"I am in the same position," concluded the Maggid. "Wherever I go people think that I must have enough money in my pockets by now, and so they save themselves the trouble of contributing to my charity. As a result, I never get any money at all."

Now the miser was not displeased with the Rabbi's words, but he was not yet ready to give up the fight. "Yes, I suppose you are right," he replied, "It would be a *Mitzvah* indeed to make a donation to the cause to which you give so much time and effort. But I am afraid I have little interest in these worldly matters. I am more at home in the study hall and you know what our sages say: *Talmud Torah k'neged kullam*—'The study of the Torah outweighs all other things.*

But the Maggid of Dubno, nothing daunted, countered the argument with another *Moshol:*

"In a certain wealthy neighborhood it became fashionable for all the rich to wear fur jackets. Those who wore such furs were considered by all to be superior in wealth and social status to those who did not.

"Now there was one poor man who had more social ambition than money. He therefore went out and had a similar fur jacket made for himself. When the garment was ready, he proudly put it on and strutted through the streets, quite certain that the people would think him to be one of the rich.

"But to his surprise, all the people in the street only laughed at him. And why should they have laughed? The answer is simple. The wealthy folk wore sumptuous garments under their furs, but it was obvious that beneath his fur jacket, this man had on not a stitch of other clothing.

"Do you see," concluded Rabbi Yaakov, "This story can be applied also to the *Mitzvoth* and the study of the Torah. The study of the Torah is like a fur jacket, a dignified complement to the garments of *Mitzvoth* that should be worn beneath. But what good is study without the observance of basic laws such as charity and humaneness? Why, it is no better than going around stark naked, covered only by a jacket of fur."

□ 4 — HAD ISAAC REFUSED TO SHOW HIS COIN...

Once it happened that Rabbi Yaakov called upon a rich man by the name of Isaac, to request a donation for a cause of great merit. Isaac, however, refused to help.

Said the Maggid of Dubno: "My friend, I must warn you that if you do not give me the money I need, I have good cause to suspect that you were born out of wedlock."

Isaac turned upon the Maggid in fury and threatened to take him to court for this impertinent aspersion on his antecedents unless he would be able to substantiate his accusation.

Said Rabbi Yaakov of Dubno: "Surely I can prove it if you will but hear me out. In the Book of Genesis (25:19) we read, '*And these are the descendants of Isaac, the son of Abraham. Abraham fathered Isaac.*' Rashi, the most illustrious Commentator of all times, explained why the Torah had felt compelled to add the statement that 'Abraham fathered Isaac.' It seems that in those days there were some cynics who said, 'Behold, Sarah has lived with Abraham for many years and yet she never had a child until now. It must be, then, that Abimelech, who had wanted her as a wife, and not Abraham, is the father.' What, then, did the Holy One, blessed be He, do to silence these rumors? He shaped the facial features of Isaac exactly like those of Abraham so that everyone seeing him had to admit that it was Abraham, and no one else, who had fathered Isaac. Now the Talmud notes that this was obvious evidence only if one could see Abraham and Isaac together. But since father and son could not be together all the time, Abraham had a metal coin made on which he had his own features engraved on one side, and those of Isaac on the other, and Isaac kept this coin with him at all times (Bava Kamma 97b). Thus, if anyone raised doubts as to Isaac's legitimacy, all that Isaac needed to do was show his coin and then no one would have any question as to his antecedents.

"Let me ask you, Isaac," concluded the Dubnoer with a gentle smile, "how could Isaac prove his legitimacy? Yes, only by showing his coin. Now if Isaac had refused to show his coin and kept his purse tightly locked instead, what do you think the people would have thought?"

The present-day Isaac bowed his head in shame and immediately gave the Maggid a generous contribution.

□ 5 — ONIONS FOR CHARITY

Unfortunately, the ignorant have no monopoly on miserliness. One day the Maggid of Dubno visited a scholar for the purpose of soliciting funds for charity and found that, despite his wealth and his erudition in our sacred literature, the man refused to comply with his request. Knowing that the scholar had a wholesome respect for what is written in our holy books, the Maggid began to lecture him on the laws of charity, interspersing commentaries and explanations which he knew would be of great interest to the man. But all that the miser did was to reciprocate with a lecture on his own on equally fine points of the Law. Rabbi Yaakov then attempted to move him with appropriate tales and parables from the *Aggadah*, but once again the niggardly scholar responded only with stories and homilies that were even more involved.

In the end the Maggid of Dubno asked permission to tell one of his own *Mesholim:*

"A hundred years ago," he began, "a man came to a distant island where onions were unkown. When he found out that the natives had no knowledge of this everyday vegetable he took out a bagful and distributed its contents among the people. They soon found out that onions tasted most delicious in salads and sauces. Therefore, as a reward, they gave the stranger the weight of the onions in silver coins.

"Delighted, the visitor returned to his home town and told a friend of his good fortune. His friend, decided that he, too, would try his luck in the same place, this time with garlic, which he felt sure would also be quite foreign to the natives. And really, the natives of the island were more than pleased with the pleasantly pungent taste of the little bulbs. Desiring to reward their new benefactor, they gave him the weight of the garlic in onions.

"But the latter was most indignant and said, 'When I brought you this valuable spice I expected that my reward would be at least as great as the one you gave my friend who introduced the onion here. I must say I am surprised at your pettiness. Onions may be a delight, but they will not help me buy food or pay my debts. What I need is money, solid gold and silver.'

"The same is true of me," said the Maggid with a smile. "Your ingenious lectures will not help my cause. What I need is ready cash."

□ 6—WHEN IS WEALTH A DISEASE?

Another time, Rabbi Yaakov came to a man who was wealthy but never gave anything to the poor. When asked what it was he wanted, the Maggid of Dubno replied: "I merely want to pay you a visit, for I understand you are seriously ill."

"Me ill? Ridiculous!" snorted the master of the house. And he continued sarcastically, "Would you be kind enough to let me know just what you think is wrong with me?"

"Certainly," said the Maggid. "We read in the Book of Ecclesiastes: 'There is an evil which I have seen under the sun, and it is heavy upon me. A man to whom God gives riches, wealth and honor, so that he lacks nothing for his soul of all that he desires, yet God does not give him the power to eat of it, but a stranger eats it; this is vanity and it is an evil disease' (Eccl. 6:1-2). Such is the fear which keeps man from enjoying what he has."

The miser could not answer. But when he saw that Rabbi Yaakov had no intention of leaving, he asked him, "And what do you want from me now? You have fulfilled the *Mitzvah* of visiting the sick; you may now leave."

Said the Maggid of Dubno, "Not quite yet. For do not our Sages say, (Baba Metzia 30a), 'He who fulfills the commandment of visiting the sick thereby helps ease his pains by taking from him one sixtieth of his illness.' Your wealth to which you so stubbornly cling has become a disease with you. If I were to leave without having relieved you of at least a small part of it, I would not have completed my *Mitzvah*."

□ 7 — THE COIN FINDS ITS MATE

הַלְעִיטֵנִי נָא מִן־הָאָדֹם הָאָדֹם הַזֶּה . . .   (תולדות)

לֹא־טוֹב הֱיוֹת הָאָדָם לְבַדּוֹ . . .   (בראשית)

Of course not every wealthy man is a miser. One day, the Maggid of Dubno visited a wealthy man and found him busily engaged in counting his money, piling up the silver coins on one side according to size, and the gold ones on the other.

When Rabbi Yaacov asked for his contribution, he absently handed him one of the silver coins. The Maggid, somewhat disappointed that the contribution was no larger, said: *"Give me, please some of this red, red thing over there."**

The wealthy man quickly understood the hint and gave Rabbi Yaakov one of the golden coins.

But the Rabbi of Dubno only smiled and quoted yet another verse. *"It is not good that 'the red one' should be alone."***

The merchant laughed in delight, "Rabbi, I like that play on the word Adom—Adam. Here, take a second gold coin for old friendship's sake."

Rabbi Yaakov accepted the second piece of gold with thanks, but then ventured to add: "You know, it takes three to make a *Mezuman.**** So if you'll give me a third gold piece the three of them can give thanks together."

Needless to say, he received the additional coin.

---

* Gen. 25:30—This actually refers to a dish of lentils.
** Gen. 2:18—A play on words: Adam—Man; Adom—Red one.
*** The quorum necessary for the recital of a slightly more elaborate "Grace after Meals."

CHAPTER FIFTEEN

□ THE MAGGID ABROAD

□ 1—THE LAWSUIT AGAINST HEAVEN

Once, on a visit to Paris, where the Jews had a reputation for laxity in religious observance, the Maggid of Dubno delivered a short speech as follows:

"Gentlemen, I fear I must institute a lawsuit against God and I would like to have my case tried in Paris. Now you may ask me why I should do it here, of all places. Why undertake so long and arduous a journey, for couldn't I have settled it in my own home town in the East? Let me give you my answer, then. Indeed, I have tried to bring my case to trial in my own homeland, but wherever I went the people would say to me, 'How dare we accept a charge against Him Who is the Supreme Master over all the world?' and they refused to have any hand in this matter. But there was one thing which they did tell me: 'Why not go to Paris? You ought to find someone there to take your case, for is it not known to you that in Paris the people don't fear God?' "

☐ 2 — TEMPLES OR "SHULS"

One day, Rabbi Yaakov of Dubno journeyed to Berlin in order to stir the hearts of his brethren there, for he had heard that many of the younger generation had conceived a slavish passion for German culture and had come to look upon their own tradition with disdain.

It happened that a group of these youthful "Reformers" invited the Maggid to visit their beautiful temple. They pointed out the magnificent style of architecture, and it was indeed an imposing structure. And they declared with pride that a house of worship like this would surely make a profound impression even on those indifferent to religion.

The men then took the Maggid into the temple and showed him the exquisite Ark and the richly embroidered curtain that screened it. The Scrolls of the Law inside were many, all enveloped in costly mantles and adorned with gold and silver.

"Now tell us, Rabbi," one of the young men asked when the tour had been completed. "Would you be good enough to answer a question for us? You claim that in your part of the world, in the East, the Jews all love the Torah and honor it much more than we do. In fact, you say they would be ready to die for it, if need be. But consider for a moment what treatment they give to the very thing they profess to love. Your 'shuls' in Poland and Lithuania are miserable shacks with no windows and no proper lighting. Your Scrolls are wrapped not in gold-embroidered velvet but in shabby cloth, and the *wimpel*, the cloth to tie the Scroll together, is not beautiful and embroidered like ours, but only a plain scrap of linen. You spend much less for the upkeep of your synagogues than we do for our temple and yet you persist in calling us atheists. Now that you have seen our beautiful house of worship, tell us, who is it that shows more respect for the Law? Is it you people in the East with your broken-down shuls, or is it we with our temple in which we all can take pride?"

And the Maggid of Dubno replied, "Since I am a Maggid, I shall answer your question with a *Moshol*":

Once there were two sisters whom fortune had not treated alike.

The elder of the two went abroad, married a wealthy man, and did not lack for fancy friends and gay rounds of travel and pleasure. The younger, however, married a poor man from their home town and had great difficulty making ends meet for her growing family.

One day the wealthy lady returned to her native town to visit her younger sister and she was horrified to see the misery in which the other woman lived with her husband and her many children.

After a while, the wealthy sister began to tell of her life across the ocean. "You cannot imagine," she said "the beautiful mansion in which we live. I am one of the most honored citizens of my town and of course I must dress the part. So I buy for myself the choicest of dresses and the most precious jewelry. I have maids and servants aplenty so that I need not trouble myself with household cares. In short, I have everything you might wish for."

"Then you must be very happy," said the other woman joyfully.

"Alas," signed her sister. "Happiness is the one thing that has eluded me thus far. My husband gives me a beautiful home and lovely gowns, but he does not love me. He takes no notice of me whatever, and sometimes weeks pass without his addressing even one word to me. He is a handsome man and he accepts the attentions of other women. This cannot go on forever, and I do not know what the end will be."

Said the poor sister: "As you see, we live in very humble circumstances and it is hard to make a living. We cannot afford servants, or beautiful clothes for me and the children. But thank the Lord, we are not unhappy. We have lovely children, healthy, pious, and studious, who all try to help us wherever they can. Certainly this does not ease our poverty, but eventually they will be self-supporting and then things will surely be better for all of us. And my husband is a good man; I have never heard one unkind word from his lips. He loves me more than he does himself."

And the wealthy woman answered, "Heaven's blessing on you, little sister. With all the hardships you must endure, you have a better chance for happiness than I who live in plenty."

"Such, too," said the Maggid of Dubno, "is the difference between yourselves and your brothers in the East. True, you give generously so that your temple may lack for nothing and that the Scrolls of the Law may be seen in a beautiful setting. But what else do you do for the Torah besides thus ornamenting it? Is your own conduct in accordance with her laws and her spirit? No, indeed. Most of you let your hearts and minds hanker after the culture and the habits of your Gentile neighbors. How, then, can you remain loyal to the Law of the Torah? Despite your sumptuous temple, you are still very far from being good Jews, and the Torah feels unloved, slighted and unhappy in your midst.

"Now behold your brothers in Eastern Europe, in Poland and in Lithuania. True, they are poor and the Torah is surrounded by poverty and squalor, but there the Jews love the Torah, they study it and never depart from its teachings. Therefore the Torah is safe in their midst, and in turn, the Torah protects them so that their little dark shul becomes a spiritual fortress, much mightier than your majestic temple will ever be. To them the Torah is truly a fountain of life, it invigorates and heartens. *"She is a tree of life to those who cleave to her, and happy are they who hold her fast"* (Prov. 3:18).

□ 3 — TRUTH AND FALSEHOOD*

On another occasion in Berlin, Rabbi Yaakov of Dubno began his sermon with these words:

"There is a great difference between Dubno, my home town, and your great city of Berlin: In our little town, we tell the truth, *emeth*, in the street and *sheker*, lies, in our synagogues. But here, in this renowned city, the situation is reversed. In the market places of Berlin falsehood prevails, yet truth is spoken in your synagogues."

When questioned about this strange statement, the Maggid replied: "Our people in Poland are honest and pious. They devote only a very few hours each day to making a living; the rest of their time is spent at study and at prayer. And when they work, they are

---

* A similar story is attributed to Rabbi Levi Yitzchak of Berditchev.

careful not to be dishonest when it comes to weights and measures, and to abide strictly by the Torah's laws of justice and righteousness. They shun falsehood like the plague. Then, on Yom Kippur, they stand in the synagogue and say to God, 'We have trespassed, we have been faithless, we have robbed...!' In their case, is this anything but utter falsehood?

"Things are different here in Berlin. The people here rush to and fro all year long to get rich quickly, and they do not take the time to consider whether they have been entirely honest in their business dealings and whether they have told the truth each time. And if they should catch themselves at any unrighteous dealing, they always have an excuse for their conduct. Therefore, when on Yom Kippur in the synagogue they beat their breasts before God and say that they have trespassed, that they have been faithless and that they have robbed, they tell the plain, unvarnished truth."

□ 4 — The Messiah Has Not Yet Come

The latter part of the eighteenth century saw vast advances in Western Europe. Industry flourished, people were prosperous, and a new spirit of liberalism was making itself felt. People spoke of a new world where all men, regardless of religion or nationality, would be brothers, and some Jews, too, came to believe that a glorious Messianic era had dawned.

One day the Maggid of Dubno had occasion to address a meeting of Jews in Germany. This particular group had among its members many who, feeling that a new day had dawned for them all, had gradually abandoned much of our sacred tradition, and the Maggid came before them with the hope of winning them back to the paths of God's Torah.

While the Maggid was in the midst of a fiery oration against the evils that were still rampant even in this supposed day of new freedom, he was suddenly interrupted by a young man who rose and said:

"Old man, why preach to us about evil? Do you not know that

there's a new world a-dawning? The nations are awakening; the Dark Ages are over. As far as we are concerned, the Messiah has come. Soon all evil will be at an end, with or without your ranting. Do you think that we still should be waiting for a Messiah in a white cloak, riding on a donkey and sounding the Shofar? Who needs Jerusalem? Who needs a Messiah? Aren't we living in the best of all possible worlds right now?"

The Maggid of Dubno was silent for a moment. Then he turned to the questioner with a smile and asked permission to answer him with a *Moshol:*

"It seems that a fox, passing through a forest, saw a raven perched in the branches of a tree. The cunning fox tried every trick to entice the bird to come down but to no avail. Finally, he called out, 'My dear raven, will you not come down and join me? It is only proper, you know, that we should be friends.' But the bird only answered, 'How could we ever live in friendship, for are we not of two different worlds?' Said the fox, 'Why, do you not know that the Messiah has come? At long last the time has arrived where the wolf shall dwell with the lamb and the leopard shall lie down with the kid (Isaiah 11:6). Why, then, should the fox and the raven not be friends?'

"But at that very moment the silence of the forest was pierced by the loud barking of dogs. The fox dashed off at once, leaving the raven behind. And the raven cried out, 'But Master Fox, did you not tell me that the Messiah is here and that all living things are now brothers? Why, then, should you run away from the dogs?' But the fox never ceased to run and did not even turn around as he shouted in reply, 'What else can I do? Those dogs are an ignorant lot; they don't know yet that the Messiah has come.'

"Do you see, young man?" concluded the Maggid. "The same is true now of ourselves and the nations. The times are good, and people believe that the days of the Messiah have come at long last. Therefore the other nations are willing now to extend the hand of friendship even to the homeless and defenseless people of Israel. But what does evil know of friendship and brotherhood? Not much more than dogs do about the Messiah. Wait and see what will become of these protestations of good will, if there should be a war, or a bad harvest, or lack of work. When bad times will come, Israel will be the first to be made to feel it. No, I fear the Messiah has not yet come."

□ 5 — THE EVIL IMPULSE AND POVERTY

Another time, Rabbi Yaakov had been invited to address a debating society in Berlin whose members were reputed to be somewhat lax in their religious observances.

He began the discourse with a strange statement. He said to his audience: "You have cast the Evil Impulse from his high station and so have deprived him of his powers."

Surprised, one of the audience rose and replied: "Coming from you, this certainly is an unusual thought. Do you rabbis not consider us the most ardent followers of the Evil Impulse? After all, what you call the Evil Impulse is nothing but the desire for the things that make life easy and pleasant, and is this not the aim of all modern movements?"

The Maggid of Dubno, amazed at the speaker's frankness, replied: "Before I go further, I should like to tell you of a strange dream I had the other night. It seems that the Evil Impulse had a most interesting conversation with Poverty.

"The Evil Impulse asked Poverty: 'My poor friend, how are you getting along in this world? Can you make headway there now?'

"And Poverty replied: 'I manage quite well, thank you. Indeed, my progress is most satisfactory. In days gone by, I was confined to the slums, to attics and basements. But gradually, I have begun to move into the homes of the better classes. In fact, you might say I've even become something of a snob. But how are you getting on, O Evil One?'

" 'Not very well, I am afraid," answered the Evil Impulse with a sigh. 'In the olden days I had much work to do; true, I had to struggle hard, but after a while I saw the fruits of my labors. It was through me, and through me alone, that my customers came to transgress the Law. But those days are gone forever, I am afraid. When I saw that business was getting slow, I decided to travel to a big city, to see if I could not find work there, and my choice fell on Berlin. Imagine my dismay when I found out that here, too, I remained unemployed. Whenever I tried to tempt people in Berlin to sin and to act contrary to the Torah, they merely smiled and said, 'Why, you have nothing original to offer. None of the sins you have to sell are new to us Berliners; we've known and practiced them all for a long, long time.' "

CHAPTER SIXTEEN

□ MORE TRAVELS AND HOMILIES

□ 1—THE CITY WITHOUT SCHOLARS

תַּלְמִיד חָכָם אַל יֵצֵא יְחִידִי בַּלַּיְלָה מִפְּנֵי הַמַּזִּיקִין.

Once, when walking at night through the dark streets of the city of Constantinople, where he had come for a brief visit, the Maggid of Dubno was stopped by a group of "enlightened" people who recognized him.

"We are surprised," they said to him, "to see a great scholar like yourself deliberately acting contrary to a precept of our Sages. For does not the Talmud say that a Jewish scholar should not go out at night unescorted, because of the demons that dwell among the ruins (Berachoth 43)?"

Replied Rabbi Yaakov: "Have no fear. I do not think it will ever occur to the demons of Constantinople that I may be a scholar, for I am quite sure that they have never seen one in this city."

□ 2 — "NO QUOTATIONS FROM THE SCRIPTURES, PLEASE"

(בא)   וּלְכֹל בְּנֵי יִשְׂרָאֵל לֹא יֶחֱרַץ־כֶּלֶב לְשֹׁנוּ.

232

"But against all the children of Israel not one dog will whet his tongue." *(Exod. 11:7)*

On one of his journeys through Germany, the Maggid of Dubno came to a place where the entire Jewish community had long since turned away from tradition. But they all had heard of the great preacher from the far-away town of Dubno whose parables both edified and delighted his listeners, and therefore the Maggid was invited to speak to them in the community hall.

Before the Maggid began his address, however, the president of the congregation told him that the audience was definitely not religiously inclined. Therefore, he specified, the Maggid was to refrain from using Hebrew words or phrases. Furthermore, the worldly gentleman said, "We are anxious to hear your famous parables, but we shall insist on one thing — no quotations from the Scriptures, please."

Rabbi Yaakov paused for a moment in deep thought, then ascended the pulpit and began:

"My dear brothers and sisters, I shall begin with a most appropriate *Moshol:*

"Once there was a teacher, who, much like the great philosopher Aristotle, delighted in holding his classes out of doors rather than in a closed classroom. One day, just before beginning his lesson, the teacher said to his students: 'If dogs should come, my children, do not be afraid. All you need to do is recite the verse from the Book of Exodus which reads, *"But against all the Children of Israel not one dog will whet his tongue."* If you will do as I have taught you, then not one dog will dare bark at you, much less bare his teeth, for his mouth will be sealed as if by magic.'

"The teacher had hardly finished talking when a pack of wild dogs rushed out from a neighboring forest and made straight for the little group. The children, obedient students that they were, remained rooted to the spot and recited the verse from the Scriptures which their teacher had just taught them. It was only then, when the dogs had vanished as if by magic, that the children noticed that their teacher had taken to his heels. After a long search they finally found him hiding in a safe place, surrounded by a strong fence. And they asked him, 'Rabbi, why did you run away? Why did you not stay and recite the verse from the Bible which you taught us?

"Replied the teacher, 'Your question is fully justified. But what could I do if the dogs had the nerve to prevent me from reciting the verse from the Bible?'"

With that, the Maggid bowed to his audience, turned round and stepped down from the pulpit.

□ 3 — "No Parables, Please"

One time the Maggid of Dubno came to a town where the head of the Jewish community took a dim view of the method of teaching by parable. He decided to permit Rabbi Yaakov to preach, but only on the condition that he not bring in a *Moshol.* Should the Maggid disregard this stipulation, he would be requested to leave the platform at once.

Rabbi Yaakov ascended the pulpit and addressed his audience as follows:

"My dear brethren, once it happened that I was walking on foot toward the city of Lemberg. On my way I saw a horse without a rider and I asked it where it was going. The animal replied, 'I am going to Brody.' I tried every means to persuade the horse to take me to Lemberg, but with no success. In the end I said to the horse, 'I am tired from my long journey. Therefore I would even go to Brody with you if only you will give me a ride.' To this the animal agreed at once.

"Once I was in the saddle, however, I pulled at the reins of the horse and headed it for Lemberg. When the animal noticed that we were approaching the outskirts of Lemberg, it became very angry and asked, 'What is the meaning of this? Did you not tell me that you would be willing to go with me wherever it was that I wanted to go?'

" 'You are right,' I replied, 'I did agree to go with you to Brody.

But that was before I settled on your back and had your reins in my hand. Is it not obvious to you that, once you let me sit in your saddle, I can head for whatever place I please?'

"My brethren," said the Maggid. "Once you let me stand on your platform, do I not have the same privilege? Let me, therefore, begin with a *Moshol!*"

□ 4 — THE MAGGID'S MORAL SERMON

Said the Maggid of Dubno:

"Once there was a man who had an only son, and the two were united by a strong bond of tender affection. But the father was growing old, and one day he was taken ill and died. The son's grief and mourning were beyond description and he could not cease lamenting his great loss.

"But the father, too, suffered greatly from this forced separation. After a few years in the World of Truth, he asked permission from the Heavenly Authorities to go down to earth in order to see how his son was faring. His request was promptly granted.

"When father and son met again on earth, their bliss knew no bounds. They fell into each other's arms and wept for sheer joy. All too soon the time came for the father to return to heaven. But the young man wept and said:

" 'O my father, you are the pride of my heart. You must never leave me again. Take me with you! I'll follow you wherever you go.'

"The father replied that this was hardly possible, since he belonged to the realm of the departed, and a living person could not be brought into the World to Come. But the son insisted, pleading that he could not face a lifetime on earth alone.

"In the end, the father said: 'My son, I must tell you that if I were to take you with me, your eyes would behold mysteries without number, and your soul would yearn to understand them. You would want to ask many questions but in the World of Truth the asking of all questions is forbidden and he who attempts to question anything he sees there would be expelled from Heaven and cast down to the

nethermost depths. But I can see that you would indeed be most unhappy if you had to remain on earth without me. Do you think, my
son, that you would be able to restrain yourself and ask no questions, regardless of what you might see in the World Above?'

" 'Ah, yes, dear father,' the son cried out eagerly.

" 'Then I shall guide you heavenwards,' said his father.

"Delightedly, the son promised that he would conduct himself in
keeping with the rules; he would keep his eyes open and his ears attentive, but would not utter even one word of question or inquiry.

"Thus the two of them went up together until they reached the
First Sphere of Heaven. It was a Sabbath Day. Imagine the young
man's shock when he saw a host of angels offering up incense. He
was about to go up to one of the heavenly beings and remind him
that he was violating the Sabbath by this act, but he remembered
his father's admonition and withstood the temptation to ask questions.

"Thereafter they ascended further still, until they reached the
Second Heavenly Sphere. It was now the Day of Atonement. To his
horror, the young man saw that the angels there were eating a
sumptuous dinner, and forbidden food at that."

Here the Maggid paused and looked at the congregation seated
before him in awed silence. Then he continued:

"But this was not yet all. He saw heavenly beings dishonoring
their elders, and leading lives that contradicted all he had learned
about family life..."

The congregation sat shamefacedly before the Maggid, for many
of them recognized their own sins in this long list of misdeeds.

And the Maggid continued:

"Now the son could no longer restrain himself and he cried out,
'My father, my father! I can remain silent no more! When such hor-
rors can happen even in Heaven above, restraint is not a virtue but
a crime! I must expose the evil I see here, no matter what the consequences. Ah, sinful beings, I shall not mince words with you. How
dare you do such evil? Why will you not obey the commandments of
Him Who is the Ruler over all the Universe? You profane the Sabbath, you violate even the holy Day of Atonement, you eat forbidden

food, you behave like beasts rather than like creatures made in the image of the Lord! Why? Why? Answer me! I admit, I may have overstepped my bounds. Then do with me whatever pleases you! I dare you! Kill me, shatter me into a thousand pieces! Truth will out, lest it burn my tongue! I must speak, and fight for truth, and not count the cost!...' "

And, concluding his oration with a wise saying of our Rabbis, Yaakov Mi-Dubno left the pulpit, leaving the congregation quiet and subdued.

□ 5 — Do Clothes Make the Man?

מִפְּנֵי מָה תַּלְמִידֵי חֲכָמִים שֶׁבְּבָבֶל מְצוּיָּינִים ? לְפִי שֶׁאֵינָם בְּנֵי תּוֹרָה . . .
בְּמָתָא שְׁמָאי וּבְלֹא מָתָא תּוֹתְבָאי. . . .   (שבת קמה:)

At one time the Maggid of Dubno had the occasion to visit a city far from his home town. He was dressed in his most elegant robes. An acquaintance of his, who happened to find him there, asked him: "Rabbi, why the fine attire? After all, this is not a Sabbath or even a New Moon."

"I think I can answer you with the help of the Gemara," replied Rabbi Yaakov. "It is written there, '*Why are the scholars in Babylonia attired in distinctive dress? Because they are not learned*'" (Sabbath 145b).

"This seems a paradoxical statement, for how can scholars be scholars if they are not learned?

"But the Talmud should help us find the solution. Here it is written, '*At home it is my name* (that counts); *abroad, it is my dress*' (ibid). In a place where one is well known for his merits he need not put on distinctive dress, because a good name counts more than fine clothes. But in a strange place, where he is unknown, he must take care to don the most distinguished robes he has, for there the people do not know who he is and they will pay attention to him only if he is attired in such garb as will command respect wherever he goes.

"This is what the Gemara means by saying that the scholars in

Babylonia are attired in distinctive dress 'because they are not learned.' The pronoun 'they' refers not to the scholars but to the people of Babylonia. The Babylonians were not learned; therefore they could not appreciate a scholar for his erudition and knowledge alone. Hence it behooved a scholar traveling through Babylonia to take great care of his outer appearance so that in this manner he might gain the attention and respect of the ignorant populace.

"I, Yaakov of Dubno, must do likewise. In Dubno I need not go out in fancy dress, because there they know of my achievements, such as they are. But here, where I am unknown, I must take care to wear the most princely garments I possess, if the people are to pay attention to what I have to say to them."

□ 6—ON THE ALERT

וַיְהִי־שָׁם עִם ה' . . . לֶחֶם לֹא אָכַל וּמַיִם לֹא שָׁתָה.   (כי תשא)

"And he (Moses) was there with the Lord forty days and forty nights; he neither ate bread nor drank water." *(Exod. 34:28)*

Rabbi Yaakov of Dubno once came to a small town. It was evening and he was hungry and weary, so he immediately went to the Jewish inn and asked for a meal and a bed for the night. The innkeeper gave the traveler a room, but told him that there was no food at all in the house, not even bread or water, so he could not provide him with a dinner.

Since there was no other place in the town where he could have obtained kosher food, the Maggid had to go to bed without having eaten. After he had been in his room for about an hour he heard steps and talking downstairs, and delicious aromas from the kitchen drifted up to the attic chamber where the Maggid lay. He got up, went downstairs and, behold, the dining room was lit up and the table set with the most sumptuous dinner imaginable. The owner of the inn and his family were enjoying their supper. Naturally they were surprised and somewhat embarrassed to see Rabbi Yaakov, for they had waited to prepare the meal until they thought he would be asleep.

The Maggid, however, greeted them all with a friendly smile:

"I am not angry. In fact, I have every reason to be grateful to you, for you have helped me understand a passage from the Bible and from the Gemara which I could never understand before. In the Torah, we are told of Moses, *"and he was there with the Lord forty days and forty nights; he neither ate bread nor drank water"* (Exod. 34:28). And the Talmud explains this verse with the remark, *'A man should never deviate from the customs that prevail in his surroundings. This we can learn from Moses, who did not eat while he was with God for forty days and forty nights, in deference to the angels, who never eat or drink.'*

"Comes the question: Why did the Torah single out Moses' fasting as the one example of his courtesy in conforming to the rule we have just mentioned? Why wasn't it mentioned also that, since the angels of Heaven never sleep, Moses, too, remained awake all the time that he was in their midst, receiving the Torah for his people? Is it not well known that it is much more difficult to keep from sleeping than it is to abstain from food?

"Now, with your help, I have come to understand the reason why the Torah does not explicitly record that Moses had not slept at any time during that entire forty-day period. It is considered enough to say that Moses fasted during those forty days, for from this it can readily be deduced that he could not have slept. It is logical to assume that Moses remained on the alert all the time to see whether it was really true that angels never eat; in this way he could find out whether he, courteous as he was, would also have to keep a strict fast while in Heaven. Had Moses ever attempted to go to sleep, the angels might very well have used that time to partake of food. So, naturally, Moses had to keep awake!"

□ 7 — "IT WAS NOT FOR NOTHING"

וִידַעְתֶּם כִּי לֹא חִנָּם עָשִׂיתִי אֵת כָּל־אֲשֶׁר־עָשִׂיתִי בָהּ נְאֻם ה'.(יחזקאל י״ד, כ״ג)

Once, when he was still very young, the Maggid of Dubno was hired by a small congregation to serve as preacher. This meant that, every day, between Afternoon Services and Evening Prayers, he would deliver a lecture to the congregation on weighty questions of Torah and Talmud, and follow this daily lesson with a brief sermon on morals and ethics. But the pay he received in return was so miserably small that it barely sufficed for bread and water.

To add insult to injury, as it were, an official of the congregation came up to him after he had delivered a brilliant moral sermon, and said to him: "Maggid, I must say I am amazed! Do you really think you are entitled to receive payment for your activities in this congregation, and for your religious functions in particular? It certainly seems strange to me."

Rabbi Yaakov replied without a moment's hesitation: "All I do in this congregation is emulate the example of God Himself of Whom the Prophet Ezekiel said: *'And you shall know that it is not for nothing that I have done all that I have done in it, says the Lord God.'* "*

□ 8 — THE BOON OF YIDDISH

וְדִבַּרְתָּ בִדְבָרַי אֲלֵיהֶם.   (יחזקאל ג', ד')

"Go, come to the House of Israel and speak with my words to them."   *(Ezek. 3:4)*

Yiddish, which is not to be confused with Hebrew, is actually not one language but a peculiar mixture of languages, composed principally of the German spoken during the Middle Ages (1100-1500), which was the language employed also by the Jews who lived in the German states and provinces at that time. When, due to oppression and persecution during and after the Crusades, these Jews migrated

---

* Usually rendered: *"And you shall know that I have not done without cause all that I have done in it, says the Lord God"* (Ezekiel 14:23).

east to Poland, Russia and the countries now known as Lithuania and Latvia, they took their language with them. Even before that, the speech of these Jewish emigrants was no longer pure, but mixed with fragments of colloquial Hebrew. Now that they had come to Eastern Europe the language gradually absorbed scraps of local dialects. Eventually, centuries later, when the masses came west once more, this time to England and America, English words, too, became part of what by then had come to be known as "Yiddish" (Jewish) or affectionately as "Mama-loshen" ("our mother tongue"). This was the language which, with only slight variations from region to region, was employed by Jews for centuries at home and in the market place as well as for study in the synagogue and at the house of learning. And since the common folk did not use Hebrew except for prayer, it was Yiddish that came to be the language that forged strong bonds between the great Jewish communities of Eastern Europe. Thus equipped with a universal language of their own, most of the Jews of Eastern Europe had little interest in learning the dialects of the nations in whose midst they lived, and which, at the time, did not have much to offer in the way of great or inspiring literature. As the years passed, the Yiddish language took on an aura of sanctity, rendering Jewish life even more pronouncedly Jewish. It thus proved an insulating barrier, too, against cultural influences from the non-Jewish world, and so was a most effective agent for the preservation of a way of living permeated with Judaism and Jewishness.

But we must not forget that there are many countries where Yiddish has remained unknown. In the "Sephardic" countries such as Italy, Yugoslavia, Turkey, and Greece the place of Yiddish was occupied by Ladino, an ancient Spanish dialect intermingled with fragments of Serbian, Turkish, Greek and Hebrew. In Germany and France, Yiddish was spoken only by Jewish immigrants from Eastern countries. For in Germany the Jews had kept pace with the evolution of the German language from medieval to modern, and looked down on Yiddish as an impure language, a kind of "jargon" or dialect suited only to the Jews of Eastern Europe who for centuries had been shut off from all worldly culture.

Thus when Rabbi Abraham Berush Flamm, the most famous disciple of the Maggid of Dubno, went to Germany late in the eighteenth century to have his books printed, he found that while he and the Jews of Eastern Europe had come to venerate and cherish the Yiddish language as a vital part of their Judaism, the Jews of Germany had no interest at all in learning Yiddish and, in fact, boasted of their ignorance of the "jargon."

In his book *Shemen Ha-Mor,* Rabbi Flamm wrote: "I entered one of their synagogues to preach but I talked to the winds, for no one seemed to understand my words of teaching and exhortation. The elders of the congregation then came up to me and demanded that I speak in a proper German since my 'jargon' was unintelligible to them. While I was talking to these illustrious officials I found that, actually, German and Yiddish were not so very different from one another. Nevertheless they insisted that I use their language, which I considered strange and unsuitable for a meeting of this nature. Therefore I told them as follows:

"Listen to what God Himself has told you through the prophet Ezekiel: '*And He said to me: O son of man, go, come to the House of Israel and speak with My words to them. For you are not sent to a people of an unintelligible speech and a slow tongue, but to the House of Israel; not to many peoples of an unintelligible speech and a slow tongue, whose words you cannot understand. Surely, if I sent you to them, they would listen to you. But the House of Israel will not consent to listen to you, for they do not consent to listen to Me'* (Ezekiel 3:4-7).

"I then began my discourse, addressing myself to the man who had criticized me for speaking in Yiddish: I must tell you of something that happened to a great Maggid from the East, from Lithuania, to be exact. He made a journey through Germany and Italy and wherever he went he preached words of wisdom and exhortation, but the people said to him: Your sermons mean nothing to us, for we do not understand Yiddish. You had best go back to the people of your own country and speak to them; we can do without this jargon which no one here cares for. As a result, the Maggid stepped down from the platform, got into his waiting carriage and drove away.

"On the way out of the town he stopped at an inn, where he saw many different kinds of goods offered at tempting prices. He went over to the counter and bought bundles of flax, and wool, furs, candles and other salable articles which he then loaded onto his carriage. He changed his clothing and disguised himself completely so that no one could possibly have recognized him as the country preacher who had just been sent away from the synagogue.

"Now, when the Jews of the town saw the carriage crammed full of merchandise standing in the open marketplace, they crowded around it, seeking to buy the goods on display. The Maggid, disguised as a merchant, quoted his prices, and the customers bargained with him and finally made purchases.

"After a few hours of bargaining and selling, the Maggid suddenly said, 'Let us go to *Shul* together so that I may speak to you words of exhortation and wisdom.' And suddenly the people around him all gaped and said to one another in tones of surprise, 'What's that he's talking about? Who can understand him?'

"Thereupon the Maggid tore off his elaborate disguise and said to them: 'Do you recognize me now? I am the rabbi who preached to you in your synagogue yesterday. At that time you said you did not understand Yiddish. But isn't it a fact that I spoke to you in Yiddish now, too, when I advertised the carload of merchandise I had to sell, and you understood every word I said to you? It is only when it is the Word of God that comes to you in Yiddish that you do not understand it, and why not? Simply because you obstinately refuse to let God come into your lives. You are interested neither in studying the Torah nor in improving your character. That is why you understand Yiddish only when you can derive some material gain from it, but not when a rabbi uses it to teach you the things that you should know.'"

"This," said the Rabbi, "is how I interpreted to my audience the verse from the Book of Ezekiel, *'Go to the House of Israel and speak with My words unto them';* this means go to the Jewish people and address them in that language in which the Word of God is taught the world over. *'For you are not sent to a people of an unintelligible speech and of a slow tongue, but to the House of Israel...; surely, had I sent you to them they would listen to you. But the House of Israel will not...listen to you, for they do not consent to listen to Me.'* God has sent the teachers of His Law not to people who are incapable of understanding the language but to the people of Israel in a place where, in fact, they do understand it. Had I gone to others, who might have had real difficulty with the language, they would have made every effort to listen to me and comprehend what I have to say. But these people, who, in fact, have no trouble in understanding when it seems convenient or advantageous to do so, are actually rejecting not the Yiddish language but the Word of God."

□ 9 — THE MAGGID'S MODESTY

עַל בְּשׂוֹרוֹת הַטּוֹבוֹת אוֹמֵר בָּרוּךְ הַטּוֹב וְהַמֵּטִיב וְעַל שְׁמוּעוֹת רָעוֹת אוֹמֵר בָּרוּךְ דַּיָּן
הָאֱמֶת.   (ברכות ט' ב')

"On hearing good news one says, 'Blessed be He Who is good and does good,' and on hearing bad news one says, 'Blessed be the True Judge."   *(Berachoth 9:2)*

One day, in the city of Minsk, the Maggid of Dubno chanced to meet another Maggid of renown, Rabbi Judah Leib Ha-levi Eidel, better known as "The Afikei Yehudah" after his classic work, "The Streams of Judah." It was quite natural that both rabbis should be invited to speak at the great synagogue of the city. But both were men of exceptional modesty, so that neither wanted to be the first to speak. In the end Rabbi Baruch Dayan, the rabbi of the community, was asked to decide which one of the two should be the first speaker.

Rabbi Judah was chosen to ascend the pulpit first. His sermon was most clever and original, and the entire congregation sat fascinated. When he had finally concluded his oration, Rabbi Baruch enthusiastically cried out, *"Tov! Tov!* Good! Good!"

Next came Rabbi Yaakov of Dubno, who also did not disappoint his audience. The audience again sat spellbound as he expounded to them the Word of God, and made his explanation clear with the help of ingenious *Mesholim*.

Afterwards there was some discussion as to which of the two speakers had been the better. Finally one listener asked Rabbi Baruch: "Rabbi, what did you think of this last speech?" Rabbi Baruch smiled, and said, *"Emeth! Emeth!* Absolutely true."

It was a strange remark and it did not help resolve the question. Hearing the heated discussion that went on all through the hall, Rabbi Yaakov of Dubno returned to the pulpit and said:

"I believe your question has been answered quite adequately. May I recall to you what we are taught in Tractate Berachoth of the Talmud? On hearing good news, we must recite a blessing as follows: 'Blessed be He Who is *good* and does good.' And on receiving bad tidings, we must bless the Lord, too, only this time we must say 'Blessed be the *true* Judge.' By regrouping the Hebrew words one can also translate thus: "On hearing good tidings, Baruch says, "Good Good"; on bad tidings, Baruch the Dayan (judge) says "True!""

□ 10—THE SIEVE WITHOUT HOLES

It was the custom of the Maggid of Dubno to deliver special sermons for each of the annual *Shalosh Regalim,* the three Pilgrim Festivals, basing his text on the Scriptural passages of the Holy Books that are read on these holidays. Thus his Passover address dealt with the Song of Songs, his Shavuoth lecture was on the Book of Ruth and his Sukkoth sermon was centered about the Book of Ecclesiastes.

One Passover, as he was about to begin his discourse, the officials of the congregation came up to him and said: "Worthy Rabbi, we are all anxious to hear your sermon on the Song of Songs, but we must ask of you not to use allegories or *Mesholim* at any time. Those little stories are meaningless and a waste of time."

The Maggid of Dubno, with a gleam in his eye, ascended the pulpit and promptly began to speak:

"I shall begin with a *Moshol*. Once there was a wealthy man who married his daughter to a scholar. The young bridegroom had spent all his time at the Yeshiva in study, and, as was the custom, his father-in-law promised to support the young couple so that the boy could continue to devote all his time to the study of the Torah.

"Unfortunately there came a time when the generous father-in-law lost all his money and the naive, unworldly student was faced with the urgent need of making a living for himself. His father-in-law gave him permission to use his wife's dowry, which had been on deposit in the local bank, untouched, to purchase some cheap articles and then to sell the merchandise in the city at a profit. Before the scholar-turned-businessman left, the older man said to him:

" 'You have led a very sheltered life until this day, and you know little of buying and selling. Let me, therefore, give you some advice. Do not buy everything you are offered, for there are many people who are anxious to get rid of worthless or defective goods and would exploit your guilelessness to their advantage. Before you buy, inspect the merchandise carefully for dents and holes, and if you find anything at all wrong with it, stand your ground and refuse to take it.'

"Before entering the wholesaler's store, the shy young student read over once more the list of articles his father-in-law had asked him to buy: One large tea urn, a tea pot, a tea set, and some sieves and strainers. He then made his purchases and, his errand accomplished, returned home. Looking over the merchandise, the older merchant could not find any sieves or strainers. When he asked the younger man why he had omitted these items, the latter replied, 'Father, you explicitly told me not to buy anything of inferior quality, anything that is dented or has holes. Now when I looked at the sieves and the strainers, why, I noticed at once that they could not possibly be good, for there was not one of them that was without holes.'

"The father-in-law looked at the *shlemiel* in exasperation. 'Don't you know,' he said, 'that there are certain things that must have holes in them in order to be good? Tell me, boy, is Swiss cheese ever without holes? And yet, despite the holes, it is one of the best and the most expensive of foods. Even so, too, a strainer without holes wouldn't be a strainer at all, but only a plain dish or pan, totally useless as a sieve, for unless the vessel has holes in the right places, it can never be used to separate the pure from the impure, the fine from the coarse, or the useful from the useless.'

"Now," concluded the Maggid of Dubno, "you should understand why I could never explain to you the beauty and the mysteries of the Song of Songs without resorting to allegory or *Moshol*. It may be true that in some cases allegories are out of place and may spoil a good sermon, but not here. For do you not realize that the entire Song of Songs is itself nothing but one beautiful allegory, a *Moshol* comparing the love of God for Israel to the love of a bridegroom for his bride? How, then, could I interpret it to you if I were to take pains not to resort to parables or allegories? A sermon on the Song of Songs without a *Moshol* is about as worthwhile as a sieve without holes."

□ 11 — UNCANCELLED DEBTS

One Rosh HaShanah the Maggid of Dubno was told that there were present in the synagogue a number of men who had never come there all year long and had shown no interest whatsoever in the affairs of the community. Yet, on the High Holidays, it was they who attracted the attention of the entire congregation. Each one had pulled his *Tallith* over his eyes, and continuously swayed to and fro most energetically as if their bodies, too, had joined in the prayers they were reading.

The Maggid noted this, but said nothing, at least not until he ascended the pulpit for his Rosh HaShanah sermon.

The he began his address with a *Moshol* as follows:

"A well-to-do merchant who enjoyed high esteem for his honesty and for his above-board conduct in business matters had the misfortune of having his entire business establishment burn down. As a result he could not meet his liabilities. When, just at that time, one of his suppliers demanded payment for an old debt, he was deeply grieved at being unable to do much about it.

"After discussing the matter with some good friends, he decided to call on his creditor and to tell him of his present difficulties, hoping that the latter would understand and be patient. But when he came to the door of the creditor's private office, the merchant's courage failed him and he stood outside, sighing and lamenting his fate.

"Naturally, the wholesaler inside could not help hearing him; he came out and asked him the reason for his distress. And the merchant replied: 'I have good reason for sighing, for I fear that I cannot settle my accounts with you, and my debt to you is great, thousands of rubles, in fact, and it weighs heavily on my conscience.'

"The wholesaler, seeing his customer's despair, comforted him and said, 'We have done business together for many years; therefore let bygones be bygones. I shall cancel these debts so that we may start with a clean balance sheet once you will see your way clear to buying from me again.' The agreement was sealed over a glass of wine, and the trader went home, relieved, and told his neighbors about the exceptional consideration that his creditor had given him.

"Now there was another man who, hearing the story, thought that he, certainly, was deserving of the same treatment. He went to the wholesaler's place of business, stationed himself at the office door, moaned and groaned and waited for the door to open. When the owner of the establishment came out, this man told him that he had come upon bad times and was in urgent need of a loan of a few thousand rubles. But to the man's dismay, the magnate only laughed and said, "Why, this is unbelievable. Here you are, a perfect stranger whom I have never heard of before, asking me for a loan. Frankly, of all the presumptuous people I've met...'

" 'But sir, do you think I am any less a person than the merchant to whom you were so generous only the other day?' the poor man interrupted him. 'Am I any less deserving of justice than he?'

"The wealthy merchant looked at him long and steadily, and then said: 'One of us must be insane. How can you compare your situation with that of your friend? He is a man of integrity whom I have known and dealt with for many, many years. Throughout this time I have found him to be irreproachable in his business conduct and absolutely dependable when it came to the payment of his obligations. Now that Providence has sent him misfortune—and who is immune to calamity?—it is only fair that I make allowances in his case. For I know that he would not willingly renege on his agreements, nor would he take advantage of my generosity. But you—whom I have never even seen before—what right have you to stand before my door, putting on a show and expecting me to give you money in return?'

"This," said the Maggid of Dubno, "is the difference, too, between him who is pious all year long and that man who puts on a show of devotion only on the High Holidays. The pious Jew is anxious at all times to obey the commandments of God; to this end, he goes to synagogue every day and not just three times a year. He uses all of his spare time for study and charitable works, and considers all of his life only as a 'vestibule' to the World to Come. If, therefore, unintentionally and against his will, he becomes guilty of some transgression, and he sincerely repents of it, he will be forgiven, for all the credit which he has already amassed in the Heavenly Register proves that he would never sin on purpose and that he would not seek forgiveness only to sin again the next day.

"But the 'High Holiday Jew' is like the foolish man who wept and wailed in vain before the wholesaler's office door. All year long he has little to do with God; he is never seen in the synagogue and Judaism and Jewishness hold little interest for him. Then, when the High Holidays come, he suddenly turns religious; he comes to the synagogue and makes himself conspicuous in the congregation by his show of zeal and devoutness. He covers his head with his *Tallith*, sways back and forth, beats his breast and fills the hall with his sighs and groans. But all this will be of little avail, for he has no record of good deeds with God. and his past conduct certainly does not indicate a sincere desire to do better in the future. Therefore no matter how much he weeps and wails in the synagogue on Rosh Ha-Shanah and Yom Kippur, his debt cannot be completely cancelled in the Heavenly Register."

□ 12 — TRUTH AND PARABLE JOIN HANDS

In another small town in the East some of the most devout members of the Jewish community there came to the Maggid and said to him:

"We admire you for your great scholarship and for your eloquence. Your *Mesholim,* too, are excellent, but, tell us, are they necessary? After all, is not Judaism based on plain truth? Why hide the truth in parables which, beautiful though they may be, so often serve only to obscure the facts as they are?"

The Maggid of Dubno smiled. "If we're talking about parables, then I would do well to answer you with another *Moshol* and you will see how helpful *Mesholim* can be.

"Naked Truth used to walk about bare and unadorned. Now when people saw him walk thus unclothed through the town, they turned away in disgust and refused even to look at him. Wherever he went, he was rebuffed, or, at best, ignored.

"One day, as, dejectedly, he walked down a side street, he met a friend dressed in beautiful garments. It was none other than *Moshol,* Parable. Now Truth poured out his bitter heart to Parable, and said:

" 'Why is it that you should get so much attention, while I, the actual Truth, receive none whatever?'

"Replied Parable: 'The trouble, my friend, lies in the fact that you walk about plain and unadorned. No one likes to meet the naked Truth face to face. Let me help you and you will see a change for the better in your life.'

"And, without waiting for an answer, Parable clothed him in some of his own garments, and, behold, Truth looked most elegant and attractive.

"From then on, wherever Truth appeared in his exquisite new

apparel, he was greeted and welcomed most cordially, and he prospered in all his endeavors.

"This," concluded Rabbi Yaakov, "is what I endeavor to do for truth by means of my *Mesholim*. I would not change truth, nor — Heaven forbid — obscure it. All I do is clothe it in a graceful garment. Truth will remain the same, unalterable, with our without my *Mesholim*. But most people cannot bear to come face to face with naked Truth. Therefore truth can often find its way into their hearts only when it is clothed in a parable. While the *Moshol* does nothing to change the truth, it makes it beautiful and appealing to those who would otherwise ignore it."

CHAPTER SEVENTEEN

□ THE MAGGID AND THE HASSIDIM

□ 1 — HASSIDIM

Until the days of the First World War, the dominant force in Eastern European Jewry was Hassidism, a movement which had originated in Galicia about the middle of the eighteenth century.

Hassidism was the movement of the simple Jewish masses who, though deeply religious and strictly observant, had little Jewish learning and therefore were branded by the more erudite as *Amei Ha-Aretz* or "ignoramuses." Hassidism taught that even unlearned people like them could be quite as close to God as those who were on intimate terms with the by-paths and intricacies of Rabbinic literature. In fact, Hassidism maintained that the important thing in Judaism was not so much the constant study of weighty legal tomes, but simple, genuine piety and love for God and fellow-man. Any man possessing these simple qualities of goodness, piety and sincerity could aspire to the coveted title of *"Tzaddik"* (righteous one) even if he had little theoretical knowledge of the subject matter that was taught in the great Yeshivoth.

The Hassidim ('pious ones') sought to "serve the Lord with gladness." In their worship there was song and dance, to demonstrate the joy and ecstasy a man should feel when communing with his Maker. Perhaps this was a welcome relief from the austerity and rigor that was associated with Rabbinic Judaism which had come to place overriding emphasis on learning and logic, perhaps at the expense, sometimes, of simpler, more natural piety.

Like any new idealistic movement, early Hassidism, too, was not immune to certain less welcome outgrowths and excesses. The free and joyful mode of Hassidic worship, as opposed to the Rabbinic ideal of "worship of God through study of His Law," was viewed by some as undisciplined rather than free. Though Hassidism had never so intended it, the title of *Tzaddik* became a patent of nobility that was passed on from father to son, and some *Tzaddikim* came to be the objects of blind and adulating worship by their followers.

All this was extremely disquieting to the adherents of Rabbinic Judaism, particularly to the great Gaon Elijah of Vilna, who was their spiritual leader. The Gaon feared that the Hassidic way of "serving God with gladness" might degenerate into plain laxity in the observance of set prayer ritual, that the institution of the *Tzaddik* might give rise to an un-Jewish cult of saint-worship, and that the lack of stress on the study of the Torah might lead to a distortion of Judaism. He never ceased to emphasize that, in fact, study of the Law was the very soul of Judaism and Jewishness.

Today, of course, little remains of the controversy between these two great movements in Judaism, a dispute which at one time bordered on civil war in the ranks of Eastern European Jewry. Numerous Jewish communities have come to adopt many Hassidic customs and have retained them to the present day. The Hassidim, on the other hand, became more moderate in their views and attitudes; they realized the importance of the systematic and thorough study of the Law and themselves established numerous Yeshivoth.

But in the eighteenth century, in the time of the Maggid of Dubno, the strife between the Hassidim and the adherents of Rabbinic Judaism, who were labeled *Mithnagdim*—"opponents"

—still raged unabated. Not only was Hassidism the target of much ridicule and satire, but, in 1772, the Gaon of Vilna actually pronounced a stern interdiction *(cherem)* against the movement and its disciples.

The Maggid of Dubno agreed that the ideas advanced by some of the extremists in the Hassidic ranks might prove detrimental rather than beneficial for the cause which Mithnagdim and Hassidim alike held dear — the preservation of Judaism in accordance with the Word of God. And the Maggid made no secret of his disagreement with the views of Hassidism. Yet he had no lack of respect for those leaders of the Hassidic movement whom he judged to be sincere and honest men, and he deplored the excesses of intolerance perpetrated by overzealous adherents of either movement.

□ 2 — THE DISCOURTEOUS CHAZZAN

וְהוּא רַחוּם יְכַפֵּר עָוֹן.   (תהלים עח' ל"ח)

"And He, being merciful, forgives transgression." *(Psalms 78:38)*

Knowing that the Maggid of Dubno had no great liking for their views, a certain group of narrow-minded Hassidim sought an opportunity to embarrass him. Since they happened to be in the majority in that particular Jewish community, the opportunity most readily presented itself when Rabbi Yaakov spent one Sabbath in their midst and he was asked by the officials of the congregation to preach in the synagogue after the *Mincha* service. It was arranged that the Maggid's sermon should be scheduled for a very late hour, as close as possible to the Conclusion of the Sabbath. It was then planned that at the very moment when the Maggid would ascend the pulpit to speak, the *Chazzan,* the Reader, would rise and begin the Evening Service with the traditional *"V'hoo rachum..."* ("And He, being merciful,...") Psalms 78:38) so that the Maggid would never have a chance to preach his sermon.

Everything went as scheduled, and the Maggid of Dubno stood dumbfounded on the pulpit as the Reader of the congregation launched into the Evening Service for the Conclusion of the Sabbath. But when the Chazzan had finished the first four words of the service *V'hoo rachum yechaper avon,* "And He, being merciful, forgives transgression...," the Maggid cried out, "Pray, stop for a moment, for I must thank you for helping me understand the connection between this verse from the Psalms which you have just recited and the two verses which precede it. There the Psalmist says, *'And they beguiled Him with their mouth, and lied to Him with their tongue. For their heart was not steadfast with Him, neither were they faithful in His covenant'* (Psalms 78:36, 37). Now these words quite apply to the narrow, spiteful and discourteous conduct which you have shown this afternoon. Therefore, my dear Chazzan, it is only proper that, now, you should recite for these people the verse that follows. *"And He, being merciful, forgives transgression...."* May God indeed have mercy upon you and forgive you."

□ 3 — THE WORLD TURNED UPSIDE DOWN

Another time, the Maggid was sitting in his room in the inn of a small town, preparing the sermon which he was to deliver to the Jewish community there that Sabbath, when he was suddenly disturbed by noisy shouts and raucous singing. Looking out of the window, he found a large band of Hassidim, wildly dancing around their master, Rabbi Ber, the Maggid of Mezeritch. When he saw that they were preparing to enter the inn, Rabbi Yaakov began to feel somewhat uneasy, for he immediately suspected that they had come on purpose to annoy him and to make him appear ridiculous in the eyes of the community. And he was right.

Now Rabbi Ber was actually a man of tolerance and moderation. When his Hassidim told him that, at last, they had caught the Maggid of Dubno and would give him the treatment they felt he deserved, Rabbi Ber quickly sent for the Maggid and said to him,

"You are not of our camp, but I still think you are a great Jew. You must know what my followers want to do with you here. I will protect you from their hands, but first you must tell me, immediately, some allegory or parable which would be appropriate for a situation like the one in which you are now."

Replied the Maggid of Dubno, "I would be glad to do this for you, but I am afraid it would only kindle the wrath of your Hassidim. But if you give me your word of honor that you will let no harm befall me at the hands of these rowdies, I will let you hear my allegory."

When Rabbi Ber had given him the promise that he would not be molested, Rabbi Yaakov said. "Your community's turned upside down. All over the rest of the world it's the gypsies who play and the bear dances, but here it is the other way round: it's the Ber that plays, while his wild gypsies dance."

☐ 4 — "And a Redeemer Shall Come to Zion"

וּבָא לְצִיּוֹן גּוֹאֵל . . .

Despite their violent disagreement with his views, the Hassidim had to admit that the Maggid of Dubno was a man of exceptional wit and intelligence and they greatly enjoyed his words of wisdom. It came to pass in one small town where the Maggid happened to visit that from among a group of Hassidim a young Hassid stepped up to him, looked him squarely in the eye and insolently demanded, "We want to hear some of your witty sayings, and that right quickly."

The Maggid smiled, and, without hesitation, began:

"You know that all of us Jews anxiously await the Messiah. Every day, in fact at every moment, we hope for his coming. All our prayers, hopes and yearnings are summed up in the words *'And a Redeemer shall come to Zion.'* And what is the purpose of all the lectures and sermons that are delivered in Israel? It is not so much to make those who listen feel the prick of conscience, as it is to come to the concluding sentence, 'And a Redeemer shall come to Zion.'

"Now what about you yourselves? You asked me to give you some wise and witty saying to remember, but what you really want to hear from me is the gladsome news that the Messiah is indeed about to come. Tell me, why is it that the Messiah is not yet here?

"You do not know? Then I shall tell you. For a long time now the rich and the poor have each been blaming the other for delaying the coming of the Messiah. The poor tell the rich, 'The Talmud says *The Messiah will not come until every purse is empty* (Sanhedrin 97a). But you misers would rather die than part with your money, and that is why we are still languishing in exile.' And the rich say, 'Is it not also written in the Talmud, that *in the period before the coming of the Redeemer impudence will prevail* (Sota 49)? But you poor people are so meek. Therefore, how can the Messiah come?"

"But as for you, my friends," said the Rabbi with a smile, "I can proclaim to you with full confidence and justification the message you have really come to hear — '*And a Redeemer shall come to Zion!*' For, unlike the rich, you have no money at all, but at the same time, unlike the poor of the rest of the world, you have enough impudence to make up for your lack of wealth. Therefore, if the Messiah has not yet come, it is certainly not you who are to blame."

□ CHAPTER EIGHTEEN

□ IMPOSTORS AND WOULD-BE COMPETITORS

□ 1 — THE HEATHENS ALSO WORSHIP GOD

גָּדוֹל שְׁמִי בַּגּוֹיִם וּבְכָל מָקוֹם מֻקְטָר מֻגָּשׁ לִשְׁמִי.   (הפטרת תולדות)

"My Name is great among the nations, and in every place offerings are made to My Name."   *(Malachi 1:11)*

At first glance we may well wonder at this statement, for is it not obvious that there are nations around us who worship false gods?

Said the Maggid of Dubno:

"I shall tell you a *Moshol*. One day someone came to me and told me that a certain man was touring the provinces, pretending to be the Maggid of Dubno, and wherever he chanced to go he was received with great honors and lacked for nothing.

"But I was not angry. Why should I have been disturbed? For if a person who dresses as I do, and assumes all my own peculiarities and mannerisms, receives such honor and adulation wherever he goes, is this not an indication that the people love and venerate the Maggid of Dubno whom this impostor represents to them?

"And I believe I may humbly apply this personal experience of mine also to the words of the great Prophet Malachi. The heathens do not deny the existence of God. It is only their conception of the nature and essence of God that is wrong, and therefore they make for themselves idols to represent to them the Almighty Power to Whom all of us pray. Therefore, even when they bow down before stone, clay and wood, they actually intend to worship the One God, the Ruler of all the Universe. And the day will come when their eyes will be opened and they will recognize the figures they have made as worthless impostors, infinitely far from the Supreme Being they had been made to represent.

"The Prophet Malachi, in this one verse, has set down for us an eternal truth. He declares that, even now, the Name of God is great among the nations, and in every place offerings are made to His Name, for even the heathens who kneel before idols believe in all sincerity that they are thereby doing honor to the One True God."

□ 2 — A BLUNT LESSON

Yet, despite the Maggid's modesty, there were times when he could not help being incensed at the audacity of those who passed off his *Mesholim* as their own without even properly understanding the message that the parable originally had been intended to convey.

One such incident occurred in a town where the Jewish community, though large, was not noted for the culture and refinement of its members. It seems that another Maggid had come to the town at the same time as Rabbi Yaakov of Dubno, and both of them were asked to speak in the synagogue on that Sabbath. The Maggid of Dubno was the first to ascend the pulpit and acquitted himself marvelously well.

Now the other Maggid was fearful lest his prepared speech might be received as an anti-climax to the sermon that had gone before. Therefore, instead of launching into the moral lesson he had intended to give, he began his remarks with a *Moshol.* Unfortunately, he neglected to tell his listeners that the *Moshol* was not his own but had been composed by the Maggid of Dubno. However, the latter, modest man that he was, sat quietly without saying one word of protest. But when the country preacher began to twist the *Moshol* to suit his own purposes and compounded the felony by distorting its true meaning and intent beyond recognition, the Maggid of Dubno could no longer contain himself. He quietly rose from his seat near the pulpit and left the synagogue. Some of the officers of the congregation ran after him and asked him to explain his strange behavior. The Maggid of Dubno promised to comply with their request once the service would be over.

When the prayers had come to an end, a crowd of eager listeners gathered outside the synagogue, anxiously waiting for the Maggid's explanation. The Maggid looked at the crowd of simple country folk who stood before him, and he began:

"Once upon a time there were two brothers. One was very wealthy and lived in luxury, but the other was miserably poor and never got a decent meal.

"Now it came to pass that the daughter of the wealthy brother was betrothed, and of course the less fortunate brother was invited to the wedding festivities. In avid anticipation of the wedding dinner, the poor man decided to eat nothing at all at home on the day of the wedding, so that he might be able to enjoy the festive fare all the more.

"But when he came to the wedding he found that no one was in any hurry to start dinner. As the hours crept slowly by, the uncle of the bride found that he could no longer stand the pangs of hunger and decided to rush home for some refreshment prior to the wedding feast. Now all the food that he had at home was the tail piece of a fish, onions, and some carrots left over from the Sabbath. The poor man fell upon the food and quickly devoured it as it was. Then he hurried back to the wedding hall where, an hour later, the dinner began. First there was a plate of tasty chopped liver, then a thick and hearty soup, followed by delicious roast beef and succulent turkey. These were accompanied by a veritable garden of appetizing salads and pickles. The climax of the meal was a rich and most elegant dessert the like of which the humble wedding guest had never seen before. It was quite natural that he should gorge upon all these delicacies, but three or four helpings of each course of the meal proved to be too much for the man to accommodate and what was bound to happen happened. The food returned the way it had gone, but in reverse order, first the dessert, then the salads, then the meat and fish. When, finally, the chopped liver came forth, the father of the bride, who had stood by solicitously, supporting his brother's head over the basin, sighed in relief and said, 'Well, I trust that finishes it.' But much to his dismay his unfortunate brother now gave forth remnants of fish, carrots and onions. By this time the father of the bride had lost his patience and he asked, 'What is this? Until this point I understood the sequence. But I can no longer be held responsible for what comes now. It's not my food.'

"The same was true in the case of the speech of this afternoon," concluded the Maggid to his gaping audience. "Up to a certain point I understood. But beyond that, I felt compelled to dissociate myself publicly from what the speaker gave forth thereafter, for the conclusion he delivered was not mine."

□ 3 — PROVING HIS IDENTITY — THE HALF-HOUR MOSHOL

לֹא־יָבֹא עַמּוֹנִי . . . בִּקְהַל ה'. (כי תצא)

מִי שֶׁעָנָה לְאַבְרָהָם אָבִינוּ בְּהַר הַמּוֹרִיָה הוּא יַעֲנֵנוּ. (סליחות)

"An Ammonite or a Moabite may not enter into the assembly of the Lord."
(Deut. 23:4)

"May He Who answered Abraham our father on Mount Moriyah answer us."
(Selichoth prayers)

One Friday afternoon Rabbi Yaakov of Dubno arrived at a certain town. It was the first time that he had ever been there and he had not told anyone of his coming. Imagine his surprise, then, when at the inn he heard a man say to a group of people, "Do you know that the famous Maggid of Dubno is going to speak at the synagogue tomorrow? He's here even now; he arrived yesterday."

Hearing this, Rabbi Yaakov at once suspected that an impostor had preceded him into the town. However, he made no attempt to reveal his identity at the inn, and the next day he came to the synagogue and took his place in the congregation, curious to see and hear the man who had been passing as the Maggid of Dubno for the past two days.

He did not have long to wait. The "Maggid of Dubno" was introduced, and a man wrapped in a long *Tallith* ascended the pulpit and began to speak. Rabbi Yaakov could not restrain a smile as he watched the speaker imitate his own gestures and mannerisms with amazing accuracy. But as the would-be "Dubnoer" went on, quoting Rabbi Yaakov's *Mesholim* as his own and mutilating them beyond recognition, the Maggid's annoyance grew. Finally, when the man's harangue had come to an end, Rabbi Yaakov asked leave to speak, strode to the pulpit and proclaimed in a firm voice:

"Gentlemen, I feel it my duty to announce publicly that the preacher whom you have just heard is not the Maggid of Dubno, but simply a shameless impostor. And who should know it better than I? For, gentlemen, it is I, and not he, that is in fact the Maggid of Dubno.

"Now I have no wish to embarrass this man, and I certainly have no desire, Heaven forfend, to sing my own praises. But the very verse in the Book of Proverbs which tells us not to boast of our achievements, *Y'hallelcha zar v'lo picha, 'Let another man praise you, and not your own mouth'* (Prov. 27:2), has implicit in it the one situation in which it is permissible, nay, mandatory, for us to speak up for ourselves: '*Y'hallelcha zar v'lo*... 'When another man should praise you, but there is none (to do it), then *picha*, the wisdom of your own mouth must do it for you, You must speak up for yourself.

"Besides, I can truly say to you in the words of our Patriarch Abraham '*I am a stranger in your midst*' (Gen. 23:4). You have never met me before. Therefore I feel it is only right and proper that I should prove to you that I am indeed the Maggid of Dubno, the preacher who makes his point with *Mesholim.*

"How can I prove it? Let me make a suggestion. Here before me there are two holy books: the one is a *Siddur,* a prayer book; the other is a *Chumash,* a copy of the Five Books of Moses. Now let one of your congregation come forward and open both books, at random, and then it shall be the task of this preacher and myself to expound the first verses on top of the right hand page of each book together in such a manner that the verse from the prayer book and that from the *Chumash* be correlated in one and the same *Moshol.* You will agree, I think, that the one of us who will be unable to meet this challenge is not the Maggid whose name has spread even to your town."

The proposal was unanimously accepted. The President of the community stepped forward. First he opened the prayer book to the *Selichoth,* the penitential prayers that are recited on various occasions. The first verse on the right-hand page was *"May He Who answered Abraham our father on Mount Moriah answer us."* He then opened the *Chumash* and the choice fell upon the Book of Deuteronomy, the fourth and fifth verses of the twenty-third chapter: *"An Ammonite or a Moabite shall not enter into the assembly of the Lord ...Because they did not meet you with bread and with water on the way, when you came forth out of Egypt, and because they hired against you Balaam the son of Beor from Pethor of Aram Naharaim, to curse you..."*

Now the President turned to the man who had preached from the pulpit and said: "Proceed with your *Moshol* that will explain both of these verses." The response, however, was nothing but embarrassed silence. When it was obvious that the would-be Maggid was unable to meet the challenge, Rabbi Yaakov of Dubno began his homily as follows:

"Let us begin with the verse from the prayer-book, '*May He Who answered Abraham our Father on Mount Moriah answer us*' and my *Moshol* will show not only the problems this verse presents but also the answer to these questions.

"Once there was a rich man who was renowned not only for his wealth but also for his charity and his generous support of Jewish learning. When the time came for his only daughter, a girl of great beauty, to marry, he went to the head of a famous Yeshiva and brought home with him the star pupil of the institution as a bridegroom for the young woman. He was more than happy to find so learned a man for his daughter and was quite willing to support the young couple so that the scholar could devote all of his time to the study of the Law.

"Of course none but the best would do for his daughter, and the most sumptuous satins and laces were procured for the girl's bridal gown. When the gown was almost finished the seamstress found that more material was needed. The father of the bride, therefore, sent his clerk to a store, whose proprietor was a good friend of the family, to get the extra lace. That merchant was delighted to see the clerk and attended to his request personally and with dispatch. The clerk then paid five pieces of gold for the material. He was about to leave when the merchant took him aside and asked him to convey his heartfelt congratulations to his employer. The storekeeper then produced twenty-five gold coins which he gave to the clerk with a smile. 'Here's my small gift for the bride and groom,' he said in a low voice.

"A stranger, dressed in shabby garments, had watched the proceedings with some interest. When the clerk had left, he came forward and asked the storekeeper whether he, too, could buy some lace. The storekeeper called over one of the salesmen and ordered him to wait on the customer. The latter paid the five pieces of gold and then remained standing at the counter with a look of expectancy on his pale features. 'Is there anything you are waiting for?' inquired the merchant after a few moments. 'Is there anything else I can do for you?' 'Certainly,' replied the customer. 'I am waiting for my twenty-five pieces of gold!'

" 'What twenty-five pieces of gold?' asked the merchant in some surprise.

" 'Why, the man who just left here bought the same amount of lace as I did, and he received twenty-five pieces of gold in return. Am I not entitled to the same gift?'

"The shopkeeper could no longer restrain himself and burst into loud laughter.

" 'One of us must be a fool,' he exlaimed. 'Do you really think that whenever a customer comes and buys five gold pieces' worth of goods I can give him a present of twenty-five gold coins in return? I suppose you do not know who that customer was. It so happens that he is the clerk of a wealthy merchant with whom I have had close business connections for nearly forty years. He's brought me thousands of thalers of profit each year. It is quite natural, therefore, that I should be able and willing to give him a gift when his daughter gets married. But who are you? I don't know you at all; in fact, I never even saw you before you entered my store ten minutes ago. How can you, then, expect me to give you a donation of twenty-five gold coins simply because you bought five gold pieces' worth of lace from me?'

"This," said the Maggid of Dubno, "illustrates the question we may well ask in connection with the prayer in which we beseech Him Who answered our father Abraham on Mount Moriah long ago to answer us now. Is this not an arrogant request? Abraham had been close to God; he had known Him well. He had shown hospitality to the angels, he had given fatherly care to his nephew Lot, and his love for all of mankind had impelled him to plead with God to spare even the wicked inhabitants of Sodom and Gomorrah. Not only did he risk his own life for others; he was even ready to sacrifice to God his only son, whom he loved better than life itself. It stands to reason that a man such as Abraham would have his prayers answered by the Almighty. But what about us? Are we not like the stranger who foolishly asked the storekeeper for twenty-five pieces of gold? What merits can we cite in our support before the Lord?

our *Selichoth* prayers that He should accord us the same favor that he bestowed upon Abraham our father?"

"This, then, is our first problem. Now let us turn to the verse from the Bible and the question it presents. You will remember, it read, '*An Ammonite or a Moabite shall not enter into the assembly of the Lord . . . Because they did not meet with bread and with water on the way, when you came out of Egypt, and because they hired against you Balaam the son of Beor from Pethor . . . to curse you.*'

"To show the second problem, let us continue with our story.

"The wedding of the young couple was to be held in the native town of the bridegroom, where his aged parents resided. However, this trip was not considered a difficult one for the bride and her family to make, since the two communities were only a few miles apart; besides, it was winter and the river that separated the two districts was icebound so that the bride's carriages could easily cross it without having to hire a ferry-boat. The other members of the family preceded the bride across the river and arrived safely on the other side. Unfortunately the bride and her mother, who rode in a carriage filled with wedding presents, family heirlooms and household goods, were not so lucky. The ice cracked and broke, and the carriage fell into the freezing water below. Some bystanders who saw the accident rushed over to help. The baggage, of course, was beyond rescue, but after much effort the bride, her mother and the coachman were rescued and revived. The coachman, who was the first to recover from the shock, ran to the home of the bridegroom where the father of the bride was anxiously awaiting the arrival of his wife and daughter. Seeing the look on his servant's face, the master sensed at once that something terrible must have happened.

" 'What's wrong?' he asked the coachman, alarmed.

" 'O master,' the coachman managed to gasp. 'All of the bride's heirlooms — her jewelry — everything is gone. In the river — the ice broke . . .'

" 'And what else . . . .' whispered the father, his face white with terror.

" 'All the money you spent on the bride's clothes is gone — all her gowns — her linens — it's all in the river . . .'

"The father sat down heavily in a chair, trembling. Finally, he forced himself to ask, 'And my wife and daughter...?'

" 'They were rescued. They're resting on the bank of the river. I suppose they are not hurt,' the coachman answered.

"My friends," said the Maggid of Dubno, "When the stupid coachman in our story told his master of the accident, he first bewailed the loss of the bride's baggage. That which was most important to the father of the bride, namely, the news that his wife and daughter had been saved, he left to the very last. This can most aptly be compared with the difficulty we have in explaining the Biblical verse your president has selected. There, where we read of the sins of the Ammonites and the Moabites, we are told first only of their discourtesy, that they had not met the Children of Israel with bread and water. It is only at the very end that we read of the actual transgression for which they were to be punished so severely; that is, the sin of which they were guilty in hiring Balaam to curse the Israelites. Why was this, the greatest sin of them all and the most important for our purposes, mentioned only at the end of the sentence and not in the beginning?"

"Let us answer this question by taking up our story once more. After the wedding, the young couple took up residence at the home of the bride's father and all their needs were provided for so that the young husband might be able to devote all his time to the study of the Law without having to concern himself with earning a living. The bridegroom, however, carried his zeal for study so far that he hardly had any time to spend with the woman he had married. The bride begged him to give her more attention, and tried every means to distract him from his studies until, finally, he moved to a room in the town, leaving his wife with her parents. Hoping that the couple would eventually come to some understanding, the wife's parents continued to support him and even sent him his meals. But when it became obvious that the man was content to continue this arrangement indefinitely, his parents-in-law asked him to give their daughter a divorce. They promised that, in return, they would pay him a generous allowance. However, the young scholar would not hear of a divorce. The father-in-law then decided gradually to decrease the man's food rations to see what he would do then. Eventually only bread and water were sent over to the room where his unworldly son-in-law sat and studied day and night.

"But even this attempt at slow starvation did not move the overzealous student. Finally, in desperation, the unhappy father went to the village soothsayer who was reputedly capable of eliminating undesirables. The old man paid this person a large amount of money in return for which the soothsayer was to use his 'occult powers' to liquidate the son-in-law.

"Luckily the student heard of his father-in-law's plan, moved back to the shelter of his old Yeshiva, and told the dean of the institution the whole story. Shortly thereafter the father-in-law was called to the Yeshiva. When the dean asked him why he had kept the young scholar on a bread-and-water diet, the father replied:

" 'The reason that I was compelled to do this is that I have suffered business reverses and had to cut down even on my own household budget. To tell the truth, I can no longer afford to support the young man in the same style as I could when he first married my daughter.'

" 'I am afraid this is a transparent excuse,' replied the venerable rabbi. 'For if indeed you could no longer support this boy, how is it that you could affort to give large quantities of silver to the soothsayer who, you hoped, would rid you of his presence permanently?'

"This," said the Maggid of Dubno, "should explain to you the wording of our verse from the Book of Deuteronomy. We are told that the Ammonites and the Moabites must not enter into the assembly of the Lord. The first reason given is that 'they did not meet you with bread and water on the way.' This is an argument which their defenders might seek to refute by claiming that these nations had fallen on evil days and had to lower even their own living standard in order to survive, so that one could hardly have expected them to give food to strangers. Let it be remembered: what kept them from extending this welcome to Israel was not poverty but simply the desire to destroy the Jewish people. For how else could it be explained that, when it came to paying Balaam huge amounts of money to curse the people of Israel, neither Ammon nor Moab pleaded poverty as an excuse not to hire Balaam?"

"Here, then," said the Maggid, "is the answer to the problem presented by the Biblical verse. Now let us return to the prayer which we discussed in the beginning. Why should it be proper for us to demand that God answer our prayers even as He answered our father Abraham whose merits were infinitely greater than any which we might accumulate in our own lifetime? Let us explore our story further and we shall find the answer.

"Eventually the rich man's daughter was divorced from the youthful scholar. In time the student, with the learning he had accumulated, became a most erudite and respected rabbi. Although there had been no rabbis or scholars among his simple ancestors, his reputation came to be such that distinguished familes were anxious to acquire him as a son-in-law. So it came to pass that the scholar married once again and soon thereafter he was elected Chief Rabbi in the community where he now lived with his new wife. In due time the couple had a son. By that time the entire community had come to love and revere its spiritual leader and had long been waiting for the opportunity to convey these sentiments to him. When the rabbi celebrated the new baby's circumcision, the officers of the congregation came to him and handed him an unusual contract. According to this contract, the congregation promised the rabbi that, once he would retire, his son and no one else would be taken as his successor; that is, providing that the son would be equal to his father in both erudition and piety. This promise, they felt, was a proper token of the reverence and affection in which they held their rabbi.

"But the rabbi, who was not in the habit of mincing words, said to them, 'I thank you for your good intentions, but I am afraid this promise of yours is a tribute not to me but only to the great scholarship which you hope my son will possess some day. If by some chance he will not measure up to the standards you have set, the contract will not be valid. Now had you promised to accept my son as my successor unconditionally, for no other reason but simply because he is my son, ah, that would have been different entirely!

That would have been great tribute indeed to the merits which have earned me your affection.'

"This applies also to our prayer," concluded Rabbi Yaakov. "Our father Abraham, though descended from a family of idolators, was a man of great piety and Godliness. Now if God were to save us, his descendants, only if we, too, were deserving of being saved, it would be a wondrous favor, but not a tribute to our noble ancestor. Seeing that Abraham had been so close to God, we feel that we are not too presumptuous if we come before the Lord and humbly say, 'Behold, our father Abraham was good and pious, more than we ourselves could ever be. Therefore You singled him out and answered his prayers, though his own father had still been an idol worshipper. Now, therefore, will You not pay tribute to his blessed memory by saving us, not because of any merits of our own, but simply because we have the honor to be descended from him?' May the *Z'chus Avoth*, the merits of our fathers, ever stand at our side and may He Who answered Abraham on Mount Moriah answer us today."

□ 4 — PARABLES AND DARK SAYINGS

אֶפְתְּחָה בְמָשָׁל פִּי אַבִּיעָה חִידוֹת מִנִּי־קֶדֶם. (תהלים ע"ח ב')

Once it happened that when Rabbi Yaakov of Dubno came to a town to speak on the Sabbath, he met at the synagogue another Maggid who had also come to the town to speak before the Jewish community. After the service the beadle went up to the *Bimah* and requested both Maggidim to address the congregation.

It was agreed that the first speaker would be the other rabbi, who promptly ascended the pulpit and opened his remarks with the above quotation from the Book of Psalms, which is translated in English editions of the Bible in these words, *"I will open my mouth with a parable; I will utter dark sayings concerning the days of old"* (Psalms 78:2).

The speaker then continued. "I shall now give you the true interpretation of this verse. It means: *If I were to begin my sermon with a parable,* I would need *my mouth,* the gift of glib talk, to explain and to embellish it. To avoid such idle chatter *I shall utter dark sayings* instead. I shall tell you wondrous tales *of the past* which should not be forgotten. This is what teachers and preachers should do rather than waste time on complicated parables. This is the reason why I never quote *Mesholim* but confine my sermons to secret sayings dating back to the glorious days of old. For as regards parables—there are many books that are filled with them from cover to cover. Why increase their number?"

Of course this introduction was obviously an attack aimed at the Maggid of Dubno and his method of instruction.

After the rabbi had completed his sermon, the Maggid of Dubno strode up to the pulpit and began his address with these words:

"I beg leave to differ from the views just expressed by my colleague on this verse from the Book of Psalms. My friends, here is my own interpretation of this verse. *I shall open my remarks with a Moshol,* because the *Moshol is my mouthpiece,* my means of presenting to my people the wisdom of our fathers. *If I were to expound dark sayings,* if I were merely to recite obscure phrases and verses in which these eternal truths are often couched without attempting to make them clear to my listeners, that would be nothing out of the ordinary and a poor recommendation for me, because, *ever since the days of old,* books have been filled with these teachings. The art of education is to explain them properly; as for me, I can do it best with a parable. Therefore, whatever my colleague may think of me, I will open my sermon with a *Moshol.*"

□ 5 — THE TWO THIEVES

לְפוּם צַעֲרָא אַגְרָא.   (פרקי אבות ה' כ"ו)

"The reward is commensurate with the effort."   *(Avoth 5:26)*

Once, after he had completed a particularly inspiring sermon and received a rousing tribute from his audience, the Maggid of Dubno was stopped by another Maggid who said to him:

"Rabbi, I have listened to your sermon and I enjoyed it greatly. You are indeed deserving of honor and admiration. But I would ask one question of you. Both of us base our sermons on the same Torah; both of us expound a passage from it for one full hour; therefore both of us have a right to expect some recognition for our efforts. Now you have received much applause, but I, alas, have had no thanks at all for my pains. Why is it that I of all people should have so little luck?"

The Maggid of Dubno thought for a moment, and then replied:

"With all respects to you, and with all due honor to the Torah, let me compare the two of us to two thieves who have each stolen a pair of shoes. Each pair was the same value—eight thalers. Now the one thief re-sold his pair at once, and received two thalers for it. Not much profit, is it? But not so the other thief. He went home with his loot in his bag, and then went to work. He opened all the seams, and with the help of his skill, he re-designed the shoes and re-finished them according to his own concept of beauty and craftsmanship. When he was done he polished the shoes until they shone like mirrors. Thus, when he went out to sell them, he could ask twelve silver thalers and got them, too.

"The same is true of our work. We both took precious merchandise from the same source. But the returns we will receive from it will depend on how much work we put into the fashioning, the skillful interpretation of the wisdom we have taken out of our sacred Torah. Our Rabbis said (Avoth 5:26), *'The reward is commensurate with the effort.'* The praise we reap for our sermons can only be in direct proportion to the time we have spent on their preparation."

☐ IN CONCLUSION

We have come to the end of our anthology of the wise parables and homilies of the Maggid of Dubno. We have seen for ourselves how he managed to convey to his listeners, in simple words that all could understand, the eternal truths of our Torah and our sacred tradition. His endeavors to render the lofty ideals of Judaism understood even by the unlearned masses have earned him a place alongside the famed commentators and Rabbinic authorities who have expounded the Word of God to the people of Israel through the centuries of its history.

It would be a mistake to remember Rabbi Yaakov of Dubno solely as a teller of tales. Indeed a great many of his teachings contain no parables. To him the *Moshol* or parable was not an end in itself but only an aid in accomplishing the task to which he had devoted all his days. Perhaps the best way for us to illustrate Rabbi Yaakov's concept of the function of the parable would be to cite another one of his classic *Mesholim*.

Once there was a wealthy man who had only one son. Naturally, he adored the child. One day the boy was taken seriously ill. His distraught father sent for the most famous physician in the land.

The learned doctor examined the patient and then prescribed some very potent pills which he said would surely bring the boy relief within a week's time. Since the pills were quite bitter, the physician had them coated with a thick layer of chocolate so that the child would take them.

A week later the father came to the physician in despair. The pills seemed to have had no effect whatsoever. The doctor then took the boy to task and asked him whether he had really taken the drug three times each day as he had been told to do.

"Yes," the child answered, "and I took not only three, but even extra pills to make up for the part I spat out."

The doctor raised his eyebrows in amazement. "What part did you spit out, boy?" he demanded.

"Why, the bitter part, or course," the boy replied.

With that, the cause of the mysterious failure of the medicine to effect a cure became quite clear.

The function of the *Moshol* in education is the same as that of the coating of chocolate around the pill in medicine. Even as medicine is often bitter, the moral and ethical teachings of our tradition often seem difficult to understand. Yet, without them, there can be no Jewish education, no cure for the ills of our spirit, even as without medicine there can be little hope of healing for the body. Therefore the Maggid of Dubno enclosed these hard truths in the sugar-coating of the *Moshol* to make it easier for us to assimilate them in our hearts and minds. But it is obvious that the sugar-coating alone does not present the entire story. Even as it is not enough merely to eat the chocolate covering of the potent medicine, so it is not sufficient merely to read and enjoy the *Moshol.* Our minds must penetrate through the sweet outer layer to the precious, though often difficult, lessons that are enclosed within.

Rabbi Yaakov's *Mesholim* of classic simplicity, by means of which he sought to achieve this end, have become immortal. Even today, the mere mention of any one of them, or even of his name, conjures up in the mind the image of a man who became great not merely by virtue of his scholarship and erudition, but also through nobility of both mind and spirit.

His tombstone bears the following brief epitaph.

יבא יעקב שלם* לפ״ק

הדרשן הגדול המפורסם

אשר שמעו הלך בכל המדינות

לפניו לא היה ואחריו

לא יקום כמוהו איש

אשר רוח א־להים דובר בו

מ״ו ר׳ יעקב מגיד מ׳

דפה בן מ״ו ר׳ זאב ז״ל

יעקב מגיד

"And Yaakov shall come in peace*"

    A great and outstanding orator,

Whose fame spread through all the lands of the world

    His like did not exist before him,

Nor will such another rise after him,

    A man from whom spoke the Spirit of the Lord

Our Teacher, Rabbi Yaakov the Maggid (of Dubno)

    The son of our Teacher, Rabbi Z'ev of blessed memory

       Yaakov the Maggid

---

* An allusion to the first three words of *Genesis* 33:18: "And Jacob came in peace," the letters of which combine to form the numerical value of 565, an allusion in turn to the year of the Maggid's death which was 5565 (1804).

☐ BIBLIOGRAPHY

Hebrew:

Kranz, Rabbi Yaakov ben Z'ev: *Ohel Yaakov.* Anthology of writings on the Torah. Edited by Rabbi Abraham Dov Berush Flamm and Rabbi Yitzchak Kranz.

Kranz, Rabbi Yaakov ben Z'ev: *Kochab Mi-Yaakov.* Writings on the Haftaroth.

Kranz, Rabbi Yaakov ben Z'ev: *Kol Yàakov.* Writings on the Five Megilloth. Edited by Rabbi Yitzchak Kranz.

Kranz, Rabbi Yaakov ben Z'ev: *Emeth Le-Yaakov.* On the Passover Haggadah.

Kranz, Rabbi Yaakov ben Z'ev: *Sefer Ha-Middoth.* A book of moral sermons, on the order of the classic *Chovoth Ha-Levovoth* (Duties of the Heart) by Bachya ibn Pakudah. This was the only book by the Maggid of Dubno to be ready for publication at the time of his death. It was published after his decease by his disciple, Rabbi Abraham Dov Berush Flamm, and annotated with the latter's commentary *(Shurei Ha-Middoth).*

Mandelbaum, Jacob Dov: *Ha-Maggid Mi-Dubno: Zsamosc, Bigeonah U-Be-Shivra,* edited by Moshe Tamar.

Other Pertinent Literature:

Kantorowicz, S.S.: *Mishlei Ha-Maggid Mi-Dubno.* Warsaw, 1923. An anthology of the parables of the Maggid of Dubno, for young people.

Lipson, M.: *Mishlei Ha-Maggid Mi-Dubno.* Published in serial form in *Hatzofeh*—a daily newspaper. Tel Aviv, 1945-1946.

Neches, Dr. S.M.: *Veyerd Mi-Yaakov.* Explanations on Ethics of the Fathers. Los Angeles, 1949.

Nussbaum, M.: *Mishlei Yaakov.* Selection of parables from the Maggid of Dubno. Cracow, 1886.

Steinman, Eliezer: *Kithbei Ha-Maggid Mi-Dubno.* 2 vols. Kneseth, Tel Aviv, 5712.

Yiddish:

Mishlei Chochmah. A compilation of parables and explanations from *Ohel Yaakov, Kochab Mi-Yaakov and Kol Yaakov.* Vilna, 1913.

Balaban, Pessel: *Sefer Ohel Yaakov Ve-Kol Yaakov.* Anthology of parables and explanations from *Ohel Yaakov, Kochab Mi-Yaakov* and *Kol Yaakov.* Lemberg, 1884.

Zevin, Israel J.: *Alle Mesholim fun Dubner Maggid,* 2 vols. New York, 1925, Tashrak Publishing Co.

□ GLOSSARY

Abram — Abraham's original name before it was changed.

Agadah — Part of the Talmud not aimed at treatment of traditional law.

Agra — (Aramaic) remuneration, reward.

Agunah — A woman whose husband is missing, but not proven dead.

Am Haaretz — (lit. people of the land) those ignorant of Jewish matters.

Amud — Reader's desk at the synagogue.

Ashkenazic — Pertaining to Central and Eastern European Jews (opp. to Sephardic).

Avinu Malkenu — (lit. "Our Father, Our King") High Holiday prayer in which each verse begins with these words.

Bar Mitzvah — (lit. son of the commandment) Jewish boy attaining the age of thirteen.

Baal Haturim — Jacob b. Asher (1269-1343). Author of Code of Laws, and commentary on the Pentateuch.

Badchan — Professional buffoon.

Balaam — Biblical heathen prophet.

Bentch Mezuman — Say the grace after meals prayer when at least three have eaten together.

Beth Hamidrash — House of study.

Beth Hamikdash — Holy Temple.

Bethuel — Father of Laban and Rebecca.

B'hemah temeah — Unclean beast.

Bima — Pulpit.

Birchath Kohanim — The priestly blessing.

Bitachon — Faith, trust.

Brith — Covenant.

Brith Milah — Circumcision.

Chacham — Wise one.

Chassidim — v. Hassidim.

Chaye Haolam Habba — Life in the world to come.

Chazzan — Cantor.

Chefetz — Instinctive desire.

Cherem — Interdiction.

Cheshek — Reasoned desire.

Chet — Sin.

Cheth — Heathen inhabitant of Canaan. Descendants known as Hittites.

Chukim — Statutes.

Chumash — Pentateuch.

Days of Awe — Ten days commencing with the New Year and terminating with the Day of Atonement.

Divrei Torah — Words of Torah; Commentaries.

Elai — "to me".

Eliezer — Servant of Abraham.

Elul — Sixth month of Jewish year; preceding the New Year.

Emeth — Truth.

Eretz Canaan — Land of Canaan, later became the "Land of Israel."

Eretz Yisrael — Land of Israel.

Eth — Particle used in conjunction with object; with.

Ethics of the Fathers — Tractate Avoth.

Gaon — Genius, Excellency.

Gaon of Vilna — R. Elijah b. Solomon (1720-1797) Lithuanian scholar, regarded as greatest authority of his age.

Gashmiuth—Physical, materialistic.

Gemara—Talmud.

Golus—Diaspora, Exile.

Guf—Body.

Hagar—Daughter of King of Egypt and maid to Sarah.

Haggadah—Traditional text read on Passover eve.

Hakol Kol Yaakov—"The voice is that of Jacob" (Gen. 27:22).

Hassidim—(lit. pious ones) Adherents of Hassidism.

Hassidism—a pietistic movement founded by R. Israel Baal Shem Tov, eighteenth century.

Hetter—Rabbinical dispensation.

Hillel—(ca. 70 B.C.E.) Famous Rabbi of Mishnah.

Joshua—Leader of the Israelites, successor of Moses.

Kehilloth—pl. of Kehillah. Jewish community, congregation.

Kethuvim—(lit. writings) The Holy Writings (Hagiographa) in the Sacred Scriptures, beginning with Psalms.

Kilayim—Mixture of two sorts.

Klaus—House of study and prayer.

Kohanim—pl. of Kohen.

Koheleth—The biblical book of Ecclesiastes, written by King Solomon.

Kohen—Priest; descendant of Aaron.

Korach—Biblical Levite who contested the authority of Moses.

K'toreth—Type of incense.

Laban—Brother of Rebecca, father of Rachel and Leah.

Lashon Hara—Evil language; gossip.

Lashon Nekiyah—Clean language.

Levites—Descendants of Levi, son of Jacob.

L'shem Shamayim—In honor of God.

Lulav—Palm branch. One of the four species of plants used on the Feast of Tabernacles.

Maaser—Tithe.

Maaser Sheni—Second Tithe, eaten by owner in Jerusalem.

Maasroth—pl. of Maaser.

Maggid—Preacher, to attract the masses.

Maggidim—pl. of Maggid.

Mattan—A grant.

Megillah—Scroll; the Book of Esther.

Mesholim—Parables.

Messiah—(lit. anointed) Future final deliverer of Jewry from exile and tribulations.

Mezuman—Summoned.

Mezuzah—(lit. doorpost) Small scroll of parchment attached to the doorpost, containing biblical verses.

Midrash—Explanation of the text of the Bible according to tradition.

Mikvah—Ritual bath of purification.

Mishnah—Oral Law, formed basis for Talmud.

Mitzvah—Law, commandment.

Mitzvoth—pl. of Mitzvah.

Mitzvoth Chukioth—Statutes.

Mitzvoth Sichliyoth—Universally accepted laws.

Moshol—Parable; simile.

Mussar—Reproof, ethics, morals.

Naaseh Venishma—"We will do and we will hear" (Exodus).

Nadab—Son of Aaron.

Neilah—Concluding prayer on Yom Kippur.

Nes—Miracle, supernatural.

Neshamah—soul

Neshamah Yetherah—Additional soul which comes on Sabbath and Holidays.

Neviim—Prophets.

New Moon—Rosh Chodesh, minor holiday each month at New Moon.

Olam Haemeth—The true world, the world to come.

Ol Mitzvoth—The yoke of the commandments.

Ol Torah—The yoke of the Law.

Oneg Shabbath—delight in the Sabbath.

Pesach—Pascal lamb; Passover holiday on the fifteenth day of Nissan.

Purim—Joyous holiday on the fourteenth day of Adar.

Rabbothai—(lit. my teachers) A polite salutation.

Rasha—Wicked man.

Rashi—R. Solomon b. Isaac (1040-1105). Outstanding commentator on Bible and Talmud.

Rebecca—Wife of Isaac.

Ruchniuth—Spirituality.

Sabbath—Seventh day of week; day of rest.

Sagi Nahor— (lit. much light) Blind man.

Sarah—Wife of Abraham.

Sarai—Sarah's name before it was changed.

Selichoth—Forgiveness prayers.

Sephardic—Pertaining to Jews of Spanish or Portugese origin (opp. to Ashkenazic).

Shaatnez—Material woven of wool and linen.

Shabbath—Hebrew for Sabbath.

Shadchan—Marriage broker.

Shalom—Peace.

Shalosh Regalim—The three Pilgrim Festivals; Pesach, Shavuoth, Sukkoth.

Shammash—Beadle.

Shavuoth—Pentecost holiday on the sixth day of Sivan.

Sheker—Falsehood.

Shemitah—Sabbatical year; seventh year.

Shlemiel—(Yiddish) Person beset by misfortune; hapless, clumsy individual.

Shofar—Horn; ram's horn blown on Rosh Hashana.

Shoresh—Root.

Shul—German and Yiddish for synagogue.

Sidroth—pl. of Sidra; weekly portions of Torah read on the Sabbath.

Siddur—Prayer book.

Simcha—Rejoicing.

Simchath Torah—Holiday of rejoicing in the Law—follows Sukkoth.

Sodom and Gemorrah—Two cities destroyed because of sin.

Shofar—Horn; Ram's horn blown on Rosh Hashana.

Shool—German and Yiddish for synagogue.

S'udah — Meal, dinner.

Sukkah — Ritual hut used on Sukkoth.

Sukkoth — Festival of huts on fifteenth day of Tishri; Tabernacles.

Tallith — Four-cornered garment with Tzitzith: worn especially for prayers.

Talmidey Chachamim — (lit. students of the wise) learned men.

Talmud — Encyclopedic explanation of the Mishnah; oral law.

Talmud Torah — (learning of Torah): elementary Hebrew Schools.

Tamei — Spiritually unclean.

Taryag Mitzvoth — Six hundred and thirteen (613) commandments embodied in the Pentateuch.

Tefillin — Phylacteries, worn on head and upper arm especially during prayer.

Tekioth — Long sounds emitted from the Shofar.

Teruah — Short sounds emitted from the Shofar.

Terumoth — Heave offerings.

Tikkun — Order.

Tikkun Chatzoth — Ordered prayers recited at midnight.

Tikkun Lel Shavuoth — Book studied on the night of Shavuoth.

Torah — Law, Pentateuch.

T'shuva — Repentance.

Tzaddik — Righteous one.

Tzitzith — Fringes on the corners of the Tallith.

Ulai — Perhaps, maybe.

V'hoo Rachum — 'And He being merciful,' beginning of evening prayer.

Wimpel — (German) Cloth to tie the scroll together.

Yalkut — An anthology of selections from the Midrash.

Yetzer Hara — The evil inclination.

Yom Kippur — Day of Atonement.

Yom Tov — Festival; holiday.

Yomim Tovim — pl. of Yom Tov.

Yovel — The Jubilee year, fiftieth year.

Z'chus — Merit.

Z'chus Avoth — The guarding merit of our Patriarchs.

Zohar — A Cabbalistic work by R. Shimon B. Yochai.

☐ INDEX TO PORTIONS OF THE WEEK AND SPECIAL OCCASIONS